Table of Content

1	Roles and Responsibilities of the Project Monitor	1 - 3
2	Characteristics of Asbestos and Asbestos Containing Materials	4 - 13
3	Federal Asbestos Regulations	14 - 31
4	Understanding Building Construction and Building Systems	32 - 59
5	Asbestos Abatement Contracts Specification and Drawings	60 - 65
6	Response Actions and Abatement practices	66 - 74
7	Asbestos Abatement Equipment	75 - 81
8	Personal Protective Equipment	82 - 95
9	Air Monitoring Strategies	96 - 110
10	Safety and Health Issues other than Asbestos	111 - 129
11	Air Sampling Protocols, Requirements & Data Interpretation	130 - 148
12	Legal Responsibilities and Liabilities of the Project Monitors	149 - 155
13	Recordkeeping and Report Writing	156 - 157
14	Glossary of terms	158 - 165

OBJECTIVES of this course:

1. To become familiar with accreditation requirements for project monitor.
2. To gain an overview of the monitoring process.
3. To conduct visual inspections
4. To do final clearance monitoring
5. To become knowledgeable of asbestos abatement and control techniques
6. To become familiar of pertinent regulations,
7. To become knowledgeable and understand building construction systems
8. To become familiar and determine the effectiveness of air filmizing fiber release
9. To become knowledgeable and familiar with asbestos abatement equipment
10. To become knowledgeable of proper selection of respiratory protection
11. To become familiar with AHERA TEM protocol
12. To become familiar with NISOH 7400
13. To perform air monitoring to assess exposure levels and sampling to ensure adequacy of containment
14. To become knowledgeable of Safety and Health issues
15. To become knowledgeable of recordkeeping and report writing
16. To check work activities for compliance with federal, state and local regulator requirements
17. To work with consultants, industrial hygienists, journeymen, engineers and housing specialists to develop the project specifications.

Asbestos Project Monitors must be accredited by completing a Project Monitor Course (refer to applicable for specific regulations). The course is designed for individuals who serve as the on-site representative of the building owner to oversee the asbestos abatement work and to insure that all work is performed in accordance with specification, and in compliance with all federal, state, and local laws.

A one hundred (100) question, multiple-choice examination will be administered on the last day. A score of 70 percent or higher is recognized as a passing grade. Successful completion of the course leads to eligibility to apply for a state Project Monitor certification through the state.

NOTE: According to the NY State Industrial Code Rule 56 - 2.2c(8), any individual serving in the capacity of a Project Monitor shall have such certificate or, a copy thereof, in their possession at all times while working on the project. This is modeled for a five (5) day format which includes twenty-four (24) hours of classroom instruction and sixteen (16) hours of hands-on training.

QUALIFICATIONS

The Asbestos Hazard Emergency Response Act (AHERA) Model Accreditation Plan recommends that states develop minimum requirements and qualifications for the accreditation of Project Monitors in accordance with 40 CFR 763, part E.

Some of the Suggested Prerequisites

Project Monitors

High School Diploma
Certified as a Supervisor
Have Completed a National Institute for Occupation Safety and Health (NIOSH) 582 Course
BS in Engineering or Industrial Hygiene
Working Knowledge of HVAC systems
4 Years Experience

Each state may require specialized licenses to be maintained for specific areas of work. To maintain their state license, they must attend an initial and annual refresher course. It is important to note that each state has the option of requiring persons to complete additional training, and pass re-accreditation examinations at specific intervals.

For an example, to become a NY State Asbestos Project Monitor a course is designed for individuals who serve as the on-site representative of the building owner to oversee the asbestos abatement work and to insure that all work is performed in accordance with specification and in compliance with all federal, state, and local laws. According to the NY State Industrial Code Rule 56 - 2.2c(8), any individual serving in the capacity of a Project Monitor shall have such certificate or a copy thereof in their possession at all times while working on the project. This is a five (5) day program which includes twenty-four (24) hours of classroom instruction and sixteen (16) hours of hands-on training.

Below is the text of the regulations that specifies the training accreditation of Project Monitor (EPA regulation -40 CFR 763)

EPA recommends that States adopt training and accreditation requirements for persons seeking to perform work as project monitors. Project monitors observe abatement activities performed by contractors and generally serve as a building owner's representative to ensure that abatement work is completed according to specification and in compliance with all relevant statutes and regulations. They may also perform the vital role of air monitoring for purposes of determining final clearance. EPA recommends that a State seeking to accredit individuals as project monitors consider adopting a minimum 5-day training course covering the topics outlined below. The course outlined below consists of lectures and demonstrations, at least 6 hours of hands-on training, course review, and a written examination. The hands-on training component might be satisfied by having the student simulate participation in or performance of any of the relevant job functions or activities (or by incorporation of the workshop component described in item ``n" below of this unit).

EPA recommends that the project monitor training course adequately addresses the following topics:

(a) **Roles and responsibilities of the Project Monitor.** Definition and responsibilities of the Project Monitor, including regulatory/specification compliance monitoring, air monitoring, conducting visual inspections, and final clearance monitoring.

(b) **Characteristics of asbestos and asbestos-containing materials.** Typical uses of asbestos; physical appearance of asbestos; review of asbestos abatement and control techniques; presentation of the health effects of asbestos exposure, including routes of exposure, dose-response relationships, and latency periods for asbestos-related diseases.

(c) **Federal asbestos regulations.** Overview of pertinent EPA regulations, including: NESHAP, 40 CFR part 61, subparts A and M; AHERA, 40 CFR part 763, subpart E; and the EPA Worker Protection Rule, 40 CFR part 763, subpart G. Overview of pertinent OSHA regulations, including: Construction Industry Standard for Asbestos, 29 CFR 1926.58; Respirator Standard, 29 CFR 1910.134; and the Hazard Communication Standard, 29 CFR 1926.59. Applicable State and local asbestos regulations; regulatory interrelationships.

(d) **Understanding building construction and building systems.** Building construction basics, building physical plan layout; understanding building systems (HVAC, electrical, etc.); layout and organization, where asbestos is likely to be found on building systems; renovations and the effect of asbestos abatement on building systems.

(e) **Asbestos abatement contracts, specifications, and drawings.** Basic provisions of the contract; relationships between principle parties, establishing chain of command; types of specifications, including means and methods, performance, and proprietary and nonproprietary; reading and interpreting records and abatement drawings; discussion of change orders; common enforcement responsibilities and authority of project monitor.

(f) **Response actions and abatement practices.** Pre-work inspections; pre-work considerations, pre-cleaning of the work area, removal of furniture, fixtures, and equipment; shutdown/modification of building systems; construction and maintenance of containment barriers, proper demarcation of work areas; work area entry/exit, hygiene practices; determining the effectiveness of air filtration equipment; techniques for minimizing fiber release, wet methods, continuous cleaning; abatement methods other than removal; abatement area clean-up procedures; waste transport and disposal procedures; contingency planning for emergency response.

(g) **Asbestos abatement equipment.** Typical equipment found on an abatement project; air filtration devices, vacuum systems, negative pressure differential monitoring; HEPA filtration units, theory of filtration, design/construction of HEPA filtration units, qualitative and quantitative performance of HEPA filtration units, sizing the ventilation requirements, location of HEPA filtration units, qualitative and quantitative tests of containment barrier integrity; best available technology.

(h) **Personal protective equipment.** Proper selection of respiratory protection; classes and characteristics of respirator types, limitations of respirators; proper use of other safety equipment, protective clothing selection, use, and proper handling, hard/bump hats, safety shoes; breathing air systems, high pressure v. low pressure, testing for Grade D air, determining proper backup air volumes.

(i) **Air monitoring strategies**. Sampling equipment, sampling pumps (low v. high volume), flow regulating devices (critical and limiting orifices), use of fibrous aerosol monitors on abatement projects; sampling media, types of filters, types of cassettes, filter orientation, storage and shipment of filters; calibration techniques, primary calibration standards, secondary calibration standards, temperature/pressure effects, frequency of calibration, recordkeeping and field work documentation, calculations; air sample analysis, techniques available and limitations of AHERA on their use, transmission electron microscopy (background to sample preparation and analysis, air sample conditions which prohibit analysis, EPA's recommended technique for analysis of final air clearance samples), phase contrast microscopy (background to sample preparation, and AHERA's limits on the use of phase contrast microscopy), what each technique measures; analytical methodologies, AHERA TEM protocol, NIOSH 7400, OSHA reference method (non clearance), EPA recommendation for clearance (TEM); sampling strategies for clearance monitoring, types of air samples (personal breathing zone v. fixed-station area) sampling location and objectives (pre-abatement, during abatement, and clearance monitoring), number of samples to be collected, minimum and maximum air volumes, clearance monitoring (post-visual-inspection) (number of samples required, selection of sampling locations, period of sampling, aggressive sampling, interpretations of sampling results, calculations), quality assurance; special sampling problems, crawl spaces, acceptable samples for laboratory analysis, sampling in occupied buildings (barrier monitoring).

(j) **Safety and health issues other than asbestos**. Confined-space entry, electrical hazards, fire and explosion concerns, ladders and scaffolding, heat stress, air contaminants other than asbestos, fall hazards, hazardous materials on abatement projects.

(k) **Conducting visual inspections**. Inspections during abatement, visual inspections using the ASTM E1368 document; conducting inspections for completeness of removal; discussion of ``How clean is clean?'' (l) Legal responsibilities and liabilities of project monitors. Specification enforcement capabilities; regulatory enforcement; licensing; powers delegated to project monitors through contract documents.

(m) **Recordkeeping and report writing**. Developing project logs/daily logs (what should be included, who sees them); final report preparation; recordkeeping under Federal regulations.

(n) **Workshops** (6 hours spread over 3 days). Contracts, specifications, and drawings: This workshop could consist of each participant being issued a set of contracts, specifications, and drawings and then being asked to answer questions and make recommendations to a project architect, engineer or to the building owner based on given conditions and these documents. Air monitoring strategies/asbestos abatement equipment: This workshop could consist of simulated abatement sites for which sampling strategies would have to be developed (i.e., occupied buildings, industrial situations). Through demonstrations and exhibition, the Project Monitor may also be able to gain a better understanding of the function of various pieces of equipment used on abatement projects (air filtration units, water filtration units, negative pressure monitoring devices, sampling pump calibration devices, etc.).

Conducting visual inspections: This workshop could consist, ideally, of an interactive video in which a participant is ``taken through'' a work area and asked to make notes of what is seen. A series of questions will be asked which are designed to stimulate a person's recall of the area. This workshop could consist of a series of two or three videos with different site conditions and different degrees of cleanliness.

Chapter 2 Characteristics of Asbestos and Asbestos Containing Materials

INTRODUCTION

Many factors must be evaluated before deciding to conduct an asbestos abatement project. This Chapter is intended to provide the Project Monitor with insight into a variety of asbestos-related issues that ultimately influence the air monitoring process. These considerations range from the fundamentals of locating and identifying asbestos-containing materials to the tasks of assessing the potential hazard by the Project Monitor.

The Project Monitor will be coordinating efforts with the Building Owner, Project Designer and Contractor, who is responsible for the planning to control the asbestos abatement project.

DESCRIPTION OF ASBESTOS

Asbestos is a generic term that includes a number of fibrous minerals. The various types of asbestos minerals occur predominantly in metamorphic rock where they crystallize in narrow veins as parallel bundles of tiny fibers. A fiber bundle may contain as many as a million of the minute fibrils. When dispersed into the air, these fibrils may remain airborne for several hours or longer. Three distinctive characteristics of asbestos fibers are apparent when viewed under a microscope. **Asbestos fibers are very small; they are much longer than they are wide and, there is a noticeable variation in diameter of the individual fibrils.**

The different types of asbestos are placed into two mineralogic categories termed serpentines and amphiboles. Minerals in these groups are distinguished by their chemical composition and their crystalline structure. **Serpentines and amphiboles exhibit different physical properties, which are important from a Project Monitor's viewpoint.** For example, the amphiboles do not wet as easily as the serpentines. Therefore, it may be more difficult to keep airborne fiber levels down when removing materials containing amphibole asbestos material.

The only fibrous asbestos in the serpentine group is **chrysotile**, sometimes referred to as white asbestos. It comprises more than 90 percent of all the asbestos that has been used in commercial products in the United States. The primary elements in chrysotile are silicia and magnesium. Chrysotile also usually contains impurities of iron, nickel, aluminum, chrome and some other minerals. The chrysotile fibril is a spirally wound hollow tube. The combination of fibrils bound together gives the fiber the appearance of having curly split ends. Chrysotile fibers have high tensile strength and good spinnability, but are not as resistant to acids as the amphiboles.

Chapter 2 Characteristics of Asbestos and Asbestos Containing Materials

The fibrous asbestos minerals in the amphibole group are actinolite, amosite, anthophyllite, crocidolite, and tremolite. They are characterized by a wide variation in chemical composition including calcium, sodium, aluminum, ferrous and ferric iron. **Amosite and crocidolite**, sometimes referred to as brown and blue asbestos, respectively, are the only commercially significant varieties. When compared to chrysotile in appearance, amosite and crocidolite fibers are larger in diameter, solid as opposed to hollow and straight instead of curly. The amphiboles are more resistant to acids than chrysotile and can withstand higher temperatures without breaking down.

ASBESTOS-CONTAINING PRODUCTS

To obtain asbestos for commercial use, asbestos ore is extracted from open pit or underground mines. The ore is crushed and the asbestos fibers are separated from the rock layers by vibrating screens and an air-lifting process. The fibers are bagged in bulk for incorporation into various products at manufacturing facilities or through on-site mixing. **Asbestos-containing materials, which are batch-mixed on the construction site, such as structural fireproofing, usually have a wider variation in percentage of asbestos content than those that are incorporated into manufactured products, such as floor tile**. The type of material and method of production have a bearing on the number of samples that must be collected for a given suspect material in a building survey.

The various types of asbestos have been incorporated into an estimated 3,000 commercial products. The inherent physical characteristics such as resistance to heat and chemicals, abrasion resistance, insulating capabilities and high tensile strength along with low cost and availability, resulted in the widespread use of asbestos-containing materials (ACM). Asbestos was commonly used on steam pipes and boilers of ships during the early 1900's. It was used widely in American ships and shipyards in the 1940's and was expanded to sprayed-on insulation materials in the 1950-1970's. Use of asbestos in the United States did not begin to decline until the 1973-1978 bans by the Environmental Protection Agency (EPA) on spray-applied and pre-molded friable building materials.

Asbestos Abatement Project Monitors will be primarily involved with several common asbestos materials that were incorporated into building products. These products can be described in terms of use such as fireproofing, thermal and acoustical insulation, decorative application, product reinforcement, and acid resistance. For the purposes of evaluating asbestos in buildings, the EPA has defined three categories of asbestos-containing building materials based upon application.

- **SURFACING MATERIALS**. ACM sprayed or troweled on surfaces (walls, ceilings, and structural members) for acoustical, decorative, thermal insulation or fireproofing purposes.

- **THERMAL SYSTEM INSULATION (TSI)** – Insulation used to inhibit heat transfer or prevent condensation on pipes, boilers, tanks, ducts, and various other components of hot and cold water systems, and heating, ventilation, and air conditioning (HVAC) systems. This includes pipe lagging, pipe wrap; block, batt and blanket insulation; cements and "muds;" and a variety of other products such as some gaskets and ropes.

- **MISCELLANEOUS MATERIALS** – Materials not included in the other two categories such as floor tile, ceiling tile, roofing felt, concrete pipe, outdoor siding and fabrics, sheetrock "mud," glazing putty, various mastic products and caulking products. Frequently, non-building ACMs such as material in ovens and laboratory counter tops must be addressed in the project design.

The terms friable and nonfriable are used to further describe the cohesiveness and consistency of asbestos-containing materials. **Friable ACM, when dry, can be crumbled or reduced to powder by hand pressure.** Friable materials generally release fibers into the air more readily than do nonfriable materials. However, many types of nonfriable ACM can become friable and release fibers if they are substantially broken, cut, drilled, sanded, sandblasted, crushed, pulverized, or abraded.

COMMON TYPES OF ACM

The materials most likely to be involved in an asbestos abatement design project are spray-applied fireproofing, acoustical plaster, ceiling tile, thermal system insulation, floor tile and associated mastic. A brief discussion of these materials follows, and a listing of a wide variety of asbestos-containing products follows.

Spray-Applied Fireproofing – A one-half to two-inch thick layer of friable asbestos-containing insulation was commonly spray-applied to the structural steel in a building to prevent buckling and collapse during a fire. Sometimes it was also spray-applied to the floor and roof decks. **Chrysotile, in quantities of 1 to 95 percent (25 percent on average), is the most common type of asbestos found in fireproofing insulation. Occasionally amosite or rarely crocidolite was used.** Other materials typically used in conjunction with chrysotile-included vermiculite, cellulose fibers, gypsum and binders such as calcium carbonate and portland cement.

Asbestos-containing fireproofing was usually spray applied to the structural steel before the installation of other building components, and may be located in hard-to-access places such as elevator shafts, fresh-air ventilation shafts and beams covered up by duct work. There is usually overspray on everything that was present at the time of application. It may be on the inside of some electrical and/or air conditioning ducts, if they were partially in place when the fireproofing was applied. Overspray may be found on exterior walls behind insulation on gypsum board and finish materials. Asbestos-

Chapter 2 Characteristics of Asbestos and Asbestos Containing Materials

containing fireproofing ranges from white, to gray, to brown as it was applied, but sometimes may be coated or encapsulated with a clear or colored sealant.

* REPRESENTATIVE LIST OF MATERIALS LIKELY TO CONTAIN ASBESTOS

Asbestos Cement Insulating Panels
Asbestos Wallboard
Asbestos Insulating Panels
Asbestos Chalkboards
Roofing
- Asphalt Saturated Asbestos Felt
- Reinforced Asbestos Flashing Sheet
- Asbestos Base Felt
- Asbestos Finishing Felt
- Flashing
- Paint

Sheet Metal Work
- Plastic Cement

Membrane Waterproofing & Dampproofing
Putty
Fire Door Insulation
Fire Dampers
Flooring
- Asphalt Tile
- Vinyl Asbestos Tile (VAT)
- Vinyl Sheet Flooring Backing

Mastic
Plaster
Ceiling Tile
Insulation
- Thermal, sprayed-on Fireproofing

Paints
Textured Coatings
Taping Compounds
Elevators, Brake Shoes
Insulation, Plumbing
- Piping Insulation
- Pipe Gaskets
- Equipment Insulation

Insulation, HVAC
- Boiler Block
- Breeching Insulation
- Boiler Wearing Surface Gaskets
- Duct-work Taping

Laboratory Hoods, Gaskets, Bench Tops

* Any product manufactured prior to 1978 is subject to bulk testing.

Chapter 2 - Characteristics of Asbestos and Asbestos Containing Materials

<u>Acoustical **Plaster**</u> – Acoustical plaster typically containing 10 to 30 percent chrysotile has been commonly troweled or sprayed onto walls or ceilings for soundproofing. The material is typically one-fourth to one-half inch in thickness, friable, and varies in color from white to gray. Acoustical material is usually accessible, because it is used to reduce noise levels in frequently occupied areas such as hallways, auditoriums and cafeterias, but may also be inside electrical ducts, conduits and air conditioning ducts that were in place when the material was installed or inside of walls. **Even in accessible locations where the acoustical ACM has been painted, it is still a friable material, which would need to be addressed upon renovation or demolition and in the operations and maintenance program.**

<u>Thermal System Insulation</u> – Thermal system insulation (TSI) is the category which contains the largest amount of ACM. In commercial buildings and schools, most of the material is generally limited to closed, restricted access areas rather than offices or highly used space. However, in industrial facilities, accessible TSI is much more predominant. The average percentage of asbestos in TSI ranges from 65 to 75 percent. It often contains crocidolite and amosite as well as chrysotile.

Insulation on thermal systems is typically wrapped with an outer canvas jacketing and may be applied as: a corrugated cardboard-type pipe wrap; a white chalky pipe wrap; <u>cementitious</u> mud around pipe fittings; block insulation on boilers; white batt insulation on boiler breeching; or as black batt insulation inside ducts. On tanks and boilers, there may be layers of other materials such as wire mesh sandwiched between the layers of insulation. Removal of TSI may pose special problems if it is insulating high-temperature lines, high-pressure lines, or lines containing toxic chemicals. TSI used in occupied spaces such as insulation on exposed pipe risers in public areas is more accessible and may require surveillance and preventative maintenance to ensure the material remains in good condition.

<u>Floor Tile and Mastic</u> – Floor tile and the underlying mastic are generally considered to be nonfriable materials when they are in good condition. However, these materials may need to be abated when damaged, or as part of a larger renovation project. Refer to the discussion of the National Emission Standard for Hazardous Air Pollutants (NESHAP) in the Chapter on Regulations for further information on regulated materials.

Relatively low percentages (10 to 15 percent) of asbestos were used in floor tile and floor tile mastic. The dimensions of the asbestos fibers that were used in floor tiles and mastic are sometimes too small to be detected with a polarized light microscope, which is the analysis prescribed in the EPA's Asbestos Hazard Emergency Response Act (AHERA) and National Emissions Standard for Hazards Air Pollutants (NESHAP) regulations. **A higher resolution transmission electron microscope (TEM) may be needed in order to detect asbestos fibers in floor tile**. Vinyl cove base and cove base mastic is a subset of this class of materials and is also a candidate for TEM analysis.

Ceiling Tile – Chrysotile and amosite were occasionally used in various types and sizes of ceiling tiles. If asbestos is present, the percentage usually ranges from 5 to 10 percent. Other components include mineral wool and cellulose. Like floor tile, ceiling tile may contain very small fibers, which cannot be detected with the polarized light microscope. Often the asbestos is restricted to a specific layer in the ceiling tile. **It is important to note that nonasbestos-ceiling tile may become contaminated if it is below friable asbestos fireproofing**.

BUILDING SURVEY PROTOCOL AND SAMPLE ANALYSIS

Because the Project Monitor will need to rely on written design specifications by the Project Designer, an overview of how a survey is conducted, how samples are analyzed, and a brief discussion of data interpretation follows.

A building survey for asbestos is conducted by determining where suspect materials are located, quantifying materials that appear to be the same (homogeneous materials), collecting a statistically reliable number of random samples for each suspect material identified ,and assessing the potential each material has for fiber release. This process has been formalized in the regulations for schools promulgated under the Asbestos Hazard Emergency Response Act (AHERA).

The AHERA method of assessment and prioritization incorporates the factors of current material condition and potential for damage into a decision-tree framework. The criteria evaluated for each functional space such as hallways, auditoriums, and classrooms include the extent of deterioration, physical damage, water damage, accessibility, vibration and airflow. Each suspect material found to contain asbestos is classified into one of three categories: significantly damaged, damaged, or good condition. Then, depending on the accessibility factors, the confirmed ACM is assigned a hazard ranking number, which corresponds to the degree of risk posed by the ACM including the potential for future damage.

Samples collected for EPA compliance purposes are analyzed for asbestos content by polarized light microscopy (PLM) using the "Interim Method for the Determination of Asbestos in Bulk Insulation Samples" found at Appendix A to Subpart F in Title 40, Code of Federal Regulations (CFR) Part 763. With this method, the presence of asbestos in a sample is determined by optical mineralogy using a light microscope with polarizing filters. Asbestos identification is achieved by examining the structure of the fibers and optical properties of the sample. Quantification is obtained either by visual estimation or point counting. Results are reported as percent asbestos by type (e.g., chrysotile, crodidolite). Additional information, such as other fibrous components in the sample and the nonfibrous sample matrix may also be obtained.

EPA standards define a material that contains greater than one percent asbestos, as asbestos containing. The referenced EPA method refers to percent by weight. However, the laboratory results are actually reported as percent by area. The analyst determines the amount of asbestos present by an area visual estimation. If the analysis by the standard PLM procedure indicates less than 10 percent asbestos is present, the NESHAP regulation requires verification of the percent asbestos by point counting using PLM, or by analyzing the sample three times by PLM to verify the asbestos content to <1%. Point counting is a more precise quantification procedure and, generally, the reported percentage of asbestos is lower by point counting than the standard method. As discussed earlier, the limitation to this analytical technique is the resolution of the polarized light microscope. Even under optimum conditions, fibers less than 0.25 tm in diameter cannot be detected by PLM. The size of the asbestos fibers incorporated into some materials, such as floor tile, may be too small to be detected by PLM.

ELAP provides evaluation and accreditation of environmental testing laboratories to ensure the quality of analytical data used for regulatory purposes to meet the requirements of the State's drinking water, wastewater, shellfish, food, and hazardous waste programs. The State agencies which monitor the environment use the analytical data from these accredited laboratories. The ELAP-accredited laboratories have demonstrated capability to analyze environmental samples using approved methods. The National Institute of Standards and Technology (NIST) administers the **National Voluntary Laboratory Accreditation Program (NVLAP).** NVLAP is comprised of laboratory accreditation programs (LAPs) which are established on the basis of requests and demonstrated need. Each LAP includes specific calibration and/or test standards and related methods and protocols assembled to satisfy the unique needs for accreditation in a field of testing or calibration. NVLAP accredits public and private laboratories based on evaluation of their technical qualifications and competence to carry out specific calibrations or tests. Accreditation criteria are established in accordance with the U.S. Code of Federal Regulations (CFR, Title 15, Part 285), NVLAP Procedures and General Requirements, and encompass the requirements of ISO/IEC 17025. Accreditation is granted following successful completion of a process which includes submission of an application and payment of fees by the laboratory, an on-site assessment, resolution of any non-conformities identified during the on-site assessment, participation in proficiency testing, and technical evaluation. The accreditation is formalized through issuance of a Certificate of Accreditation and Scope of Accreditation and publicized by announcement in various government and private media.

NVLAP accreditation is available to commercial laboratories; manufacturers' in-house laboratories; university laboratories; and federal, state, and local government laboratories. Laboratories located outside the United States may also be accredited, if they meet the same requirements as domestic laboratories and pay any additional fees required for travel expenses.

NVLAP provides an unbiased third-party evaluation and recognition of performance, as well as expert technical guidance to upgrade laboratory performance. NVLAP accreditation signifies that a laboratory has demonstrated that it operates in accordance with NVLAP management and technical requirements pertaining to quality systems; personnel; accommodation and environment; test and calibration methods; equipment; measurement traceability; sampling; handling of test and calibration items; and test and calibration reports. NVLAP accreditation does not imply any guarantee (certification) of laboratory performance or test/calibration data; it is solely a finding of laboratory competence. A laboratory may cite its accredited status and use the NVLAP term and symbol on reports, stationery, and in business and trade publications provided that this use does not imply product certification

OPTIONS FOR CONTROL

Based on the information from the building survey and laboratory analyses, a decision is made on how to properly handle asbestos-containing materials. The options for controlling exposure to ACM are referred to as response actions in the EPA AHERA regulations. Response actions range from in-place management with an operations and maintenance (O&M) program if the material is in good enough condition, to removal if the material is severely damaged and cannot be repaired. Building renovation, demolition or modernization may also make ACM removal necessary.

<u>In-Place Management</u> - An Operations and Maintenance program is a formal set of standard operating procedures to minimize asbestos exposure in the building. Two useful reference documents for asbestos Operations and Maintenance programs are the EPA publication "Managing Asbestos In Place - A Building Owner's Guide to Operations and Maintenance Programs for Asbestos-Containing Materials", also known as the "Green Book"; and the National Institute of Building Sciences' "Guidance Manual: Asbestos Operations and Maintenance Work Practices".

The purpose of an Operations and Maintenance program is to clean up any asbestos-containing dust or debris that may have been previously released, maintain the ACM in good condition, and prevent inadvertent disturbance to in-place

Chapter 2 Characteristics of Asbestos and Asbestos Containing Materials

asbestos-containing materials. This is achieved through a series of program elements, which include:

- Asbestos Program Manager appointment and training,
- Written, building-specific Operations and Maintenance Program,
- Notification to building occupants, staff and outside vendors about the presence and location(s) of ACM,
- Training staff on special work practices for handling or working around ACM,
- Respirator, medical surveillance and hazard communication programs.
- Special maintenance procedures.
- Special cleaning procedures,
- Work order/permit system for outside vendors,
- Periodic re-inspection and re-cleaning,
- Recordkeeping.

One of the measures for maintaining the material in good condition is repair, which involves limited replacement and/or patching.

Another control option, termed enclosure, involves the installation of an airtight (or nearly airtight) barrier between the ACM and the building environment. This measure has limited applicability and is typically only used for small amounts of material on isolated columns or beams.

Another option for in-place management is encapsulation of the material with a liquid that, after proper application, surrounds or embeds asbestos in an adhesive matrix to prevent fiber release. However, encapsulants are limited in their applicability and may make eventual removal of ACM more difficult and costly. For example, encapsulation should only be considered for ACM that is in good condition, not highly accessible, and granular or cementitious. If the material is not in good condition, the encapsulant may cause the ACM to delaminate. Also, if fireproofing is encapsulated, the Underwriters Laboratory (UL) fire rating may be voided.

Removal - If in-place management of ACM is not feasible or effective in protecting human health and the environment, the remaining control option is removal of the ACM. This option is often selected when renovation activities make it impossible to control asbestos fiber release. Partial removal of ACM in an area or on a floor-by-floor basis may be performed in conjunction with activities such as wall relocation, sprinkler installation, and ceiling, light, or duct replacement. From a building owner's perspective, the critical issues which must be considered in selecting any control option include the potential health risk, legal liability, regulatory compliance, economic factors and the owner's long-term concerns.

If the decision is made to remove ACM, it is imperative that the project be designed and executed properly to protect the safety and health of workers and building occupants, to avoid further contamination of the building and the environment and to minimize legal liability. This curriculum provides the fundamental concepts, which will assist the Project Monitor in achieving this goal. The Project Monitor must then supplement these fundamentals with a wide range of project experience, and continue to remain current in the various technical and regulatory issues associated with asbestos materials.

SUMMARY

Asbestos Abatement Project Monitors must be familiar with a wide variety of asbestos-related issues that impact the project and air monitoring process. They should know that the various types of asbestos are minerals that are in a fibrous form. The fibers are very small and can remain airborne for several hours or become airborne again. The different types of asbestos exhibit different physical properties, which may affect the design strategy. Asbestos was incorporated into more than 3,000 products. Asbestos abatement projects typically focus on spray-applied insulation, acoustical plaster, thermal system insulation, ceiling tile, floor tile and floor tile mastic. A Project Monitor should be able to review the building inspection, management plan and project designer specifications. Data, including the survey protocol and the analytical methods is used to determine if the information is adequate for design specifications. Asbestos removal is one of a variety of options for asbestos hazard control. A well written project design, accompanied by careful project management is the key to successfully removing asbestos from a facility without contaminating the building environment.

Objectives: To provide an overview of the major asbestos-related regulations affecting asbestos.

> **EPA 40 CFR part 763 AHERA**
> **OSHA 29 CFR 1910.1101 Asbestos**
> **EPA 40 CFR part 61m NESHAP**
> **OSHA 29 CFR 1910.134 Respirator Protection**
> **State Regulations**

Learning Tasks: Information in this chapter should enable participants to:

- Become familiar with the general provisions of major federal asbestos-related regulations.

- Learn details of the major regulations pertaining to abatement projects and/or personnel.

INTRODUCTION

Two federal agencies have been principally responsible for generating regulations for asbestos control. These two agencies are the U.S. Occupational Safety and Health Administration (OSHA) and the U.S. Environmental Protection Agency (EPA).

Other federal agencies promulgating regulations on asbestos include the Department of Transportation (DOT) – MSHA, and NIOSH regulations regarding the transport of asbestos; the National Institute of Standards and Technology (NIST) – establishing standards and protocols for laboratory accreditation, and the Consumer Product Safety Commission – banning asbestos in some products. Exhibit 1 presents a chronology of major federal initiatives regarding asbestos. These initiatives span the period of the early 1970's through the present.

A summary of OSHA and EPA regulations follows. Specifically covered are the OSHA Asbestos Standards; the EPA Worker Protection Rule; the National Emission Standards for Hazardous Air Pollutants (NESHAP); the Asbestos Hazard Emergency Response Act (AHERA), the Asbestos Ban and Phase-Down Rule, and the Asbestos School Hazard Abatement Reauthorization Act (ASHARA).

U.S. OCCUPATIONAL SAFETY AND HEALTH ADMINISTRATION ASBESTOS STANDARDS

The (OSHA) Occupational Safety and Health Administration has established three sets of regulations that address asbestos exposure:

29 CFR 1910.1001	-	General Industry
29 CFR 1926.1101	-	Construction Industry
29 CFR 1910.134	-	Use of Respirators (General)

The construction-industry standard covers employees engaged in demolition and construction, and the following related activities are likely to involve asbestos exposure:

- removal;
- encapsulation;
- alteration;
- repair;
- maintenance;
- installation;
- spill/emergency clean-up;
- transportation;
- disposal;
- storage of ACM.

The general-industry standard covers all other operations where exposure to asbestos is possible, including exposure to occupants of buildings that contain ACM. In most cases, however, levels of airborne asbestos are not expected to reach the exposure standards in these buildings.

In general, OSHA coverage extends to all private-sector employers and employees in the 50 states and all territories under federal jurisdiction. Those not covered under the standard include self-employed persons, certain state and local government employees, and federal employees covered under other federal statutes. Persons engaged in inspection, management planning, and other asbestos-related work fall under OSHA's construction industry standard.

To enforce its standards, OSHA is authorized to conduct workplace inspections. In addition, employees have the right to file an OSHA complaint without fear of punishment from the employer. In turn, employees have the responsibility to follow all safety and health rules. OSHA may not conduct a warrantless inspection without the employer's consent. Citations are issued by OSHA during an inspection if the compliance officer finds a standard being violated. The citation informs the employer and employees of the regulations or standards alleged to have been violated and of the proposed length of time for correction. Monetary penalties may also be imposed.

OSHA CONSTRUCTION INDUSTRY STANDARD

The following highlights of 29 CFR 1926.1101 are condensed for easy reference. Participants are encouraged to become familiar with the OSHA standard as it appears in the *Federal Register*.

Exposure Levels

- Permissible Exposure Limits (PEL) – comprised of an 8 hour TWA (time weighted average) of 0.1 f/cc (fibers per cubic centimeter)
- and a 30 minute Excursion Limit (EL) of 1.0 f/cc

Asbestos-containing material is any material containing more than 1% asbestos.

Asbestos work classifications:

Class I: activities involving the removal of TSI and/or surfacing ACM/PACM

Class II: activities involving the removal of ACM, which is not TSI or surfacing material

Class III: repair and maintenance operations where ACM, including TSI and surfacing materials, is likely to be disturbed

Class IV: maintenance and custodial activities during which employees contact but do not disturb ACM/PACM, and activities to clean up dust, waste and debris resulting from Class I, II, or III activities

Asbestos Terminology:

Competent Person is one who is capable of identifying existing asbestos hazards in the workplace, capable of selecting the appropriate control strategy, and having the authority to take prompt corrective measures. Personnel must be trained to meet the criteria of EPA Model Accreditation Plan for project designers or contractors/supervisors for Class I and II work, and training covering the topics listed in EPA's 16-hour O&M training program for Class III and IV work.

Negative exposure assessment is a demonstration by an employer that an employee's exposure during an operation is expected to be consistently below the PELs.

Presumed asbestos-containing material (PACM) is TSI and surfacing material found in buildings constructed no later than 1980.

Regulated area is an area established by an employer to demarcate where Class I, II, and III asbestos work is being conducted, and any adjoining area where debris and waste accumulate. It also includes any area where airborne asbestos levels are anticipated to exceed the PELs.

Exposure Assessment and Monitoring

Initial Monitoring

Employers who have a workplace or work operation covered by this standard must perform initial monitoring to determine the airborne concentrations of asbestos to which employees may be exposed. This assessment must be conducted by a competent person before or at the initiation of the work or activity. If employers can demonstrate that employee exposures are below the excursion limit by means of:

- objective data, or
- personal air sampling results collected from the previous 12 months, or
- initial monitoring for the current job

The former "initial monitoring" provisions allowed use of historic data. OSHA now requires the evaluation of data from earlier asbestos jobs to estimate exposures and new jobs. However, the "data" reviewed are more than air monitoring results. This record has convinced the Agency that consideration of factors in successfully controlling asbestos exposures needs to be a part of the assessment. In addition to measurement results, the assessment must review relevant controls and conditions, factors that influence the degree of exposure. These include, but are not limited to, the degree and quality of supervision and of employee training, techniques used for wetting the ACM in the various circumstances encountered, placing and repositioning the ventilation equipment, and impacts due to weather conditions.

The assessment, therefore, must be based on the competent person's review of all aspects of the employer's performance doing similar jobs. Only if similar controls are used and the work supervised by the same or similarly trained personnel, may past data be relied on. In addition, the results of initial monitoring required if feasible, must inform the competent person's assessment. Judgment of the "competent person" is required when reviewing records of past work. For example, even where an employer's earlier glove bag removals produced some exposures above the PEL, if more recent glove bag removals by the same crew show no exceedances, the "competent person" may be warranted in predicting that the current job performed by the same crew will be well controlled and exposures will not exceed the PELs.

Periodic Monitoring

Periodic monitoring is required to be conducted daily within a regulated area for all Class I and II work, unless:

- a negative exposure assessment has been made, or
- all employees in a regulated area are wearing supplied air respirators operated in the pressure demand mode, or other positive pressure mode respirator.

However, if Class I work is performed using a control method not listed by OSHA in the regulations, or if a listed method is modified, periodic monitoring must be conducted regardless of the type of respirator worn.

If daily monitoring indicates that employee exposures are below the PEL/EL, then no further monitoring is required. Employees must be given the chance to observe the monitoring, and all monitored employees must be notified of the monitoring results as soon as possible.

Regulated Areas

The employer must establish a regulated area in those areas where 1) Class I, II, or III activities will occur, or 2) where airborne asbestos concentrations exceed, or there is a reasonable possibility that airborne concentrations of asbestos will exceed the PEL and/or EL. Only authorized personnel may enter regulated areas.

The following requirements apply to a regulated area:

- mark the area to minimize the number of persons within the regulated area and to protect persons outside the area;
- limit access to authorized personnel only;
- use respirators in accordance with paragraph H of the OSHA Construction Standard;
- prohibit eating, drinking, smoking, chewing, and the application of cosmetics in the regulated area;
- competent persons must supervise work within the regulated area.

Warning signs must be displayed and must be posted at all approaches to regulated areas. These signs must bear the following information:

> **DANGER**
> **ASBESTOS**
> **CANCER AND LUNG DISEASE**
> **HAZARD**
> **AUTHORIZED**
> **PERSONNEL ONLY**

In addition, where respirators and protective clothing are required within the regulated area, the warning signs must include the words:

Respirators and protective clothing are required in this area.

The employer shall ensure that employees working in and contiguous to regulated areas comprehend these warning signs. This may be accomplished through the use of foreign language wording, pictographs, and graphics.

Warning labels must be affixed on all asbestos products and to all containers containing asbestos products, including waste containers. The label must include the following information and must be black, white, and red in color:

> **DANGER**
> **CONTAINS ASBESTOS FIBERS**
> **AVOID CREATING DUST**
> **CANCER AND LUNG DISEASE**
> **HAZARD**

Multi-Employer Worksite

When an asbestos project is being conducted at a multi-employer worksite, the employer performing work requiring the establishment of a regulated area must inform other employers of:

- the nature of the work,
- the existence/requirements of regulated areas,
- measures to protect the other employers' personnel.

Methods of Compliance

To the extent feasible, engineering and work practice controls must be used to reduce employee exposure to below the PEL and/or EL. Regardless of exposure levels, the following control methods must be used for all activities:

- HEPA vacuums to collect debris and dust;
- wet methods; and
- prompt cleanup and disposal of waste and debris.

In addition to the methods above, the following control methods must be used to comply with the PEL/EL:

- local exhaust ventilation,
- enclosure or isolation of the work process,
- ventilation of the regulated area,
- other feasible work practices or engineering controls.

Work practices that are prohibited include:

- the use of high speed abrasive disk saws,
- compressed air,
- dry sweeping,
- employee rotation to reduce exposures.

<u>Class I Requirements:</u>

In addition to the work practices and control methods presented above, the following methods of compliance shall be used:

- all work must be supervised by a competent person;
- isolate the heating, ventilation, and cooling system;
- use impermeable drop cloths beneath all removal activity;
- cover all non-movable objects
- ventilate the regulated area to move dust away from the employee;

Chapter 3 – Federal Asbestos Regulations

- use critical barriers or other isolation system in combination with perimeter air monitoring if:
  - the job involves >25 linear feet or >10 square feet of TSI/surfacing material;
  - where a negative exposure assessment has not been done, or
  - where employees are working adjacent to Class I activity.

One or more of the following specific control methods must be utilized when conducting Class I asbestos activities:

- enclosures
- glove bags
- negative pressure glove bag
- negative pressure glove box
- water spray process
- small, walk-in enclosures
- alternate control method certified by a CIH or PE who is a project designer.

Class II Requirements:

- competent person supervision
- indoor removals without a negative exposure assessment must:
  - use critical barriers
  - other feasible barrier/isolation methods
  - listed work practices for each type of work
  - employees must be trained and use work practices/controls specifically outlined in the standard based on the type of material involved (i.e., flooring, roofing, gaskets, etc.)

Class III Requirements:

- minimize exposure to individual performing work and bystanders
- use local exhaust when feasible
- use mini-enclosures or glovebag systems when cutting, drilling, abrading, sanding, chipping, breaking, or sawing TSI and/or surfacing material
- if exposures are above the PEL/EL or a negative exposure assessment was not performed:
  - contain area using drop cloths and plastic barriers, or
  - isolate area using negative pressure enclosure, glovebag, etc
- use respirator if:
  - disturbing TSI or surfacing material
  - PEL/EL exceeded
  - a negative exposure assessment is not available

Class IV Requirements

Work practices required include:
- use of wet methods
- use of HEPA vacuums
- prompt action to clean up ACM/PACM debris
- following paragraph H respirator requirements
- assume waste and debris in areas with accessible (friable) TSI and surfacing materials contains asbestos

Respiratory Protection

An employer must provide respirators and ensure they are used:

- during all Class I work;
- during all Class II work where ACM is not removed substantially intact;
- during all Class II and III work that is not performed wet;
- during all Class II and II work where TSI or surfacing ACM/PACM is disturbed;
- during all Class IV work within a regulated area where other employees are required to wear respirators;

19

- during all work where exposures exceed the PEL or EL; and in emergencies.

Respirators must be selected according to the provisions of 30CFR Part 11. The employers must develop a respiratory program in accordance with the Respirator Standard for General Industry (29 CFR 1910.134).

Employees who use a filter respirator must change filters whenever an increase in breathing resistance is detected. Employees who wear respirators must be allowed to wash their face and respirator facepiece whenever necessary to prevent skin irritation associated with respirator use. An employee must not be assigned to tasks requiring the use of respirators if a physician determines that the employee is unable to function normally while wearing a respirator, or that the employee's safety and health or that of others would be affected by the employee's use of a respirator. In this case, the employer must assign the employee to another job or give the employee the opportunity to transfer to a different job that does not require the use of a respirator. The job should be with the same employer, in the same geographical area, and with the same seniority, status, and rate of pay, if such a position is available.

Employers must assure that a respirator issued to an employee fits properly and exhibits minimum facepiece leakage. Employers must perform quantitative or qualitative fit tests at the time of initial fitting and at least every six months for each employee wearing negative-pressure respirators.

Protective Clothing

An employer must provide and require the use of protective clothing such as coveralls or similar full-body clothing, head coverings, gloves, and foot coverings:

- for any employee exposed to airborne concentrations of asbestos that exceed the PEL and/or EL;
- in situations where a negative exposure assessment was required and not performed; and
- for Class I work involving TSI or surfacing material in amounts exceeding 25 linear feet or 10 square feet.

Wherever the possibility of eye irritation exists, face shields, vented goggles, or other appropriate protective equipment must be provided and worn.

Asbestos-contaminated work clothing must be removed in change rooms and placed and stored in closed, labeled containers that prevent dispersion of the asbestos into the ambient environment. Protective clothing and equipment must be cleaned, laundered, repaired, or replaced to maintain their effectiveness.

The employer must inform any person who launders or cleans asbestos-contaminated clothing or equipment of the potentially harmful effects of exposure to asbestos. Contaminated clothing and equipment taken out of change rooms or the workplace for cleaning, maintenance or disposal must be transported in sealed impermeable bags, or other closed impermeable containers and be appropriately labeled.

Hygiene Facilities and Practices

The requirements for hygiene facilities and practices differ based on the class of work activity involved.

Class I Work (>25 linear feet or 10 square feet)

- the employer must provide clean change areas equipped with separate storage facilities for protective clothing and street clothing;
- the employer must provide lunch areas in which the airborne concentrations of asbestos are below the PEL/EL;
- the employer must establish a decontamination area for the decontamination of asbestos-contaminated employees that is adjacent and connected to the regulated area.

Clean rooms must be equipped with a locker or appropriate storage container for each employee. Equipment rooms must be supplied with impermeable, labeled bags and containers for the containment and disposal of asbestos-contaminated protective clothing and equipment. Where feasible, shower facilities must be contiguous to the equipment room and the clean change room. When contiguous decontamination facilities are not feasible, the workers must remove contamination from suits or put on clean protective clothing, then proceed to the shower. Employers must ensure that employees enter and exit the regulated area through the decontamination area.

Class I, II, and III Work

The following hygiene facility and practice requirements apply to Class I work involving less than 25 linear feet or 10 square feet of material, and Class II and III work if exposures exceed the PEL or if a negative exposure assessment has not been done:

- establish equipment room adjacent to the regulated area;
- all equipment/containers and clothing must be cleaned prior to removal from the equipment room;
- employees must enter and exit through the equipment room.

Class IV Work

- employees cleaning up TSI or surfacing materials must be provided an area to decontaminate equipment and personnel;
- employees working in a regulated area must meet hygiene practices requirements of the regulated area.

An employer shall ensure that employees do not smoke in work areas where they are occupationally exposed to asbestos because of activities in that work area.

Information and Training

An employer must provide training, at no cost to the employee, for all employees who install asbestos-containing products, or who perform Class I, II, III, or IV asbestos operations. Training must be provided prior to or at the time of initial assignment and at least yearly thereafter. OSHA bases its training requirements on the type of activity being conducted.

- training for Class I operations must be the equivalent of the 4-day asbestos abatement worker training outlined in the EPA Model Accreditation Plan;
- training for Class II operations which involve asbestos-containing roofing materials, flooring materials, siding materials, ceiling tiles, or transite panels must include training topics outlined by OSHA, including hands-on, for a minimum of 8 hours. Other Class II activity training must cover OSHA-required topics, include hands-on training, and cover the OSHA work practices and engineering control requirements detailed for Class II work.
- training for Class III operations must be the equivalent of the 16-hour maintenance and custodial training detailed in the AHERA regulations;
- training for Class IV operations must be equivalent to the requirements for EPA 2-hour awareness training outlined in AHERA.

All training programs must inform employees about the:

- methods of recognizing asbestos,
- health hazards of asbestos exposure,
- relationship between asbestos and smoking in producing lung cancer,
- operations that could result in asbestos exposure,
- importance of necessary protective controls to minimize exposure including, as applicable, engineering controls, work practices, respirators, housekeeping procedures, emergency procedures, and waste disposal procedures,
- purpose, proper use and limitations of respirators,
- the medical surveillance program,
- a complete review of the OSHA standard(s) including appendices.

The employer is also required to inform all employees concerning the availability of self-help smoking cessation program material and to provide the names, addresses and phone numbers of public health organizations that provide information, materials and/or conduct programs concerning smoking cessation. Appendix J of the construction standard, which contains a list of such organizations, may be used to comply with this requirement.

The training must also cover the requirements for posting signs and affixing labels and the meaning of the required legends for such signs and labels.

If an employer's Class II work involves only the removal and/or disturbance of one generic category of building material, for example roofing materials, flooring materials, siding, etc., the employer is required to provide training that includes all the information listed above, including a "hands-on" component, and be at least eight hours in length.

All training materials must be available to the employees without cost and, upon request, to the Assistant Secretary for OSHA and the Director of the National Institute for Occupational Safety and Health (NIOSH).

Housekeeping

Vacuuming equipment, when used, must have HEPA filters. Dust and debris in areas with accessible TSI, surfacing material or visibly deteriorated ACM must be HEPA vacuumed and **not** dry swept. Asbestos waste, scrap, debris, bags, containers, equipment, and asbestos-contaminated clothing consigned for disposal must be collected and disposed of in sealed, labeled, impermeable bags or other closed, labeled impermeable containers.

Medical Surveillance

The employer must establish a medical surveillance program, prior to assignment, for all employees who 1) will be required to wear respirators, 2) will be engaged in Class I, II, and III work for 30 or more days per year, or 3) will be exposed to airborne concentrations of asbestos at or above the PEL and/or EL.

All examinations must be performed under the supervision of a licensed physician and shall be provided without cost to the employee and at a reasonable time and place.

Examinations conducted pursuant to the Asbestos Standard for the Construction Industry must include:

- completion of a respiratory disease questionnaire;
- a medical and work history;
- a physical examination with special emphasis directed to the respiratory, cardiovascular, and gastrointestinal systems;
- a pulmonary function test.

A chest xray may be administered at the discretion of the physician. These examinations must be made available annually, or more often if the physician deems it necessary.

The employer must give the examining physician a copy of the standard, a description of the employee's duties relating to the employee's asbestos exposure; the exposure level or anticipated exposure level; a description of any personal protective and respiratory equipment used or to be used; and information from previous medical examinations. Also, employers must obtain a written signed opinion from the physician that contains: the results of the medical examination and the physician's opinion as to whether the employee has any detected medical conditions that would place the employee at an increased risk from exposure to asbestos, any recommended limitations on the employee or upon the use of personal protective equipment such as clothing or respirators, and statements that the employee has been informed by the physician of the increased risk of lung cancer attributable to the combined effects of smoking and working with asbestos and the results of the medical examination. The physician is not to reveal in the written opinion given to the employer specific findings or diagnoses unrelated to occupational exposure to asbestos. Finally, the employer must provide a copy of the physician's written opinion to the affected employee within 30 days from its receipt.

Recordkeeping

Employers must keep an accurate record of all measurements taken to monitor employee exposure to asbestos. This record should include the date of measurement, operation or activity involving exposure, sampling and analytical methods used and evidence of their accuracy; number, duration, and results of samples taken; type of respiratory protective devices worn; and name, social security number, and the results of all employee exposure measurements. These records must be kept for 30 years.

Employers who have relied on objective data as a negative exposure assessment must establish and maintain an accurate record of this data in support of the monitoring exemption. This data must include the product qualifying for the exemption; the source of the data; the testing protocol, results of testing and/or analysis of the material for release of asbestos; a description of the operation exempted and how the data support the exemption; and other data relevant to the operations materials, processing, or employee exposures covered by the exemption. These records shall be maintained for as long as the employer relies on the data for exemptions.

Likewise, the employer must maintain an accurate record for each employee subject to medical surveillance. The record must include: the name and social security number of the employee; a copy of the employee's medical examination results; physician's written opinions; any employee medical complaints related to exposure to asbestos; and information provided to the examining physician as described under medical surveillance. This record must be maintained for the duration of employment plus 30 years.

The employer must maintain all employee training records for one year beyond the last date of employment by that employee.

All records must be made available on request to the Assistant Secretary for OSHA, the Director of the National Institute for Occupational Safety and Health (NIOSH), affected employees, former employees, and designated representatives. When the employer ceases to do business and there is no successor employer to receive the records for the prescribed period, the employer must notify the Director of NIOSH at least 90 days prior to disposal of records.

U.S. ENVIRONMENTAL PROTECTION AGENCY
ASBESTOS REGULATIONS

NATIONAL EMISSION STANDARDS FOR HAZARDOUS AIR POLLUTANTS (NESHAP)

EPA's rules concerning the application, removal, and disposal of asbestos-containing materials were issued under NESHAP. Also included in NESHAP are rules concerning manufacturing, spraying, and fabricating of asbestos-containing material. NESHAP clarifies requirements regarding removal and disposal of asbestos-containing materials.

Bans on Asbestos-containing Material

Three bans on asbestos-containing material were set forth by the NESHAP regulations. These bans occurred in the three years as indicated below:

    1973 - Spray-applied fireproofing/insulating materials
    1976 - Pre-molded insulation, if friable
    1978 - Spray-applied decorative material

NESHAP Definitions (Selected)

Category I nonverbal ACM includes asbestos-containing packing, gaskets, resilient floor coverings and asphalt roofing products containing more than 1% asbestos. (Category I nonfriable ACM has been interpreted to include pliable asbestos-containing sealants and mastics since they exhibit many of the same characteristics of Category I nonfriable asbestos-containing material.)

Category II Nonfriable ACM includes any material, excluding Category I nonfriable ACM, containing more than 1% asbestos that, when dry cannot be crumbled, pulverized, or reduced to powder by hand pressure.

Friable asbestos material includes any material containing more than 1% asbestos that, when dry, can be crumbled, pulverized, or reduced to powder by hand pressure.

Regulated asbestos-containing material (RACM) includes

- friable ACM;
- Category I nonfriable ACM that has become friable;
- Category I nonfriable ACM that will be or has been subjected to sanding, grinding, cutting, or abrading;
- Category II nonfriable ACM that has a high probability of becoming or has become crumbled, pulverized, or reduced to powder by the forces expected to act on the material in the course of demolition or renovation operations regulated by NESHAP.

Waste Generator includes any owner or operator of a source whose act or process produces asbestos-containing waste material.

Analytical Methods

Polarized light microscopy (PLM) analysis of bulk samples is required by NESHAP to determine the asbestos content of ACM, if the asbestos content is less than 10% as determined by a method other than point counting using PLM, or by analyzing the sample three times by PLM.

Notification

Specific notification to a regional or state NESHAP Coordinator is required before a building is demolished or renovated. This written notification must be delivered by U.S. Postal Service, commercial delivery service, or hand delivery.

Some states have notification requirements for removal of RACM in amounts less than federal NESHAP, and/or regulate nonfriable materials. Check with the state agency responsible for NESHAP notification before any project begins.

NESHAP SUMMARY

	DEMOLITION		DEMOLITON BY ORDER	RENOVATION	
AMOUNT OF RACM	>260 if 160 ft2 or 5 ft3	<160 ft^2 if, 160 ft^2 or 35 ft3		> 260 lf, 160 ft^2 or 35 ft^3	>260 lf, 160 ft^2 or 35 ft^3
NOTIFICATION	Yes all requirements apply	Yes Simple Notification	Same as for demolition	Yes all requirements apply	Consider yearly (additive) amounts
HOW FAR IN ADVANCE?	10 days	10 days	As early as possible, but not later than the following day*	10 days	At least 10 working days prior to end of calendar year**

*Also include name, title & authority of government representative, date order issued and date which demolition was ordered to begin. A copy of the order shall be attached to the notification.
** Update notice, as necessary, including when the amount of asbestos affected changes by at least 20 percent.

NESHAP "days" are "working days" which include Monday through Friday except holidays which fall on any of the days Monday through Friday.

NESHAP requires the removal of all RACM from a facility being demolished or renovated before any activity begins that would break up, dislodge, or similarly disturb the material or preclude access to the material for subsequent removal.

The material must be removed using wet removal techniques unless temperatures are below freezing. (With special approval from EPA, dry removal is allowed under certain circumstances.) No visible emissions to the outside air are permitted during removal or renovation.

If a facility is demolished by intentional burning, all RACM including Category I and Category II nonfriable ACM must be removed in accordance with NESHAP before burning.

The following information is required on the notification:

(NOTE: In a facility being demolished, if the combined amount of RACM is less than 260 lf, 160 sf, or 35 cf, only simple notification requirements apply. This notification must include the information in **bold typeface** below, with the 10-day notification requirement also applying.

- **An indication of whether the notice is the original or a revised notification;**
- **Name, address and phone number of both the facility owner and operator, and the asbestos removal contractor owner or operator;**
- **Type of operation: demolition or renovation;**
- **Description of the facility or affected part of the facility including the size (square feet and number of floors), age and present and prior use of the facility;**
- **Procedures, including analytical methods, employed to detect the presence of RACM and Category I and Category II nonfriable ACM;**
- **Estimate of the approximate amount of RACM to be removed from the facility; also estimate the approximate amount of Category I and Category II nonfriable ACM in the affected part of the facility that will not be removed before demolition;**
- **Location and street address (including building number or name and floor or room numbers, if appropriate), city, county, and state of the facility being demolished or renovated;**
- Scheduled starting and completion dates for asbestos removal work (or any other activity, such as site preparation that would break up, dislodge, or similarly disturb asbestos material) in a demolition or renovation; planned renovation operations involving individual nonscheduled operations shall only include the beginning and ending dates of the report period;
- **Scheduled starting and completion dates of demolition or renovation;**
- Description of planned demolition and renovation work to be performed and methods;
- Description of work practices and engineering controls to be used to comply with the requirements of NESHAP, including asbestos removal and waste-handling emission control procedures;
- Name and location of the waste disposal site where the asbestos-containing waste material will be deposited;
- A certification that at least one on-site representative (such as a foreman or management level person) trained in the asbestos demolition or renovation provisions and the means of complying with them, be present when RACM is stripped, removed, or otherwise handled or disturbed as described by this notification;
- If demolition is under order form a state or local agency, the name, title, and authority of the state or local government representative who ordered the demolition, the date that the order was issued, and the date on which the demolition was ordered to begin. A copy of the order shall be attached to the notification;
- For emergency renovations, the date and hour that the emergency occurred, a description of the sudden, unexpected event, and an explanation of how the event caused an unsafe
- condition, or would cause equipment damage or an unreasonable financial burden;
- **Description of procedures to be followed in the event that unexpected RACM is found or Category II nonfriable ACM becomes crumbed, pulverized, or reduced to powder;**
- Name, address, and telephone number of the waste transporter.

Below are listed the exemptions from removal according to NESHAP:

- It is Category I nonfriable ACM that is not in poor condition and is not friable.
- It is on a facility component that is encased in concrete or other similarly hard material and is adequately wet whenever exposed during demolition.
- It was not accessible for testing and was, therefore, not discovered until after demolition began and as a result of the demolition, the material cannot be safely removed. If not removed for safety reasons, the exposed RACM and any asbestos-containing debris must be treated as asbestos-containing waste material and adequately wet at all times until disposed of.
- The material is Category II nonfriable ACM and the probability is low that the materials will become crumbled, pulverized, or reduced to powder during demolition. [NOTE: EPA has determined that any demolition operation (i.e., use of a wrecking ball, implosion, use of a bulldozer, backhoe, or other heavy machinery to knock a building over) will extensively damage Category II ACM such that it is crumbled, pulverized, or reduced to powder.

Waste Disposal
Below are listed the waste disposal provisions required under NESHAP.

- No visible emissions to the outside air are allowed during collection, packaging, transportation, or deposition of ACM waste.
- Wet ACM must be sealed in a leak-tight container.
- Containers must be labeled with OSHA warning labels.
- For waste that will be transported off the site of the facility, label all containers or wrapped materials with the name of the waste generator and the location at which the waste was generated.
- Mark vehicles used to transport asbestos-containing waste material during the loading and unloading of waste so that the signs are visible.
- Maintain waste shipment records using a form similar to Figure 4 included in the NESHAP regulations (see Figure XV-3 at the end of the *Waste Disposal* chapter). A copy of the waste shipment record must be provided to the disposal site owners or operators at the same time as the asbestos-containing waste material is delivered to the disposal site. A copy of the waste shipment record, signed by the owner or operator of the designated disposal site must be returned to the waste generator within 35 days.

Since NESHAP mandates the removal of friable ACM before a building is demolished or renovated, if the renovation will disturb the ACM, any plan for managing ACM should take into account the costs of eventual removal. Certain abatement methods, such as encapsulation and enclosure, may make eventual removal more difficult.

ASBESTOS HAZARD EMERGENCY RESPONSE ACT

In October 1986, the Asbestos Hazard Emergency Response Act (AHERA) was signed into law. Included in this Act were provisions directing the EPA to establish rules and regulations addressing asbestos-containing materials in schools. Specifically, EPA was directed to address the issues of: (1) identifying, (2) evaluating, and (3) controlling ACM in schools.

Final AHERA regulations (rules) became effective 14 December 1987.

They are found in 40 CFR 763 Subpart E sections §763.80 - §763.99 under the Toxic Substances Control Act (TSCA).

The regulations require that all public and private elementary and secondary schools (K-12) inspect for both friable and nonfriable asbestos, implement response actions, and submit asbestos management plans to state governors or designated agencies.

Schools must use accredited persons to:
- conduct inspections,
- develop management plans, and
- design or conduct response actions.

Also, the rule requires periodic surveillance and re-inspection to monitor asbestos-containing materials left in schools. Periodic surveillance requires checking these materials every six months to determine if there has been a change in condition of the material since the last inspection or surveillance. In addition, schools must have an accredited inspector re-inspect and reassess the condition of remaining asbestos-containing materials every three years and determine if the condition of the material requires new response action activity.

Schools that fail to conduct the inspections, knowingly submit false evidence to their governors, or fail to develop a management plan in accordance with regulations, can be assessed a civil penalty under the Toxic Substances Control Act (TSCA) of up to $5,000 for each day the school is in violation. AHERA also provides that civil penalties assessed will be used by schools to comply with AHERA requirements. Unspent portions of the assessed civil penalties will be deposited in a federal Asbestos Trust Fund. These monies will be made available for further asbestos abatement activities.

Schools that had previously conducted inspections consistent with this final rule, and had determined that no asbestos-containing material is present in the schools, were excluded from the inspection requirements. In addition, a school is exempt if it was built after 12 October 1988, and an architect, project engineer or accredited inspector signed a statement that no asbestos-containing material had been specified for use in construction documents. States may receive a waiver from some or all of the requirements of the proposed rule if they have established ,and are implementing (or intend to implement), a program of asbestos inspection and management at least as stringent as the requirements of the final rule.

ASBESTOS: MANUFACTURE, IMPORTATION, PROCESSING AND DISTRIBUTION IN COMMERCE PROHIBITIONS; FINAL RULE (BAN AND PHASE-OUT RULE)

On July 7, 1989, EPA announced the promulgation of its long-awaited asbestos ban and phase-down rule. This rule, which was phased in over a seven-year period beginning in 1990, prohibited the manufacture, importation, processing, and distribution of certain commercially available asbestos-containing products. This rule would have effectively banned the use of nearly 95% of all asbestos products used in the United States, with the exception of products for which no acceptable substitute has been found, and certain products for military use.

EPA had adopted separate dates for the banning of the manufacture, importation, and processing of asbestos-containing products, and for the distribution of asbestos-containing products in commerce. However, this regulation was vacated by the Fifth Circuit Court of Appeals in October, 1991. EPA appealed the court's decision and the appeal was rejected on 27 November, 1991.

The court did allow EPA to ban new uses of certain asbestos-containing products and those products that were not being manufactured, imported, or processed on the date the final rule was issued (12 July 1989). EPA issued a notice in the *Federal Register* that requested information on the status of 14 product categories included in the rule that were not being manufactured, processed, or imported when the final rule was published. Based on the research conducted by EPA, and information provided by commenters, EPA published in the 5 November 1993 *Federal Register* the following six asbestos-containing products that are still subject to the Ban and Phase-out Rule:

- corrugated paper
- rollboard
- commercial paper
- specialty paper
- flooring felt, and
- new uses of asbestos.

ASBESTOS SCHOOL HAZARD ABATEMENT REAUTHORIZATION ACT (ASHARA) [covering Public and Commercial Buildings]

Section 206 of the Toxic Substances Control Act (TSCA) mandated that EPA develop an asbestos Model Accreditation Plan (MAP). The original MAP was promulgated in 1987 and became codified as 40 CFR Part 763, Appendix C to Subpart E. Section 206 of TSCA was later amended by the Asbestos School Hazard Abatement Reauthorization Act (ASHARA). ASHARA mandated that the MAP be revised to:

- provide for the extension of accreditation requirements to the interior of public and commercial buildings for persons who inspect for asbestos-containing material, design response actions, or carry out response actions; and
- increase the minimum number of training hours, including additional hand-on training, required for accreditation of workers and supervisors performing work in schools and/or public and commercial buildings.

ASHARA does not require persons who prepare management plans in public or commercial buildings to obtain accreditation. The accreditation requirements of the ASHARA statute went into effect on 28 November 1992.

The revised MAP, which provides more information ,the meaning of the new statutory requirements and expands the length of, and/or topics addressed in the training courses, was published as an interim final rule in the *Federal Register* on 3 February 1994, and took effect on 4 April 1994.

ASHARA requires that accredited asbestos abatement contractors/supervisors and accredited workers be used to supervise or carry out:

- response actions other than a small-scale, short duration activity,
- maintenance activities that disturb friable asbestos-containing material other than a small-scale, short duration activity,
- a response action for a major fiber release episode (the accidental or unintentional falling or dislodging of greater than 3 square or 3 linear feet of ACM.)

HAZARD COMMUNICATION STANDARD
29 CFR 1910.1200

OSHA has expanded this standard to include the construction industry. The purpose of this standard is to ensure that the hazards of chemicals or materials used in the workplace are identified and that this information, along with information on protective measures, is passed on to employers and employees. Elements required under this standard include:

- Comprehensive written hazard communication program;
- Labeling of hazardous materials;
- Maintaining material safety data sheets;
- Employee training.

Employers are required to inform affected workers about hazardous chemicals they may be exposed to through:

1. A written Hazard Communication Program which must include:

   a. Plans to meet the criteria of the standard relating to the labeling, material safety data sheets, and employee training.

   b. A list of all hazardous substances found in the workplace.

   c. The methods to be used to inform employees and outside contractors of hazards of non-routine tasks.

   d. The hazards associated with chemicals contained in unlabeled pipes or vessels in the work area. This also applies to hazardous materials released while using a product.

   e. The methods to be used to inform outside contractors who may work on the premises of the hazards to their employees.

2. Material Safety Data Sheets. All chemicals used in the workplace must have material safety data sheets available which must include all health hazard exposures, as well as physical hazards and emergency procedures. All material safety data sheets must be accessible by all employees during any working time, which includes all three shifts as applicable.

3. Labels. All containers in the workplace must be labeled, marked, or tagged with the identity of the hazardous material contained and the appropriate hazard warning, and the name and address of a responsible party.

4. Employee Training. Employees exposed to any hazardous chemicals in their work environment must be educated as to:

   a. The requirements of this standard.

   b. The operations involving hazardous chemicals, the location and accessibility of the material safety data sheets, and the location and content of the written hazard communication program.

   c. The methods and observations that may be used to detect hazardous chemicals.

   d. The physical and health hazards of the chemicals in the work area.

   e. Measures employees can take to protect themselves.

   f. How employees can obtain, interpret, and use the information in the written hazard communication program.

Chapter 3 – Federal Asbestos Regulations

It is recommended that you refer to the actual standard for more detailed information.

Exposure to hazardous materials can occur in a number of tasks associated with asbestos abatement work. Examples may include: spray adhesives; surfactants; encapsulants; paints or other products used for lockdown of fibers; materials to be left in the work area; and of course, the asbestos. Training required in the asbestos standard will have to be expanded to include other hazardous materials on the job.

Information on possible hazardous exposures should be reviewed with employees before the exposure occurs so that proper precautions can be taken. Material safety data sheets are available from manufacturers, suppliers of products, and from owners of buildings where hazardous materials are handled in the removal area. Contractors fall under the umbrella of hazard communication programs of building owners who work with hazardous substances, when contractor personnel may be exposed to those materials.

STATE AND LOCAL REGULATIONS

Several provisions in AHERA and ASHARA encourage states to develop their own regulatory programs. For example, states are encouraged to establish and operate training and certification programs for the various categories of asbestos professionals, as long as the programs are at least as stringent as AHERA's Model Plan. In addition, some states have established requirements that exceed EPA's in the area of notification of abatement actions, abatement work practices, and transportation and disposal of asbestos-contaminated waste. Inspectors/management planners should consult state and local regulatory agencies in their areas.

The following exhibit outlines federal agency regulations both by year and by regulatory action.

Exhibit 1 Chronology of Major Federal Initiatives

YEAR	EPA	OSHA	OTHER
1971	Asbestos listed as hazardous Air pollutant.	Existing occupational exposure standard 5 f/cc.	
1973	Standard for milling, manufacturing and building demolition. Spray application of friable material (>1%) prohibited		
1973	No visible emissions.		
1974	Effluent guidelines for manufacturing sources (EPA/FWPCA)		
1975	No visible emissions standard Extended to waste collection, disposal and processing industries not previously covered.		
1976		Occupational exposure standard lowered to 2 f/cc	
1977			Consumer Product Safety Commission prohibition of asbestos in patching compounds and emberizing agents.
1978	All friable spray-on material prohibited, all demolition and renovation covered by no visible emissions standard (EPA/NESHAP)		Controls regarding transport of friable ACM (DOT)

Year			
1979	Technical assistance program to schools initiated to identify and control friable ACM		Controls regarding transport of friable ACM (DOT)
1982	Identification and notification of friable ACM in schools rule (EPA/TSCA).		
	Required reporting of production and exposure data on asbestos (EPA/TSCA).		
1984	EPA/NESHAP standard formally recognized		
	Asbestos School Hazard Abatement Act (ASHAA) loan and grant program to help eliminate hazards		
1986	AHERA	Construction Industry Standard issued. Permissible exposure level lowered to 0.2f/cc and action level of 0.1 f/cc established.	
1987	TSCA amended to reflect AHERA		
	Worker Protection Rule		
1988		Amendment of general and construction industry asbestos standards to include 30-minute excursion limit (1.0 f/cc)	
1989	Ban & Phase-Out Rule		
1990	Extensive NESHAP revisions including Category I & II nonfriable material definitions, point counting and waste disposal manifests.	Court-ordered amendments to asbestos standard for the construction industry regarding informing employees of the hazards of smoking and working with asbestos; employee sign comprehension.	DOT Hazardous Materials Regulations (HMR) 49 CFR Part 107 et. al. published based on UN standards. Included new asbestos classification, hazard communication, packaging and handling requirements.
1991	Fifth Circuit Court of Appeals vacates most of Ban & Phase-out Rule		
1992	ASHAA reauthorized (ASHARA), requiring accreditation of designers, inspectors, contractors/supervisors and workers involved in asbestos detection and remediation in public and commercial buildings.		DOT HRM revised with less stringent requirements when shipping friable asbestos within the United States.
	EPA issues draft list of asbestos products still covered by Ban and		

	Phase-Out Rule.	
1993	EPA published list of asbestos-containing products which are banned from manufacture, importation, processing and distribution.	
1994	ASHARA Interim Final Rule published including revisions to MAP.	Revisions to General and Construction Industry Standards and Issuance of Shipyard Standard
1996		Interpretative letters clarify bulk sample analysis of drywall or gypsum board, joint compound, & tape be performed separately (where feasible), if any of the layers contain >1% worker protection is required.
1998		Interpretative letters clarify that bulk sampling procedures are considered class III operations and hard wall/ceiling plasters and stucco are not considered surfacing materials
1999		Respiratory Protection Standard revised to require fit testing for all tight fitting masks and to be performed at least annually, the assigned protection factors for qualitative fit tests dropped to10 x's, and the approval of mobile quantitative fit testing devices.
2000	Worker Protection Rule amended to incorporate both Construction & General Industry Asbestos Standards	

Chapter 4 – Understand Building Construction and Building Systems

OBJECTIVES:

1. To understand the role of the various design professions in the construction process.

2. To understand how a building is constructed and the relationships of the various building systems.

3. To become familiar with building systems and the terms used to describe them. (HVAC, electrical, etc.)

4. To learn how to scan construction contract documents for a general understanding of a building, and for clues about ACBM in the building.

5. To become familiar with building construction basics, building physical plan layout, and organization.

6. To understand where asbestos is likely to be found in building systems.

7. To understand renovations and the effect of asbestos abatement on building systems.

INTRODUCTION

A Project Monitor should understand interrelationships among building systems, and recognize where asbestos is likely to be found. A Project Monitor should be familiar with blueprints, specifications, and other resource material which may be available for his or her use. Knowledge of how buildings are constructed and operated is vital to conducting a thorough building survey for ACM.

A **building inspection** involves (1) an investigation of records (including previous surveys, plans, specifications, and other documents) for the identification of ACBM, (2) a physical and visual inspection of the building for suspect materials, (3) sampling and analyzing suspect materials to test for asbestos, and (4) assessing the condition and location of the ACBM and other characteristics of the building. More specifically, the inspection process consists of the following steps:

- Review architectural and ―as-built‖ (record) plans, work change orders, and other records for the specification of any materials, which contain asbestos.
- Inspect the building for friable materials, and materials or products which are likely to contain asbestos.
- Delineate <u>homogeneous sampling areas</u> and develop a sampling plan for bulk samples (or assume suspect material contains asbestos).
- Collect samples and have them analyzed for asbestos by an accredited laboratory.
- Collect information on the physical condition and location of all ACBM or other characteristics of the building that may affect the likelihood that ACBM may be disturbed and those fibers may be released and disturbed.

An **Asbestos Project Monitor** is any person, other than the asbestos abatement contractor/supervisor, who oversees the scope, methodology, or quality control on an abatement project, and must maintain a valid project monitor certification. The project monitor is responsible for satisfactory operation of abatement activities. This includes those who act as a ―third party‖ and/or owner's representative capacity. Completion of this course allows an individual to also obtain an air sampling technician certification. The course incorporates extensive practical exercises, a project site visit, and concludes with a 100 question multiple choice examination.

THE INTERRELATIONSHIP OF BUILDING SYSTEMS

Each building is a combination of four basic building systems. These systems are labeled for the specialist responsible for their design and drafting.

The architect is the design professional who has overall responsibility for the project. The architect may hire three consultants -- electrical, mechanical and structural engineers -- to bring specific knowledge to the design team. In addition other consultants (e.g. acoustical engineers, interior designers, kitchen consultants, etc.) may be employed if the specific project warrants.

The structural system is the skeleton of the building and consists of the beams, columns, bearing walls and foundations, which support the loads of the building and its occupants. The mechanical systems are the heating, ventilating and air conditioning (HVAC) and the plumbing systems of the building. The electrical systems are the power and lighting systems of the building.

To provide a complete building, all of these systems must meld into a coherent and consistent facility. The architect's responsibilities are to coordinate these systems, and to choose the finishes and materials, which are not a part of the above-described engineering systems.

PHYSICAL PLAN LAYOUT

When designing a building, the design team is typically faced with limitations, notably occupant and functional requirements, a budget, and building code regulations. Consequently, the physical layout of buildings is usually very simple, with the structural systems being repetitive, and the mechanical and electrical systems being served with minimal runs of ducts, piping and conduit.

In multi-story buildings, the systems are simplified vertically. Generally a utility core runs vertically through the building. From this core, service runs branch to individual floors. Elevators are generally bundled, and stair towers run vertically through the structure.

The structural system is aligned vertically to simplify the skeletal frame. By simplifying the physical plan layout, the design team is able to achieve greater benefit within the restrictions placed upon the project.

MECHANICAL SYSTEMS

Mechanical systems are those systems designed by the mechanical engineer. They include the HVAC system, the plumbing system, and in the eastern regions of the U.S., elevators.

Heating, Ventilating and Air Conditioning (HVAC) Systems

Individual spaces or zones in a building are served by supply and return air and a thermostat to activate the HVAC system. The supply and return may be in ductwork or in a plenum. Plenums are spaces for example, the space above a dropped acoustical ceiling and below the roof or floor above. In many cases, the plenum is used for return air; that is, the air leaves the room, enters the plenum, and is drawn into the mechanical room from the plenum.

All HVAC systems consist of a means of heat transfer. The heat transfer may occur in the central mechanical space or "plant", but in large buildings or complexes it will occur in individual mechanical rooms. From the mechanical room, the supply is sent to individual spaces within the building and the return air is carried back to the mechanical room where it is filtered and re-conditioned. In addition, some make-up air is added to augment any air lost through opening of doors and windows and to provide a source of fresh, outside air to the building.

Heating and/or cooling of indoor air are both called air conditionings. For this reason, you are likely to find "Air Conditioning Plans" included in the sets of working drawings for both heating and cooling systems.

By the engineering definition, heat transfer only occurs when a warmer object gives up some of its heat to a cooler object. Exactly how the transfer occurs is dependent upon the system being used. HVAC systems can be classified as follows:

- **Air Systems**

There are two types of air HVAC systems--single duct and double duct. (This refers to supply only; return is accomplished in yet another duct.) A single duct system delivers either heated or cooled air at a constant temperature from the air conditioning equipment through ductwork. Often, a variable air volume system is used, wherein the air conditioning requirements of a space activate a damper that controls airflow based on those requirements. A terminal reheat unit, located near the point of discharge, may also be used to boost heating.

When a double duct system is used, one duct carries cooled air while the other carries heated air. The two ducts meet at a mixing box, where the amount of heated or cooled air is regulated based on the requirements of the space(s) being served.

- **Water Systems**

Heated and/or cooled water is delivered to a fan coil unit, where the air is introduced. Air is blown across coils as regulated by dampers, again activated by the requirements of the individual space. This air is introduced through a separate duct system from the mechanical or fan room, or from a direct connection to the outside, or may simply be ambient room air.

Water systems are either two or four pipe systems. A two-pipe system has a single supply and a single return pipe (thus the two pipes). With two pipes it is possible to either heat or cool at any given time, but not both at the same time. However, floors with mixed occupancy or exposure to more than one point of the compass often require heating and cooling at the same time. Conversion of a two-pipe system to the heating or cooling cycle requires a shutdown and conversion of the system. This takes a matter of hours, and thus cannot be accomplished on those days where it would be beneficial to heat in the morning and cool in the afternoon.

A four pipe system delivers both heated and cooled water (called "chilled water" as it is supplied by a chiller) at the same time. Two pipes supply and return heated water, and two other pipes supply and return chilled water. The heat transfer coil may then call for whichever water supply is required to meet the space needs.

- **Refrigerant Systems**

These are packaged units that supply heating or cooling directly to a space through a wall or roof. In general, these are used only in specialized installations in commercial buildings.

- **Radiant Systems**

Radiant systems include any number of devices, which are either embedded in the wall or floor assembly, or are set as radiators, usually along an exterior wall. They are usually used for heating and function by radiating heat directly into a space. That is, no air is blown across the heat transfer surface.

The precise HVAC system layout and distribution is a product of the architectural design and engineering analysis of the building.

Since the primary function of the HVAC system is to heat and cool building spaces, insulation is used to inhibit unwanted heat transfer. Insulation is typically found on the outside of boilers (block or board insulation) and on the breeching or the flue which conveys waste gases from the combustion process. Blanket or batt insulation is sometimes found inside ducts, and insulation is sometimes sprayed on the outside of ducts. Each of these types of insulation should be considered suspect. In addition, gasket material on boiler doors, ropes used as filler in openings, valve packing, and fire stop packing and vibration-dampening cloth connecting sections of ductwork may contain asbestos. Pipe insulation is discussed below.

HVAC Systems, which use chilled water, will typically include a cooling tower where excess heat is rejected to outdoor air. (The chilled water does not pass through the cooling tower, but rather tower water from the chiller passes through the tower.)

Cooling tower baffles and sometimes filter media (fill) are constructed with ACM; the slats are frequently transite.

Plumbing Systems

Plumbing systems include any water, gas or other fluid which is piped through a building, and in some cases disposed of as waste. Also considered part of the plumbing system is air when used in a non-HVAC manner, such as compressed air in hospitals.

Plumbing systems consist of piping. (Horizontal pipes are called runs. Vertical pipes are called risers).

The water systems in a building are of four types: consumed, circulated, static, and controlled. The consumed system is potable water for use and consumption by building occupants. Circulated water is water, which is circulated from a "plant" to the HVAC equipment in a two or four pipe system, as described above. Static water is water used for fire protection, and controlled water is water used to maintain relative humidity within the building.

The use of asbestos in plumbing systems is usually for the purpose of temperature control. Generally it can be found on the piping and equipment, which heat water and/or maintain water at a stable temperature. Insulating materials prevent heat loss from hot pipes and equipment and water condensation on the outside of cold pipes and equipment. Thus, insulating ACM is typically limited to consumed and circulated water systems.

In the consumed water system, domestic hot water (DHW) will be insulated to limit heat loss from the point of origin to the point of use. In large building complexes, a single water heater may be installed and a recirculation system will be operated to continually circulate the water from the heater to the points of use. This arrangement saves the user the inconvenience of having to wait for the hot water to arrive from the remote source. Anticipated asbestos use in these installations will be the insulation in and around the water heater and the insulation on the piping throughout the building. In the circulated water system, heating water (HW) and chilled water (CW) are circulated from the boiler and chiller to the air handling units (AHU) in various parts of the building. The temperature at which the HW and CW arrive in the AHU's directly affects the potential of heat transfer. To maintain the temperature from the source to the point of use, insulation is required along the entire pipe runs. This insulation may contain asbestos.

In addition to plumbing insulation, asbestos cement pipe may have been used in the plumbing systems, waste systems and roof drains. The pipe is concrete-like in appearance and is known by the trade name "Transite".

ELECTRICAL SYSTEMS

Electrical systems within a building may appear very complex, but are simple in their basic design. Each building includes an electric service entrance, the point where the energy enters the building. This is where the meters are located.

In large buildings, transformers will be set on site to reduce the high voltage supply from the electric company to the lower voltage used within the building. In smaller buildings, the transformer will be outside the building, either on a pad or on a pole. Once the voltage has been reduced the service is then divided into individual circuits. The size and capacity of each circuit is based on the anticipated energy requirements of items served by that circuit. The division into circuits occurs at a panel(s).

Asbestos use in electrical systems has included:

- Transite ducts for electrical cable runs;
- Partitions in electrical panels;
- Asbestos cloth to bind bare cables; and
- Insulation on stage lighting and on the wire to those lights.

Of great concern in inspecting electrical systems, is the potential hazard to the Building Inspector from unsafe inspection procedures. Some guidelines for work in and around electric equipment include:

- Whenever possible, conduct the inspection accompanied by a building operator (specifically an electrician, if possible) who is familiar with the electrical equipment, its operation and location.

- Look for and heed any 1' Danger High ~ signs.

- Ask that the system be de-energized before taking samples.

- Use extreme care not to cut into or through cables or cable insulation.

- Be wary of electrical insulation, which can flake off, with time and heat.

- Beware of exposed electrical wires and components.

- Do not use a wetting solution near an electrical system.

- When taking samples of surfacing or other suspect materials, be careful not to penetrate to electrical components that may be located underneath or behind.

- Project Monitor should be aware of the procedures followed by the Building Inspector.

CONTRACT DOCUMENTS

Contract documents, or construction documents, are the legally binding drawings and specifications, which are used to construct the building. They consist of:

- Working Drawings
- Specifications
-

Other documents including addenda, change orders, shop drawings, submittals and as-builds.

These documents are a rich source of information for Project Monitors. Building owners and/or the contractors will provide copies. If the jurisdiction has a plan check and building permit procedure, the plan check agency may have retained a set of the drawings. These drawings are often photographically reduced and stored, but even in that form, they should be valuable documents for the Project Monitor.

The working drawings or plans are a set of drawings, which indicate the finished appearance and construction of the building. They are not a set of exact instructions for the contractor. As such, they do not precisely reflect the building as it was constructed. For this reason, it is mandatory that all information gathered from the plans be verified.

A title block will appear along the right side, or in the lower right hand corner, of each sheet of the set of drawings. When beginning your review of the drawings, carefully examine the title block, for the following information:

- Abatement specifications
- The name of the architecture or engineering firm;
- The date of the drawings;
- The sheet numbers; and
- The project number.

Compare the sheet numbering to the Index of Drawings on the initial sheet to determine 1) that you have a complete set, and 2) that all the sheets have the same date. The project number and date are your clues to whether you are reviewing plans for the same project. Over the life span of a building, several renovation projects are likely to have been completed and should be considered by the Project Monitor. A Project Monitor should be familiar with each project individually.

The sheet numbering system for the entire set of drawings reflects the manner in which the drawings were prepared. Just as the design of the building is a collaborative effort of an architect and engineers, the drawings and specifications are prepared by each of these professionals. Altogether, a complete set of drawings will likely include:

- Architectural
- Structural
- Mechanical (HVAC)
- Plumbing
- Electrical

When examining the numbering of the drawings, you will find that the drawings are divided by discipline. That is, the architectural drawings are together; the structural drawings are together, and so on. The numbering is then dependent on the discipline. It is typical that the structural drawings will be identified with an S and then the sheet number, e.g. S-1, S-2, 5.3. Architectural drawings will be identified with an A, the mechanical (HVAC only) with an M, the plumbing with a P, and the electrical with an E.

There is no standardization in the production of drawings, and thus no set of rules can be given for the way that each architect or engineer prepares not only a set of drawings, but also individual items within that set. You may even find inconsistencies within a particular set of drawings, as different people in different offices develop the drawings.

Drawings can be divided into several generic types:

- Plans - drawings of the building as viewed from above. These include floor plans, foundation plans, framing plans, roof plans, electrical plans, and should not be confused with the entire set of drawings which is also referred to as the set of plans;

- Elevations - drawings of the building as viewed horizontally from outside;

- Sections - drawings cut (vertically) through the building or building parts;

- Details expanded views of small areas that can be drawn in plan, elevation or section;

- Notes - comments and explanations; and

- Schedules a tabular display of information.

As you view the drawings, be sure to check for a list of symbols. Each building material in a set of drawings is depicted, when cut in section, by a material indication. If a legend appears in the set, use it as your guide.

Symbols are also used for a variety of items on drawings, other than materials. These are called reference symbols. Again, if a legend is included in the set of drawings use it, if not, then use the reference symbol legend guide.

A drawing reference you may encounter on a set of building plans is a "revision". It is depicted by a triangle around a number; a portion of the drawing itself may also be clouded to further indicate where the revision applies. The key to the numbering is found in the area adjacent to the title block. Revisions can be added on the drawings when changes have occurred:

After the drawings have been issued for bid, or

As a result of the plan check/permitting process.

Architectural Drawings

Architectural drawings show finished surfaces and materials. Of note is the floor plan, which is cut horizontally through the building at about four feet above the floor. The floor plan is the basis for the mechanical, plumbing and electrical drawings.

Another important drawing is the demolition plan, which represents those portions of the building, which will be demolished as a part of a renovation project. In many projects, improvements include removing (demolishing) existing walls, replacing floor coverings and other changes. The existing walls, windows, doors and built-ins are all indicated much lighter in contrast to the areas to be demolished. The difference in thickness of lines on the drawing signals the areas where work is to occur.

Commercial buildings often have repetitive units; rooms, doors and windows. To organize these spaces, schedules are developed to identify and describe specific rooms, doors and windows. The specific item is referenced to the schedule with a symbol as shown on the legend in the set of drawings. If a legend does not accompany the drawings, refer to Exhibit E-2, for typical symbols used. Use extreme care when working with room, door and window designations as the same number may be used repeatedly. The only difference will be in the symbol in which the number is lettered.

Be aware of differences between the room numbering scheme in the plans and the current numbering of the rooms in the building. It may be necessary to cross-list the numbers to equate the design information with the information determined from on-site investigation.

The room finish schedule will guide the Project Monitor through the finishes, or surface treatments, used in the individual rooms. The schedules read like a graph with columns titled -- floors, base, wainscot, walls and ceilings.

When reviewing drawings, your intention should be to familiarize yourself with the layout of the building, and then examine in detail the finishes, or details at the exterior wall and other areas where you suspect ACM may be found.

Often, when referenced on the drawings, a material will be listed with the notation "OR EQUAL". This notation allows for the contractor to make a substitution of another equivalent material. The determination of what is equal is usually at the architect or engineer's discretion, as elaborated upon in the specifications. This determination is based on descriptive literature forwarded by the contractor, for the architect or engineer's review and action.

Structural Drawings

Structural drawings will consist of foundation plans, floor framing plans, roof framing plans, structural elevations, details, notes and schedules. All structural drawings are drawn without finish (architectural) materials, and are intended only to indicate the structural elements of the building.

When you review the structural drawings, you will need to be familiar with the building in general, and in particular with structural members -- beams, columns and slabs.

Many buildings use a structural grid, referenced by numbers or letters. The grid provides a way to organize the building and to communicate about specific areas.

If the building has fireproofing, it may not be indicated on the structural drawings as it is a finish or surfacing applied to the skeleton, not as part of the skeleton. Thus it is the architect's responsibility not the structural engineer's. However, to understand where the fireproofing has been applied, where the beams are located that it is applied to, and the amount of area covered; the Project Monitor will need to examine the structural drawings.

Structural notes will often include a building code reference. These codes identify the name and the year of the official building code(s) - city, county or state, which governed the design of the structural elements. This reference can be an invaluable tool. Building codes in effect when the building was erected may have specified fireproofing and other materials, which are likely to contain asbestos.

Mechanical Drawings

The mechanical engineer prepares drawings for both the HVAC system and the plumbing system. Mechanical drawings consist of mechanical plans, which are based on the building's floor plans. They indicate the routing of ductwork and piping systems (necessary for HVAC), as well as details, notes, schedules, sections, and elevations (if required). Mechanical plans may include a system schematic, or flow diagram, to indicate how the HVAC system operates.

When reviewing the mechanical drawings, the Project Monitor needs to become familiar with the kind of HVAC system used, and the location of the various parts of the system. It is necessary to verify information obtained from these drawings by field inspection.

Plumbing Drawings

Plumbing drawings include plumbing plans, which are based on floor plans, notes, schedules, riser diagrams and other required supporting drawings. When reviewing the plumbing drawings, you need to be concerned with where the various equipment is located, how the system works, and whether the information on the plans is verified upon inspection.

Electrical Drawings

Electrical drawings consist of the floor plan-based power and lighting plans, notes, schedules, details (if required) and calculations to support the load requirements. A cursory review of the electrical drawings is normally all that is required to familiarize you with the location of equipment and equipment rooms. Electrical drawings are largely schematic. The exact location of all items, excepting panels, lighting, switches and receptacles are determined in the field, and as such needs to be verified.

Specifications

The specifications (specs) for a project are a written set of standards and procedures which inform the contractor of what materials and standards are necessary for the successful completion of the facility. The specs are generally in book form and accompany the drawings as a portion of the contract documents. Just as various members of the design team are responsible for portions of the drawings, they are responsible for the corresponding portions of the specs.

Typically the drawings and specs are prepared simultaneously by different personnel in the architect or engineer's office. It is likely that some conflict between the two may occur. If that is the case, the specs take precedence over the plans.

Specifications are either proprietary or non-proprietary. Proprietary specifications require the use of a specific material from a specific manufacturer. Non-proprietary specs are essentially performance specs. They do not specify a particular manufacturer but indicate the materials or performance requirements of the material and/or equipment and allow for the selection of any number of materials or equipment, which can perform to those limits. Typically governmental projects require non-proprietary specifications, as a way of insuring that one manufacturer is not given unfair advantage in pursuing a project.

As a way to organize specifications, many firms use the Uniform Construction Index (UCI). Note that plumbing and HVAC are both included under division 15, "mechanical". This deviates from the separate manner in which they are treated in working drawings. However, plumbing and HVAC have specific subdivisions under division 15.

Addenda

Upon completion of the plans and specs, a bidding period begins. During this period, contractors estimate cost of performing the work in the hope of being awarded the contract. If changes need to be made to the plans and specs, each potential bidder is notified of those changes to insure that they are all operating with the same information. This is done through issuing an addendum to the plans and specs.

An addendum may include both drawings and specifications and is legally incorporated into the contract documents. On a complex project it is very likely that a number of addenda will be issued during the bid period. Addenda should be treated as updates to the plans.

The bid period culminates with a bid opening, following which a contract for the construction of the project is signed. The working drawings, specifications and addenda are all incorporated into the contract. The cost and time of construction are based in part on these documents.

Change Orders

A change order is a change to the construction documents after a contract for construction has been signed. A change order may include both drawings and specifications to illustrate the change. The owner, architect, and contractor as a legal change to the construction contract sign it. These items need to be consulted when investigating the building.

Shop Drawings and Submittals

During the course of construction, detailed drawings or descriptions of certain items are needed before they are installed in the building. These items are as called for in the specifications. Shop drawings and/or submittals (drawings or descriptive literature) are prepared by the contractor or his or her subcontractors, and are reviewed by the architect and/or his or her appropriate consulting engineers. If these are available, they can reveal significant information about equipment (mechanical and electrical) and may disclose the use of ACM.

Another form of submittals is operating manuals and brochures, which are transmitted to the owner after construction. These too may indicate materials containing asbestos. When available, they are a good resource for information on suspect materials.

As-Built Drawings

As noted above, numerous changes can be made to a set of construction documents during bidding and construction. Because initial plans and specs are not exact instructions, they may be substantially changed by the time that construction is completed. Drawings and specs, which reflect the way a building was actually constructed, are known as "as-builds" or record drawings. Building owners should have a set of plans and specs, which accurately represent their facility. Plans and specs often contain a provision for as-built drawings and specs to be delivered to the owner, by the contractor, upon completion of construction.

As-builds reflect the construction on the date produced and are, in part, outdated as soon as any modification, renovation, or remodeling occurs. Unfortunately, it is a rare building owner who has accurate as-builds, which are kept, updated throughout the life of the building. Project Monitors should verify the accuracy of the resource material in the field.

SUMMARY

The occurrence of asbestos in buildings can be anticipated in a number of specific locations. The Project Monitor should have knowledge of available resources, have an understanding of the interrelationships of building systems and be qualified and certified.

Persons taking asbestos bulk samples are known as Asbestos Building Inspectors who must be certified by the state and be trained by a certified trainer. A building inspection involves (1) an investigation of records (including previous surveys, plans, specifications, and other documents) for the identification of ACBM, (2) a physical and visual inspection of the building for suspect materials, (3) sampling and analyzing suspect materials to test for asbestos, and (4) assessing the condition and location of the ACBM and other characteristics of the building.

Persons taking asbestos air samples are known as Asbestos Project Monitors who must be certified by the state and be trained by an accredited trainer.

Asbestos Project Monitor -- Any person, other than the asbestos abatement contractor/supervisor, who oversees the scope, methodology, or quality control on an abatement project, must maintain a valid project monitor certification. The project monitor is responsible for satisfactory operation of abatement activities. This includes those who shall act in a ―third party‖ and/or owner's representative capacity. Completion of this course allows an individual to also obtain an air sampling technician certification. The course incorporates extensive practical exercises, a project site visit, and concludes with a 100 question multiple choice examination. NYSDOH approval is to EEA.

The Asbestos Abatement Project Monitor certification training course is five days or equivalent to (40 hours) in length. For example: New York State Industrial Code Rule (12NYCRR56) and Federal US Environmental Protection Agency and United States Occupational Safety and Health Administration asbestos regulations specify that any person, other than the asbestos abatement contractor/supervisor, who oversees the scope, methodology or quality control on an asbestos abatement project, must maintain the asbestos abatement project monitor certification. This includes those who shall act in a third party and/or owner(s) representative capacity before, during or after an asbestos abatement project. Completion of the asbestos abatement project monitor course allows an individual to also obtain an asbestos abatement air sampling technician certification. The asbestos abatement project monitor course incorporates extensive practical exercises, a project site visit and concludes with a one hundred (100) question exam. Those who complete training are permitted a thirty day working grace period to apply to the New York State Department of Labor for an asbestos abatement project monitor certificate.

Asbestos Air Sampling Technician the "Restricted Handler II" certificate applies for those individuals who perform related air sampling activities. The AST course includes information on methodology for representative quality assurance for both area and personal sampling for Phase Contrast Microscopy (PCM) and Transmission Electron Microscopy (TEM). The course includes practical exercises utilizing the various types of air sampling equipment and concludes with a 50-question multiple choice examination. NYSCOH approval is to EEA.

Asbestos Abatement Air Sampling Technician certification—New York State Industrial Code Rule (12NYCRR56) and Federal US Environmental Protection Agency and United States Occupational Safety and Health Administration asbestos regulations specify that the Restricted Handler II certificate is required for those individuals who perform related asbestos abatement air sampling activities. The asbestos abatement air sampling technician course includes information on methodology for representative quality assurance for both asbestos personal exposure assessment sampling and asbestos project area sampling for phase contrast microscopy (PCM) and transmission electron microscopy analysis (TEM).

BLUEPRINT

MATERIAL INDICATIONS

- ACOUSTICAL TILE
- BRICK
- CONCRETE
- CMU (CONC. MASONRY UNITS)
- INSULATION, LOOSE OR BATT
- INSULATION, RIGID
- METAL
- WOOD, FINISH
- WOOD, ROUGH
- PLYWOOD
- CERAMIC TILE
- GLASS
- RESILIENT FLOOR TILE
- PLASTER
- GYPSUM WALL BOARD
- ROCK
- STONE, GRAVEL, POROUS FILL
- METAL LATHE AND PLASTER
- STRUCTURAL CLAY TILE

Chapter 4 – Understand Building Construction and Building Systems

BLUEPRINT
REFERENCE SYMBOLS

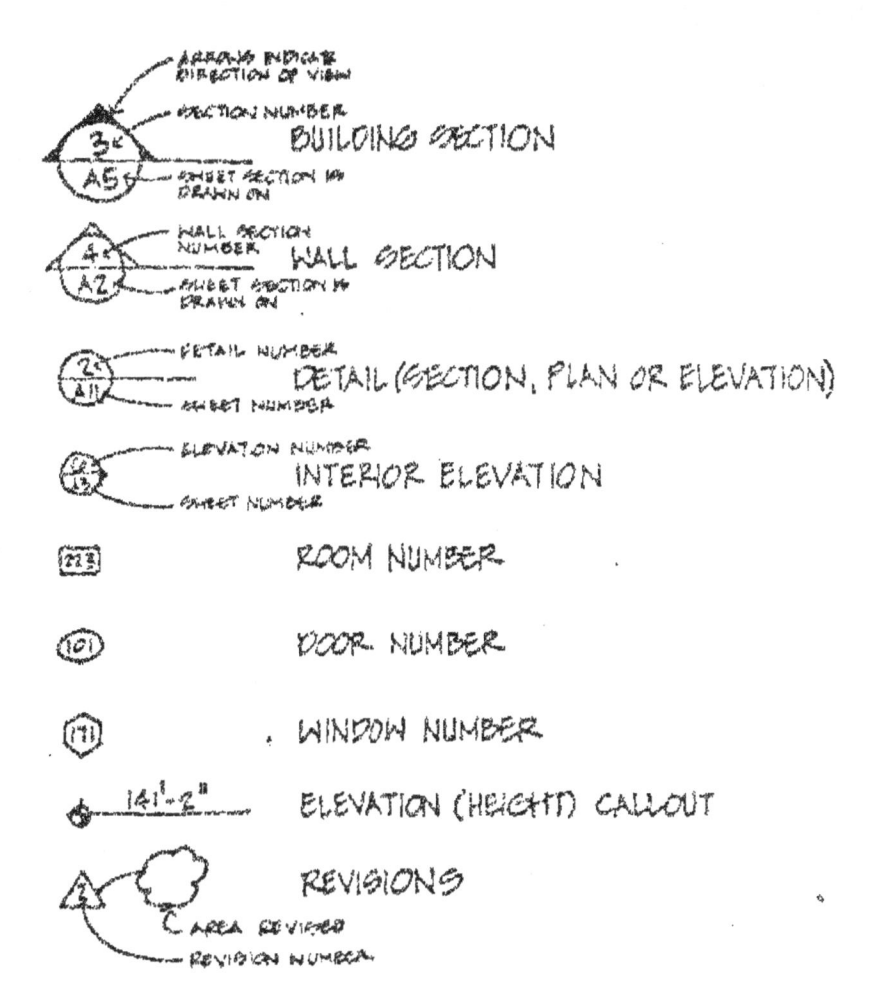

- **Building Section** — arrows indicate direction of view; section number; sheet section is drawn on
- **Wall Section** — wall section number; sheet section is drawn on
- **Detail (Section, Plan or Elevation)** — detail number; sheet number
- **Interior Elevation** — elevation number; sheet number
- **Room Number**
- **Door Number**
- **Window Number**
- **Elevation (Height) Callout** — 141'-2"
- **Revisions** — area revised; revision number

A TYPICAL STRUCTURAL GRID, THAT MAY BE USED FOR AIR AND OR BULK SAMPLING STRATERGY AND DOCENTATION

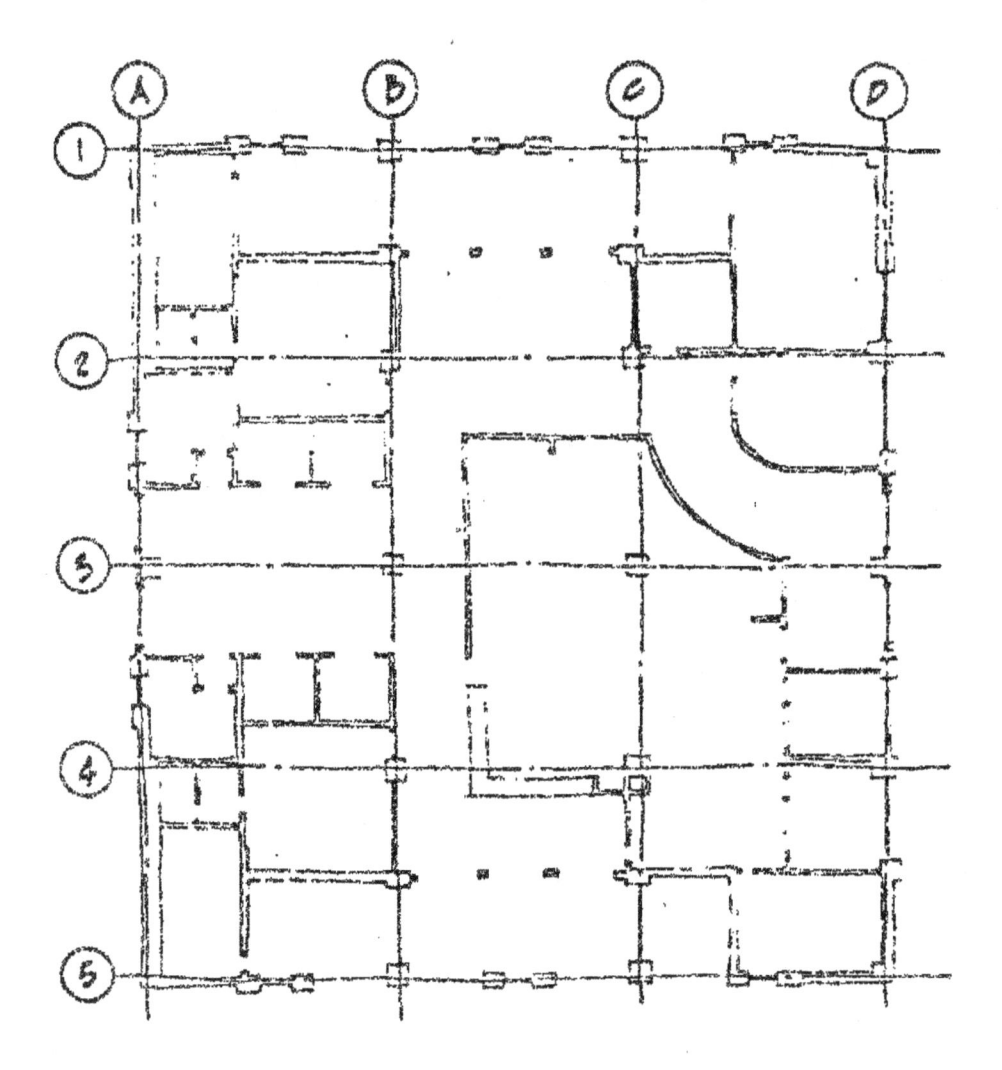

TYPES OF CEILING CONSTRUCTION

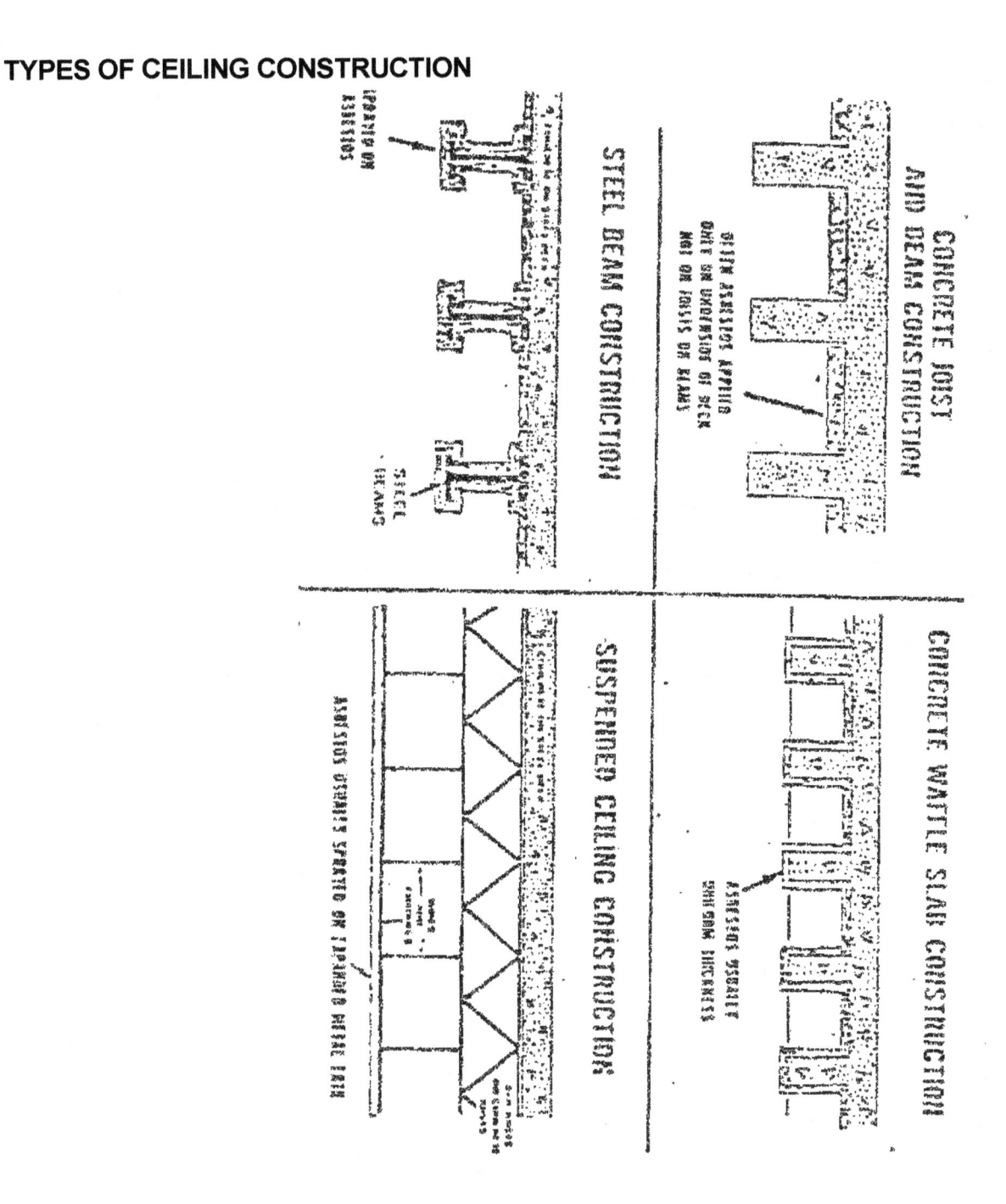

CONCRETE JOIST AND BEAM CONSTRUCTION

STEEL BEAM CONSTRUCTION

CONCRETE WAFFLE SLAB CONSTRUCTION

SUSPENDED CEILING CONSTRUCTION

SPECIFICATIONS

Proprietary

"... starting at the low edge apply one 18" wide, then over that one full 36" wide J-M (Johns-Manville) Asbestos Finishing Felt."

Non-proprietary

"Asphalt Saturated Asbestos Felt shall be 15 pound perforated complying with ASTM Designation D 250, latest edition."

Proprietary

"Insulation shall be Pyrospray Type T, by Baldwin-Ehret-Hill, Inc.; Asbestospray by Asbestospray Corporation; Sealspray by Sealtite Insulation Manufacturing Corp., Waukesha, Wisconsin; Spray Craft, Type S by Smith and Kanzler Company; or Spraydon Standard by Spraydon Research Corporation."

Non-proprietary

"Insulation shall be a quality controlled mixture of virgin asbestos fibers and mineral wool fibers blended with inorganic binders and rust inhibitors. Binder, after setting, must be unaffected by water, moisture and condensation."

REPRESENTATIVE LIST OF MATERIALS
LIKELY TO CONTAIN ASBESTOS

SUSPECT MATERIALS	MATERIAL TYPES	PLANS	SPECS
CEMENT ASBESTOS INSULATING PANELS	M	A	6
CEMENT ASBESTOS WALLBOARD	M	A	6
CEMENT ASBESTOS SIDING	M	A	6
ROOFING, ASPHALT SATURATED ASBESTOS FELT	M	A	7
ROOFING, REINFORCED ASBESTOS FLASHING SHEET	M	A	7
ROOFING, ASBESTOS BASE FELT	M	A	7
ROOFING, ASBESTOS FINISHING FELT	M	A	7
ROOF, PAINT	S	A	7
ROOFING, FLASHING (TAR AND FELT)	M	A	7
ROOFING, FLASHING (PLASTIC CEMENT FOR SHEET METAL WORK)	M	A	7
WATERPROOFING, ASBESTOS BASE FELT	M	A	7
WATERPROOFING, ASBESTOS FINISHING FELT	M	A	7
WATERPROOFING, FLASHING	M	A	7
DAMPPROOFING	M	A	7

REPRESENTATIVE LIST OF MATERIALS
LIKELY TO CONTAIN ASBESTOS

SUSPECT MATERIALS (CONTINUED)	MATERIAL TYPES	PLANS	SPECS
PUTTY AND/OR CAULK	M	A	7/9
DOOR INSULATION	M	A	8
FLOORING, ASPHALT TILE	M	A	9
FLOORING, VINYL ASBESTOS TILE	M	A	9
FLOORING, VINYL SHEET	M	A	9
FLOORING, BACKING	M	A	9
PLASTER, ACOUSTICAL OR DECORATIVE	S	A	9
CEILING TILE	M	A	7
INSULATION, THERMAL SPRAYED-ON	S	A	9
BLOWN-IN INSULATION	M	A	9
INSULATION, FIREPROOFING	S	A	9
TAPING COMPOUNDS	S	A	9
PAINTS	S	A	9
TEXTURED COATINGS	S	A	9
PACKING OR ROPE (AT PENETRATIONS THRU FLOORS OR WALLS)	M	A	9

REPRESENTATIVE LIST OF MATERIALS
LIKELY TO CONTAIN ASBESTOS

SUSPECT MATERIALS (CONTINUED)	MATERIAL TYPES	PLANS	SPECS
LABORATORY HOODS	M	A	11
LABORATORY OVEN GASKETS	M	A	11
LABORATORY GLOVES	M	A	11
LABORATORY BENCH TOPS	M	A	11
FIRE CURTAINS	M	A	12
ELEVATORS, EQUIPMENT PANELS	M	A	14
ELEVATORS, VINYL ASBESTOS TILE	M	A	14
HVAC PIPING INSULATION	TSI	M	15
HVAC GASKETS	TSI	M	15
BOILER BLOCK OR WEARING SURFACE	TSI	M	15
BREECHING INSULATION	TSI	M	15
FIRE DAMPER	M	M	15
FLEXIBLE FABRIC JOINTS (VIBRATION DAMPENING CLOTH)	M	M	15
DUCT INSULATION	TSI	M	15

REPRESENTATIVE LIST OF MATERIALS LIKELY TO CONTAIN ASBESTOS

Key to Abbreviations

Material Types:

M	=	Miscellaneous Material
S	=	Surfacing Material
TSI	=	Thermal System Insulation

Plans:

Which drawings to reference for material location

A	=	Architectural Drawings
M	=	Mechanical Drawings
P	=	Plumbing Plans
E	=	Electrical Plans

Specs:

Which division used from uniform Construction Index (EXHIBIT - 7)
Numbers 6 - 16

UNIFORM CONSTRUCTION INDEX

division	0	bid requirement
division	1	general data
division	2	sitework
division	3	concrete
division	4	masonry
division	5	metals
division	6	wood and plastics
division	7	thermal and moisture protection
division	8	doors and windows
division	9	finishes
division	10	specialties
division	11	equipment

division	12	furnishings
division	13	special construction
division	14	conveying systems
division	15	mechanical
division	16	electrical

TRADE NAMES

I. SUBSTITUTE MATERIALS FOR ASBESTOS PIPE INSULATION

TRADE NAME	MANUFACTURER	SUBSTITUTE MATERIAL
1. Aerotube	Johns-Manville	Foamed Plastic
2. Alpha-Maritex Style 1925	Alpha Associates	Fibrous Glass
3. Alpha-Maritex #311 1-RW	Alpha Associates	Fibrous Class
4. Armaflex 22	Armstrong Cork Co.	Foamed Plastic
5. C P A	Upjohn	Plastic
6. Crown	Fiberglas Ltd.	Fibrous Glass
7. Fit-Rite	Fibrous Glass Products, Inc.	Fibrous Glass
8. Flame-Safe	Johns-Manville	Fibrous Glass
9. Glo-Brite	Glo-Brite Products	Poly Foam
10. G P C	Sohos-Manville	Fibrous Glass
11. Hewflex	H. E. Werner, Inc.	Polyurethane Foam
12. Kaowool	Babcock & Wilcox	Ceramic Fiber
13. Kaylo 10	Owens Corning Fiberglass	Fibrous Glass
14. Micro-Lok 650	Johns-Manville	Fibrous Glass
15. Pabcoc Super Caltemp Type NA	Fibreboard Corp.	Diatomaceous Earth, Non-Asb. Fiber, Lime
16. PF-CG	Owens-Corning Fiberglass	Fibrous Glass
17. P M F	Jim Walter Resources Inc.	Fibrous Glass
18. Ruberoid Fiber Glass Pipe Insulation	Ruberoid	Fibrous Glass
19. Snap-On	Certain Teed	Fibrous Glass
20. TGA-1 000	Alpha Associates	Tedlar and Glass Fiber
21- Therma-K	Ehret Magnesia Mfg. Co.	Glass Fiber
22. Thermashield	Tecknit	Ceramic Fiber
23. Transifoam	Johns-Manville	PolystyTene
24. Transitop	Johns-Manville	Wood Fiber
25. Uni-lac	Pittsburgh Corning	Glass Fabric
26. Vapo-Lok	MMM Div. Insular Prods. Corp.	Expanded Polystyrene
27. VB-Vapor Barrier	Johns-Manville	Kraft Paper with Glass Fiber
28. VEL-Vapor Barrier	Johns-Manville	Fibrous Glass
29. V I	Riva and Mariani	Cellular glass
30. Z-Lock	Fibreglas Ltd.	Fibrous Glass
31. Zonolite	W. R. Grace and Co.	Vermiculite

TRADE NAMES

II. SUBSTITUTE MATERIALS FOR SPRAYED-ON ASBESTOS INSULATION

	TRADE NAME	MANUFACTURER	SUBSTITUTE MATERIAL
1.	Cafco	USM	Mineral Fibers
2.	Cafcote H	USM	Mineral Fibers (also abrasion resistant)
3.	Ceramafiber	USM	Ceramic Fiber
4.	Ceramospray	Spraycraft Corp	Ceramic Fiber
5.	Ceramwool	Johns-Manville	Ceramic Fiber
6.	Encage! V	Childers Products Co.	Urethane
7.	Ensolite	U.S. Rubber Co.	Polyvinyl Chloride
8.	Ensolite Type M	U.S. Rubber Co.	Polyvinyl Chloride
9.	K-13	National Cellulose Corp.	Cellulose

III. SUBSTITUTE MATERIALS FOR ASBESTOS-CONTAINING PANELS OR WALLBOARDS

	TRADE NAME	MANUFACTURER	SUBSTITUTE MATERIAL
1.	Sestwell	Georgia Pacific	Gypsum
2.	Cal-Shake	U.S. Gypsum	Calcium Silicate
3.	Caretemp 1500	Celotex	Expanded Perlite
4.	Ceilofoam	USM	Polystyrene
5.	Cellutron	Owens Corning	Cellulose
6.	Celot-Therm	Celotex	Perlite
7.	Ceramfab	USM	Ceramic Fiber
8.	Delta-T	Keene Corp.	Ceramic Fiber
9.	Doraspan	Owens Corning	Ceramic Fiber
10.	Dylite	Sinclair-Koppers	Molded Foam
11.	Econacouslic	Sinclair-Koppers	Wood Fiber
12.	Filomat-D	Alpha Associates	Glass Fiber
13.	Fire Stop	Cottofle Inc.	Treated Cotton
14.	Firetard Type X	Johns-Manville	Gypsum
15.	Foamyrid	USM	Polystyrene Foam
16.	Foamsil-28	Pittsburgh Corning	Glass Foam
17.	Foamthane	Pittsburgh Corning	Polyurethane Foam
18.	SE Armalite	Armstrong Cork Co.	Polystyrene
19.	Styrofoam	Dow	EPDM and Aramid
20.	Watertite Backer	Johns-Manville	Gypsum

IV. SUBSTITUTE MATERIALS FOR ASBESTOS-CONTAINING FABRICS

	TRADE NAME	MANUFACTURER	SUBSTITUTE MATERIAL
1.	Alpha-Maritex #3111-RW	Alpha Associates	Glass Fiber
2.	Alpha-Maritex #84205	Alpha Associates	Glass Fiber
3.	Aramid	DuPont	Synthetic
4.	Ceel-Tite	Ceel-Co	ABS Plastic
5.	Cerafelt	Johns-Manville	Ceramic Fiber
6.	Ceramfab	USM	Ceramic Fiber
7.	Fiberfrax	The Carborundum Co.	Ceramic Fiber
B.	Fiberseal	Pyroteka Inc.	Glass Fiber
9.	FireStop	Cotton, Inc.	TreatedCotton
10.	Flexlelt	General Insulating	Rock Wool

#	Trade Name	Manufacturer	Substitute Material
11.	Flextra	Raybestos-Manhattan	Cotton/Aramid
12.	Fyrepol	Fyrepel	Glass Fiber
13.	Glas Ply	Johns-Manville	Glass Fiber
14.	Glassbestos	Raybestos-Manhattan	Glass Fiber
15.	Glassbestos	Raybestos-Manhattan	Glass Fiber
16.	Glass Web	Steiner Industries	Class Fiber
17.	GVB Glas~Cloth Vapor Barrier	Johns-Manville	Glass Fiber
18.	Hansoquilt	Saldwin-Ehret-Hill	Glass Fiber
19.	Insulfas	Benjamin Foster	Class
20.	Kynol	American Kynol Corp.	Novoloid Fiber
21.	Nomex	DuPont	Synthetic
22.	Nor-Fab	Nitco (Armco)	Synthetic
23.	Nor-Fab	AMATEX Corp.	Synthetic
23.	Preox	Gentex Corp.	Heat-Stabilized Polyacrylonitrite
25.	Pyroglas	Raybestos-Manhattan	Glass Fiber
26.	SF 2600	Santa Fe Textiles, Inc.	Ceramic Fiber
27.	Sisalkraft	St.Regis Paper Co.	Kraft
28.	Snap Form	Certainreed	Polyvinylchioride
29.	Tempo	TempoGlove Manufacturing Inc.	Glass Fiber or Leather
30.	Terrybest	A-Best Co.	Keviar and other synthetics
31.	Thermafiber	U.S. Gypsum	Perlite
32.	Thermobest .	A-Best Co.	Keviar and other synthetics
33.	Thermo-Ceram	Garlock, Inc.	Ceramic Fiber
34.	Themoglass	Amatex Corp.	Glass Fibers
35.	Thermo-Sil	Garlock, Inc.	Glass Fibers
36.	Zonolite Dyfoam	W. F. Grace andCo.	Polystyrene

V. SUBSTITUTE MATERIALS FOR ASBESTOS-CONTAINING CEMENTS/PLASTERS

	TRADE NAME	**MANUFACTURER**	**SUBSTITUTE MATERIAL**
1.	Alumina-Hi-Temp	Carey	Alumina
2.	Careytemp 1500	Celotex	Expanded Perlite
3.	Cem-Fil	Asahi Glass Co. Ltd.	Glass Fiber
4.	Cerablanket	Johns-Manville	Ceramic Fiber
5.	Cerachrome	Johns-Manville	Ceramic Fiber
6.	Epitherm 1200	Eagle-Picher	Polyvinyl Chloride
7.	Feldina	Nonco Corp.	Non-Asbestos Mineral
8.	Fesco Board	Johns-Manville	Perlite
9.	Mono-Block	Deene Corp.	Mineral Wool
10.	MW-One Insulating Cement	Celotex	Mineral Wool
11.	MW-SO	Celotex	Mineral Wool
12.	Nonpariel	Armstrong Cork Co.	Rock Wool
13.	Pabco No.127	Fibreboard Corp.	Mineral Wool
14.	Pabco Super Caltemp Type NA	Fibreboard Corp.	Diatomaceous Eanh. Mineral Fibers. Lime
15.	Super 1900	Keene Corp.	Mineral Wool

VI. SUBSTITUTE MATERIALS FOR ASBESTOS-CONTAINING BRAKE LININGS OR DISCS

	TRADE NAME	**MANUFACTURER**	**SUBSTITUTE MATERIAL**
1.	ARAMID	Dupont	Synthetic
2.	Kynot	American Kynol Corp.	Novoloid Fiber
3.	Metal-Might	Lear Siegler, Inc.	Metallic -Fiber
4.	Premium	Euclid Industries	Synthetic

5. Scan-Pac   Scan-Pac   Metal Chips
6. Star Line   Abex Corp.   Glass Fiber

VII. SUBSTITUTE MATERIALS FOR ASBESTOS-CONTAINING PACKINGS OR FILLERS

TRADE NAME	MANUFACTURER	SUBSTITUTE MATERIAL
1. CA-S		Calcium Silicate
2- Garlite	U-S. Gypsum	Graphite
	Garlock, Inc.	
3- GFO Fiber	W. L. Gore and Associates, Inc.	PTFE and Graphite
4. Navalon	Johns-Manville	Ramie
S. Parfab	Parker Seals	Synthetic
6. Partherm	Parker Seals	Glass Fiber
7- Processed Mineral Fiber	Jim Walter Resources, Inc.	Glass Fiber
		Calciumsulfate
8. Snow White	U.S. Gypsum	Ceramic Fiber
9. Spandreline	PPG	
10. Spandrelite	PPG	Glass Fiber
11. Spinsulation	Johns-Manville	Glass Fiber
12. Style 50-50	Garlock Inc.	EPOM and Aramid
13. Synethepak	Garlock Inc.	Polymer Fiber
14. Technifoam	Celotex	Urethane

VIII. SUBSTITUTE FOR ASBESTOS-CONTAINING GASKETS

TRADE NAME	MANUFACTURER	SUBSTITUTE MATERIAL
1. Aramid	DuPont	Synthetic
2. Brue-Gard	Garlock, Inc.	Styrene Foam
3. Chevron	Garlock, Inc	Fibrous Glass
4. Fil-Tec	Fil-Tec	Glass Fiber
5. Garthane	Garlock, Inc.	Graphite
6. Gylon	Garlock, Inc.	Glass Fiber
7. Kynol	American Kynol Corp.	Novotoid Fiber
8. Marblock	Garlock, Inc.	Glass Wool
9. Nobestos	Rogers Corp.	Chioroprene, Nitrije, or Acrylic
10. Prolene	Garlock, Inc.	EPDM Rubber
11. Temp Mat	Pittsburgh Corning	Glass Fiber
12. Texo	PPG	Fiber Glass

REFERENCES

1. Sourcebook on Asbestos Diseases: Medical, Legal, and Engineering Aspects Volume 2. George A. Peters and Barbara j. Peters. Garland Law Publishing1 New York 1986. For more information on Volumes 1-3 contact: Garland Publishing, 136 Madison Avenue, New York1 NY ~0016.

TRADE NAMES OF ASBESTOS-CONTAINING PRODUCTS

Coronet	Fireguard Jacketing	Kaobestos
Covergard	Fire Halt	Kaylo
Crystal whlte	Firetard	Kearsarge
Cutno	Flamegard	K-Fac
Dtltston	Flamesafe	K&M Aircell
Designer Solids	Flexachrorne	Konnetal
Dominique	Flexboard	K Therm
Donbiex	Flexgold	Lasco
Double Sanded Asbestos	Flex-Slate	Unalbestos
Dualay	Flexstone	LK
Duplex	Flirtite	ImCA
Own-Color	Florobestos	I£k4ah
Dumform	F-WC	Marinite
Oura Shake	F.O.P.	Mastic

Dirocell	Form Pack 2	Maricove
Dii Shield	Foster	IveKirn
Ebonized Asbestos	Ernst Proof	Micabestos
Electrobestos	OAF	Mightyplate
Enduro	GanijanLine	Meico
Etemit	Gardweil	Minkote
Eternit Stonewall	Ganiwell Products	K'dernak
Excelon	Goetre b/frtallic Gaskets	b'knobess
Face Span	Gold Bond	bjbnoblock
Featherweight	Grafel	Mornasite
Felbestos	Gralam	Multi-Ply
fi-ACS	Grizzly	Mundet
Fiberock	O.T. Ring	New Era
Fiberock Asbestos Felt	GurfrBestos	Niagarite
Fiber Shake	Herto	Nicolet
Fiber-'pmy Asbestos	Hi Seal	Non-Con-Dux
Fibra Plow	Hoodex-22	Noriscell
Fibre Coating Asbestos	Hopaco	Novabestos
Fibre Kote	Homeblende	Nu Grain
Fibrocel	Hy Temp	Nu Side
FibrmCell	'fl-al	Nu Way
Fibofil	Imperial Excelon	OtnIstone
FibrFiil	'fl-al Pipe Covering	O-N.C
Fibroid	Industrial	One Cote Cement
Fibmid Stove putty	Industrial Tile	Pabco
Fil-Instil	Insulation Seal 820	Pakrnetal
Filpaco	Insulcolor	Pal-Lite
Fire Chex	Isobestos	Palmetto
FirChex	Janobestos	Palmetto Cutno
Firectad	Janos	Pairretto Super Sheet
Fire Fell	Jewen	Pamco
Firerd	John-'Manville	Paneistone

TRADE NAMES ASBESTOS-CONTAINING PRODUCTS

Permaboard	Sheedle-ctcs	Therm-Wrap
Permatherm	ShingleSeal	Thrift T
Permatone	Sirrico	mm/chip
Piedra	Sindaymo	Til-ex
Plastibest	Soundgard	Tilostore TK 33
Plastic	Spintex	Tmnshield
PlastiClad	Spiroflex	Transie
Plasticrylic	Spirutallic	Transi-Korduct
Pliaboard	Spi-ard	Transitop
Plia-F-Lex	Spray-Cote	Tm flame
Pluto	Spray Craft	Tropag
Portugese Asbestos	Sprayed Lirnpet Asbestos	U.F.P.
Powrninco	Sta Safe Long Life	Unibestos
Prasco High Temperature	Sterlbestos	Unibestos 750
	Stik4n	Unibestos 1200
Prenite	stone Chip	UniSyn
Profile	Stonewall Board	VDerrt
Pyrotx Felt	Stratalite	Ventsulattion
	Stri-Color	Victopac
Quiflorgo	Stn-N-lay	Vitribestos
Quinterra	Summit	Vitrobestos
Ranch Style	St.i,-,bestco	VUlcfrDSC
Red Mistite	Super Cinno	Weidgard
Rendezvous	Superheat	White Top Asbestos

Resiflal   Super X   Jacket

Riflg~te	Super 66	whittaker
Ripple Tone	Supradur	Wirepack
R-M or Raybestos-riM 7504	Sur-Stik	Woodflex
	Target	Zerogloss
R/M 24 H120	Tempeheck	Zeroseal
R/ME-66	Terraflex	Zetabond
Roca	Tenahex	Zip Stik
Rock Slate	Thermal Kote	
Rornanaire	Thermalon	
Rondelle	Therinatite	
Rubber Coat	Thermoeestos	
Satarrander	Therrn-Bord	
Salon	Thermofelt	
Sal-Mo	Therm-lake	
Scandiva	Thermoflex	
Sea Ring Packing	Thermomat	
Selk~lo	Thern-Pac	
Service Sheet Packing	Thermostone	
Cut Gaskets	Th-LlLvtay	
Shasta Snow	Thumotex S	

CONSTRUCTION SPECIFICATIONS INSTITUTE (CSI) MASTERFORMAT

division	0	conditions of the contract
division	1	general requirements
division	2	sitework
division	3	concrete
division	4	masonry
division	5	metals
division	6	wood and plastics
division	7	thermal and moisture protection
division	8	doors and windows
division	9	finishes
division	10	specialties
division	11	equipment
division	12	furnishings
division	13	special construction
division	14	conveying systems
division	15	mechanical

division 16 electrical

Asbestos Containing Materials in Buildings

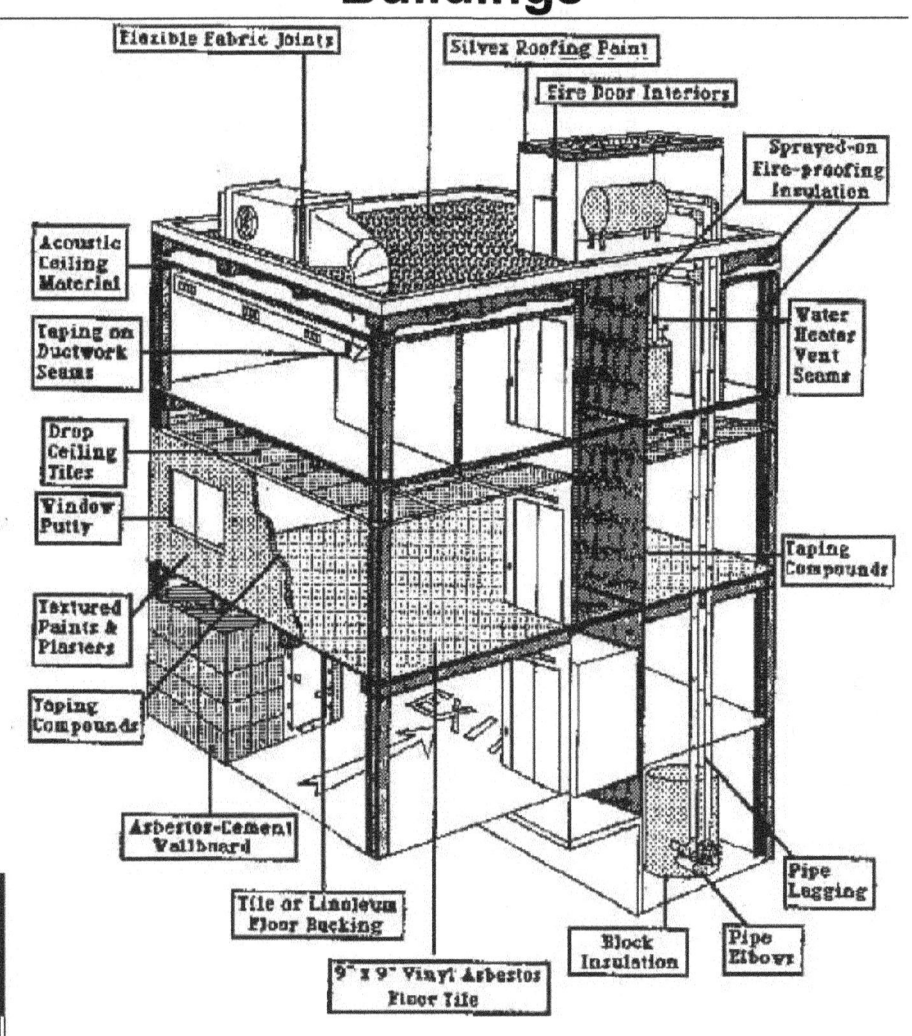

Building Structure

Chapter 5 - Asbestos Abatement Contracts Specifications and Drawings

Objective: To provide the Project Monitor with an overview of the contract specifications used for asbestos abatement projects.

Learning Tasks: Information in this section should enable participants to:

- Recognize the importance of well-designed, detailed contract specifications.
- Become familiar with the key elements of contract specifications.
- Recognize the basic components of material, equipment, and substitution specifications.
- Become familiar with the importance of detailing specification for the execution of work.
- Further recognize the need for interdisciplinary approaches to asbestos abatement.

Chapter 5 – Asbestos Abatement Contracts Specifications and Drawings

CONTRACT SPECIFICATIONS

Well-designed, detailed contract specifications provide the overall guidance for each asbestos abatement project. These specifications permit the contractor to provide the building owner or designer with an accurate estimate or bid for completing the project. With few exceptions, two contracts are required for each project. One contract is established with the contractor performing the actual abatement work, and a second contract is between the building owner (or designer) and the air sampling professional.

Poorly designed specifications will result in a poorly performed project. If details are omitted in specifications or procedures are unclear, the bids will vary tremendously. Likewise, contractors must spend the necessary time to read the specifications in their entirety before the pre-bid walkthrough of the intended job site. The National Institute of Building Sciences (NIBS) "Guide Specifications for Asbestos Abatement Projects" may be a helpful reference for individuals designing projects. With the enactment of AHERA and the issuance of the Asbestos School Hazard Abatement Reauthorization Act (ASHARA), most asbestos response actions in public and private schools (K-12), as well as public and commercial buildings, must be designed by an accredited asbestos abatement Project Designer.

CONTRACT SPECIFICATIONS

This Chapter is written primarily as a guide to preparing specifications for a large asbestos abatement project in anticipation of obtaining bids from a select group of qualified contractors. However, for small projects, many facilities obtain asbestos abatement services through a "work order" or "purchase order" system. This mechanism can work very well if the contractor is well qualified, and if work practices to be used are clearly understood. It is highly recommended that the guidelines in this section be used to develop a basic specification by which all work order projects are done at a given facility. This specification can then be used as a basis for negotiating unit prices with work order contractors.

Contract specifications (specs) are a written set of standards and procedures informing the contractors or abatement professionals of materials and operations necessary to successfully complete an abatement project. Typically, these documents cover the entire spectrum of an abatement project; from site investigation by the contractor to use and application of replacement materials. The specifications are usually prepared in book form, and with the contract drawings and any addenda or change orders, constitute the contract documents. During preparation of the contract documents, conflicts may result between specs and drawings. In a case such as this, specs will take precedence over drawings, unless otherwise stated in the contract documents.

During the bidding period, in which each contractor determines his/her cost of performing the work, quite often it is necessary for the designer to change or alter the project specs. Such a change is issued as an addendum to all bidding contractors in order to ensure that all parties are bidding on the same information. Basically, an addendum is a legally incorporated update to the drawings and/or specs prior to submittal of bids.

Should any change be necessary in drawings or specs after the contract has been awarded, a change order is issued. The owner, designer, and contractor sign this legally binding action. It may entail an increase or, rarely, a decrease in the dollar amount of the contract, and may increase or decrease the amount of time necessary to perform the work.

Information, which is often included in contract specifications, is contained on the following pages. It is important for an asbestos abatement professional to keep in mind that no two abatement projects will be identical. Various aspects of a project will be similar from job to job, but no one set of contract specifications can be used from project to project without modification or large-scale changes. Hence, the designer who will develop the specifications and most likely represent the interests of the building owner will want to become familiar with all aspects of the project.

ELEMENTS OF THE SPECIFICATIONS

Site Inspection

Contract specifications issued to bidding contractors will usually include general information on bidding requirements. Often, in order to become a qualified bidder, a site inspection will be required of the contractor. This is done to assure all parties that the contractor has become familiar with the conditions of the project, including the physical condition of the site, access to water and electricity, as well as the character and quantity of the ACM involved in the abatement project.

Chapter 5 – Asbestos Abatement Contracts Specifications and Drawings

Regardless of whether or not a site investigation is specified, a prudent contractor will want to become familiar with the project in order to present a responsible estimate for the work. Associated with the site inspection is a pre-bid walkthrough and meeting during which details of the project will be discussed, and the competing contractors can ask questions to clarify any misunderstandings.

Scope of Work

The project "scope of work" will be detailed in the specifications. This section will include a description of ACM locations and quantities to the extent they have been determined (usually also provided on drawings), the type of abatement procedures to be used in a particular area, timeframe for project completion, and any restoration requirements that may be necessary.

Description of Work

A "description of work" section will detail abatement measures for each work area. Additionally, the contractor will be required by this section to supply all labor, materials, services, insurance, equipment, etc. necessary to carry out the work in accordance with the specs and all applicable laws. Any special conditions that may be encountered on the project (i.e., high temperature steam lines, operational equipment, etc.) will be detailed. This section also may include the requirement that the contractor restore an abatement area to conditions equal to or better than original. The contractor will be held responsible for any damages caused during the course of his work and will remedy any damages at his own expense.

Submittals and Notices

Submittals and notices are important in getting the abatement project off to a smooth start. The contract specs should spell out who is responsible for properly notifying applicable regulatory agencies, in addition to securing the necessary permits for waste handling and disposal procedures. Documentation that the contractor's supervisors, foremen, and workers are properly trained licensed where required and medically certified under applicable regulations will also be submitted to the building owner. It is also important that any existing damage be documented by the contractor and submitted to the owner prior to any work commencing. This will protect both the contractor and owner from punch-list disputes at the close of the project.

Included in the contractor's submittals will be a list of equipment to be used along with any certification documents, which the specs call for. (For example: HEPA-vacuums conforming to American National Standards Institute (ANSI) standards). This will include respirators as well as other equipment for the project. During the abatement activity itself, the specs may call for weekly progress reports on abatement status, transport manifests, waste disposal receipts, project monitor logbooks, bulk and air sample results, and documentation of HEPA-filter changes.

In addition to requirements for the contractor, the project specifications will sometimes require the building owner to perform certain functions. This may include notification of building occupants of the work to be performed and making arrangements for temporary relocation. Additionally, the owner will usually have to make available to the contractor the results of any pre-abatement air sampling or bulk sampling tests.

Site Security

An area of concern for building owners and contractors alike is site security and emergency planning during the abatement project. Contract documents will specify that only authorized personnel will be allowed access to the work site (employees of the owner and subcontractor, air monitoring personnel, inspectors). This is done to limit the liability of the parties involved and to prevent any worksheet problems. Emergency planning will include written notification to police, fire, and emergency medical personnel regarding the proposed abatement activity and the proper procedures to follow if an emergency situation should arise.**MATERIAL, EQUIPMENT, AND SUBSTITUTION SPECIFICATIONS**

Material Specifications

Material specifications will include documentation of onsite storage regulations, details of material to be used (example: black polyethylene for worker decontamination units), any special materials to be used to protect objects in the work area and proper containers for asbestos waste. Materials for removal (subfactants), encapsulation, and any replacement.Chapter 5 – Asbestos Abatement Contracts Specifications and Drawings materials will be specified here. Proprietary specifications will require the use of a specific material from a specific manufacturer, whereas non-proprietary specifications will indicate materials or performance requirements and will allow the selection of materials, which will perform to those limits.

Equipment Specifications

Equipment specifications will detail the performance requirements of units such as negative air filtration units, Type-C respirators and associated compressed air systems, and protective clothing and safety equipment such as footwear, hardhats, and eye protection. Equipment used in the actual removal of ACM will also be specified, such as scaffolds, ladders, sprayers and their capacity ratings, and any other equipment deemed essential for proper completion of the job.

In the event that a substitution of materials or equipment is necessary, specifications will usually call for the submission of complete technical data and information on the substitution from the contractor to the building owner or his/her representative. The building owner will then review the information and have the authority to approve or disapprove such substitution. It is important to keep in mind that the terms "or equal" and "or equal as approved by owner" do not mean automatic owner approval of substitutions. The owner should approve any material or equipment that the contractor feels is equal to what has been specified before being used. There have been many instances where a contractor has had to redo work when unapproved substitutions were found to have been made.

SPECIFICATIONS FOR THE EXECUTION OF WORK

Procedures for preparation of the work area will be specified in the contract documents. The specs will include the shutting down and locking out of electrical power to the area, if possible. Provisions for temporary power and lighting may have to be made, and are usually the responsibility of the contractor. The HVAC system of the building will also need to be shut down or modified in the area of abatement to prevent the spread of contamination to other areas of the building. This is an especially important consideration in buildings where adjacent areas will remain occupied. Considerations will be detailed for furniture, machinery, etc., which will be cleaned, removed from the work area, and stored. Any items not able to be removed will be cleaned and sealed using specified methods.

Specifications will often detail the construction design of the decontamination facilities, including location, size of chambers, and number of airlocks. Additionally, entry and exit procedures will be set forth, with provisions for waste material removal and storage.

The work area will be prepared according to project specs, which will usually state polyethylene sheeting thickness, layers, and seam overlap. Special considerations for equipment, which cannot be shut down and removed from the work area (computers, communications switching equipment), and for work areas with adjacent occupied space will also be specified. It is vital that contractors, as well as other abatement professionals, become familiar with any special circumstances.

Once the preparation of the work area is complete, specifications will usually detail the methods and order of removal of contaminated materials in the work area. Any encapsulation or enclosure of asbestos-containing material will be specified. As removal, encapsulation, and/or enclosure operations are completed, the waste material will be taken out of the work area, transported by a permitted waste hauler, and disposed of in an approved landfill. Proper documentation and retaining of waste shipment records from disposal practices are specified to be delivered to the building owner.**RESPIRATORY PROTECTION**

Specifications for respiratory protection may vary with either the type of abatement activity or with fiber concentrations. HEPA-filter cartridge respirators may be specified for use during work area preparation and/or following complete removal of gross contamination and one or more phases of cleaning. Type-C air supplied respiratory protection is usually specified from the beginning of actual ACM removal until gross contamination has been cleaned-up and removed from the area. Powered air-purifying respirators are sometimes specified in place of cartridge respirators.

When considering airborne fiber concentrations and specifications for respirators, a general rule of thumb is to provide a protection factor that would maintain a fiber concentration of 0.01 fibers per cubic centimeter (f/cc) inside the mask. Due to daily fluctuations in fiber concentrations and analytical considerations, it is often difficult to ensure that a concentration of 0.01 f/cc is maintained. Increasingly, a combination of fiber concentrations in the work area and abatement activity is used in specifications to determine the level of respiratory protection. For example, during the second phase of cleaning, PAPRs may be acceptable if measured fiber concentrations would justify that adequate protection was achieved. Documentation that workers have received proper training in the purpose and use of respirators and that workers have been qualitatively or quantitatively fit-tested should always is specified.

CLEARANCE AIR TESTING

Specifications should include requirements that the owner's representative, an Asbestos Project Monitor, prior to final air clearance testing, conduct a complete and thorough visual examination of the work area. The procedures to be followed for final air clearance testing should always be thoroughly spelled out in the specs. Sampling locations and the number of samples to be collected will sometimes be specified. Often, however, this is left to the discretion of the air sampling professional. Sampling methods (aggressive or non-aggressive), analytical techniques (PCM or TEM), and sampling times will be specified according to applicable regulations. The specs should also state very clearly what would be considered "clean" in regard to airborne fiber levels.

WASTE DISPOSAL

Contract specifications will indicate an EPA authorized landfill that will accept asbestos waste as an acceptable dumpsite for the abatement project's waste. A recordkeeping format, whereby all waste shipment records required by the NESHAP regulations, receipts, and manifests will be retained and delivered to the building owner, will usually be included. Specific requirements for the transportation of asbestos waste will include preparation of the waste containers and truck, proper loading and unloading procedures, personal protective equipment that must be worn by waste handlers, and decontamination procedures for the transport vehicle itself.

MATERIAL REPLACEMENT

Replacement of materials, which have been removed, such as fireproofing, insulation, a drop or suspended ceiling, or any renovation work that incorporates new material will be completed following passage of clearance testing. This work may be covered under the original abatement contract and included in the same set of specs, or may be under separate contract and specifications. Following the completion of replacement, or if no additional work is to be done, the contractor will be required to remove all critical barriers, re-secure any objects or fixtures taken from the area, replace furniture and fixtures in their former positions, and re-establish the HVAC, electrical, and any plumbing systems to their proper working order. Finally, any damage resulting from the contractor's abatement activities will be repaired.

OTHER ABATEMENT PROFESSIONAL

Contract documents will specify the qualifications and responsibilities of other abatement professionals associated with the particular project. These other persons will include the Asbestos Project Manager – usually the owner or owner's representative. The Project Manager will be responsible for assisting in decision making, developing, implementing, and enforcing the contract specs, inspecting the work areas and critical barriers, and possibly coordinating bulk and air sample collection as well as other duties.

The Air Sampling Professional will be in charge of conducting air sampling in accordance with the project specifications. The types of sampling – pre-abatement, area sampling, personal, ambient – and any air volume requirements or

Chapter 5 - Asbestos Abatement Contracts Specifications and Drawings

associated sampling strategies will be outlined. The procedures to be followed for final air clearance testing will be detailed in accordance with applicable Federal and State regulations.

The laboratory services utilized will be specified as having to be accredited for both bulk and air sample analysis. Turnaround time for samples may also be specified, as well as accreditation requirements for individual analysts.

A well-designed and organized set of contract specifications will provide for a successfully completed abatement project. However, it is important for a contractor to remember that not all regulations and requirements will be included in project specs. For this reason, a contractor should become familiar with any Federal, State, and Local laws that apply to his or her situation.

Objectives: To provide instruction to participants on the most effective methods for containment of asbestos fibers during an asbestos abatement project.

Learning Tasks: Information in this section should enable participants to:

- Understand the primary methods used to contain and minimize airborne fiber concentrations during an asbestos abatement project.

- Know principles and procedures for setting up a negative air filtration system on an abatement project.

- Become familiar with the use and limitations of negative air filtration units.

- Understand the application and use of wet removal techniques.

- Become familiar with proper procedures and equipment for removal of asbestos-containing sprayed and troweled-on friable insulation material.

- Become familiar with proper procedures and equipment for removal of asbestos-containing insulation from pipes, tanks, and boilers.

RESPONSE ACTIONS & ABATEMENT

The preparation phase of an asbestos abatement project is directed toward containing the airborne fibers that will be generated during removal, primarily by constructing barriers with polyethylene sheeting. This containment effort, along with measures to minimize airborne fiber concentrations, is continued throughout the removal phase. The primary methods for contaminant control are the use of wet removal techniques and the use of negative pressure filtration systems accompanied by continuous cleanup in a work area sealed with polyethylene.

NEGATIVE PRESSURE FILTRATION SYSTEMS

The planning strategy for the use of negative pressure systems in abatement work includes two main goals.

- Changing air within the containment area at a minimum of every 15 minutes while filtering the exhausted air through high efficiency particulate air (HEPA) filters.

- Establishing conditions in which air from all portions of the sealed zone is being pulled toward the negative pressure fans and HEPA filters.

Negative pressure systems should be used on an abatement project to accomplish several positive effects.

- Containment of airborne fibers even if the barrier is ripped or punctured.

- Lower concentration of airborne fibers in the work area.

- Worker comfort and increased productivity.

- Improved efficiency in final cleanup.

Negative pressure filtration units are known by several different names including Micro-TrapTM, Red BaronTM, HogTM, micro-filter, HEPA units, and negative pressure system. Prototypes for use in asbestos abatement were developed in the latter 1970's. The concept of air filtration systems as a primary control technique on asbestos abatement projects was adopted by the EPA.

RECOMMENDED SPECIFICATIONS AND OPERATING PROCEDURES FOR THE USE OF NEGATIVE PRESSURE SYSTEMS FOR ASBESTOS ABATEMENT

This section provides guidelines for the use of negative pressure systems in removing asbestos-containing materials from buildings. The manufacturer's instructions for equipment use should be followed for negative air filtration units, as well as all other equipment discussed in this manual. A negative pressure system is one in which the static air pressure in an enclosed work area is lower than that of the environment outside the containment barriers.

The pressure gradient is maintained by moving air from the work area to the environment outside the area via powered exhaust equipment (negative air filtration unit) at a rate that will support the desired air flow and pressure differential. Thus, the air moves into the work area through designated access spaces and any other barrier openings. Exhaust air is filtered by a high-efficiency particulate air (HEPA) filter to remove asbestos fibers.

The use of negative pressure during asbestos removal helps protect against the large-scale release of fibers to the surrounding area in case of a breach in the containment barrier. A negative pressure system also can reduce the concentration of airborne asbestos in the work area by increasing the dilution ventilation rate (i.e., diluting contaminated air in the work area with uncontaminated air from outside) and exhausting contaminated air through HEPA filters. The circulation of fresh air through the work area reportedly also improves worker comfort by increasing the cooling effect, which may aid the removal process by increasing job productivity.

MATERIALS AND EQUIPMENT

The Portable, HEPA-Filtered, Powered Exhaust Unit

The exhaust unit establishes lower air pressure inside than outside the enclosed work area during asbestos abatement by moving air from the contained work area to the outside. Basically, a unit consists of a cabinet with an opening at each end, one for air intake and one for exhaust. A fan and a series of filters are arranged inside the cabinet between the openings. The fan draws contaminated air through the intake and filters and discharges clean air through the exhaust.

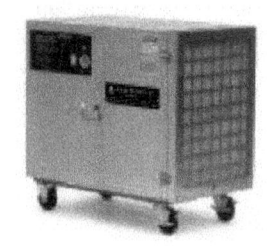

Portable exhaust units used for negative pressure systems in asbestos abatement projects should meet the following specifications.

STRUCTURAL SPECIFICATIONS

The cabinet should be ruggedly constructed and made of durable materials to withstand damage from rough handling and transportation. The width of the cabinet should be less than 30 inches to fit through standard-size doorways. Appropriate cabinet seals should prevent asbestos-containing dust from being emitted during use, transport, or maintenance. There should be easy access to all air filters from the intake end, the filters must be easy to replace. The unit should be mounted on casters or wheels so it can be easily moved. It also should be accessible for easy cleaning.

MECHANICAL SPECIFICATIONS

Fans

The fan for each unit should be sized to draw a desired air volume through the filters in the unit at a specified static pressure drop (see manufacturer's literature for this information). The unit should have an air-handling capacity of at least 1,000 to 2,000 cubic feet per minute (CFM or ft^3/min) (under "clean" filter conditions). The fan should be of the centrifugal type.

For large-scale abatement projects, where the use of a larger capacity, specially designed exhaust system may be more practical than several smaller units, the fan should be appropriately sized according to the proper load capacity established for the application, i.e.,

$$\text{Total } ft^3/\text{min (load)} = \frac{(\text{Volume of work area in } ft^3)(\text{air changes/hour})}{60 \text{ min/hour}}$$

Smaller-capacity units (e.g., 500 ft^3/min) equipped with appropriately sized fans and filters may be used to ventilate smaller work areas. The desired air flow could be achieved with several units.

Filters

The final filter must be the HEPA type. Each filter should have a standard nominal rating of at least 1,100 ft^3/min with a maximum pressure drop of 1 inch H_2O clean resistance. This pressure drop will increase as the filters load and the manufacturer's literature will indicate a clean filter pressure drop and a recommended maximum allowable pressure drop for dirty filters. The filter media (folded into closely pleated panels) must be completely sealed on all edges with a structurally rigid frame, and cross-braced as required to prevent air bypassing the filter. Exact dimensions of the filter should correspond with the dimensions of the filter housing inside the cabinet or the dimensions of the filter-holding frame. The recommended standard size HEPA filter is 24 inches high x 24 inches wide x 11 1/2 inches deep. The overall dimensions and squareness should be within 1/8 inch.

A continuous rubber gasket must be located between the filter and the filter housing to form a tight seal. The size of the gasket material is dependent upon the manufacturer. (Some manufacturers use gaskets that are approximately 1/4 inch thick and 3/4 inch wide.) This gasket should be checked periodically for cracks and gaps. Any break in this gasket may permit significant leakage of contaminated air. Leaks in the gasket or filter will be indicated by lower than normal "clean resistance" pressure.

Each filter should be individually tested and certified by the manufacturer to have an efficiency of not less than 99.97 percent when challenged with 0.3 micrometers (μm) dioctylphthalate (DOP) aerosol. Testing should be in accordance with Military Standard Number 282 and Army Instruction Manual 136-300-175A. Each filter should bear a UL 586 label to indicate ability to perform under specific conditions. Each filter should be marked with: the name of the manufacturer, serial number, air flow rating, efficiency and resistance, and the direction of test air flow.

Pre-filters, which protect the final filter by removing the larger particles, are recommended to prolong the operating life of the HEPA filter. Pre-filters prevent the premature loading of the HEPA filter. They can also save energy and cost. One (minimum) or two (preferred) stages of pre-filtration may be used. The first-stage pre-filter should be a low-efficiency type (e.g., for particles 10 μm and larger). The second-stage (or intermediate) filter should have a medium efficiency (e.g., effective for particles down to 5 μm). Various types of filters and filter media for pre-filtration applications are available from many manufacturers. Pre-filters and intermediate filters should be installed either on, or in, the intake grid of the unit and held in place with special housings or clamps.

Instrumentation

Each unit should be equipped with a Magnehelic gauge or manometer to measure the pressure drop across the filters, which would indicate when filters have become loaded and need to be changed. The static pressure across the filters (resistance) increases as they become loaded with dust, affecting the ability of the unit to move air at its rated capacity.

ELECTRICAL

General

The electrical system should have a remote fuse disconnect. The fan motor should be totally enclosed, fan-cooled, and the non-overloading type. The unit may use a standard 115-V, single-phase, 60-cycle service. All electrical components must be approved by the National Electrical Manufacturers Association (NEMA) and Underwriter's Laboratories (UL).

Fans

The motor, fan, fan housing, and cabinet should be grounded. All units should have an electrical (or mechanical) lockout to prevent the fan from operating without a HEPA filter.

Instrumentation

An automatic shutdown system, that would stop the fan in the event of a major rupture in the HEPA filter or blocked air discharge, is recommended. Optional warning lights are recommended to indicate normal operation, too high of a pressure drop across the filters (i.e., filter overloading), and too low of a pressure drop (i.e., major rupture in HEPA filter or obstructed discharge). Elapsed time meters may also be purchased to show the total accumulated hours of operation of the negative pressure units.

SETUP AND USE OF A NEGATIVE PRESSURE SYSTEM

Determining Approximate Ventilation Requirements for a Work Area

Experience with negative pressure systems on asbestos abatement projects indicates a recommended minimum rate of one air change every 15 minutes. The volume (in ft^3) of the work area is determined by multiplying the floor area by the ceiling height. The total volumetric air flow requirement (in ft^3/min) for the work area is determined by dividing this volume by the recommended air change rate (i.e., one air change every 15 minutes).

Total ft^3/min = Volume of work area (in ft^3)/15 min

The number of units needed for the application is determined by dividing the total ft^3/min by the rated capacity of the exhaust unit.

$$\text{Number of units needed} = \frac{\text{Total } ft^3/min.}{\text{Capacity of unit } (ft^3/min.)}$$

Location of Exhaust Units

The exhaust unit(s) should be located so that makeup air enters the work area primarily through the decontamination facility and traverses the work area as much as possible. This may be accomplished by positioning the exhaust unit(s) at a maximum distance from the worker access opening or other makeup air sources.

Wherever practical, work area exhaust units can be located on the floor in or near unused exterior doorways or windows. The end of the unit or its exhaust duct should be placed through an opening in the plastic barrier or wall covering. The plastic around the unit or duct should then be sealed with tape.

Each unit must have temporary electrical power (115V A.C.). If necessary, three-wire extension cords can supply power to a unit. The cords must be in continuous lengths (without splice), in good condition, and should not be more than 100 feet long. They must not be fastened with staples, hung from nails, or suspended by wire. Extension cords should be suspended off the floor and out of workers' way to protect the cords from traffic, sharp objects, and pinching.

Wherever possible, exhaust units should be vented to the outside of the building. This may involve the use of additional lengths of flexible or rigid duct connected to the air outlet and routed to the nearest outside opening. Windowpanes may have to be removed temporarily.

USE OF THE NEGATIVE PRESSURE SYSTEM

Testing the System

The negative pressure system should be tested before any asbestos-containing material is wetted or removed. After the work area has been prepared, the decontamination facility set up, and the exhaust units(s) installed, the unit(s) should be started (one at a time). Observe the barriers and plastic sheeting. The plastic curtains of the decontamination facility should move slightly in toward the work area. The use of ventilation smoke tubes and an aspirator bulb is another easy and inexpensive way to visually check system performance and direction of air flow through openings in the barrier. For example, smoke emitted on the inside of the work area at a barrier should not leak outward. Smoke emitted in the shower room of the decontamination unit should move inward to the work area. Smoke tubes can also be used to check if air flow is moving inward at high and low levels of the work area.

EXAMPLES OF NEGATIVE PRESSURE SYSTEMS

DF, Decontamination Facility, EU, Exhaust Unit; WA, Worker Access; A. Single-room work area with multiple windows; B. Single-room work area with single window near entrance; C. Single-room work area with exhaust unit placed on the outside of the building; D. Large single-room work area with windows. Arrows denote direction of air flow. Circled numbers indicate progression of removal sequence.

SCHEMATIC REPRESENTATION OF NEGATIVE AIR HEPA SYSTEM IN PLACE

Another test method for negative pressure is to use a Magnehelic gauge (or other instrument) to measure the static pressure differential across the barrier. The measuring device must be sensitive enough to detect a relatively low pressure drop. A Magnehelic gauge with a scale of 0 to 0.25 or 0.50 inch of H_2O and 0.005 or 0.01 inch graduations is generally adequate. The pressure drop across the barrier is measured from the outside by punching a small hole in the plastic barrier and inserting one end of a piece of rubber or Tygon tubing (be sure to seal around tubing if tube is left in place). The other end of the tubing is connected to the "low pressure" tap of the instrument. The "high pressure" tap must be open to the atmosphere. The pressure is read directly from the scale. After the test is completed, the hole in the barrier must be patched. Instruments are also available that monitor the pressure drop continuously. These units can be connected to a strip chart recorder to provide continuous documentation of negative pressure. An audible and/or visible alarm may be used to alert the project manager of a severe drop in pressure. Typically, a pressure drop of 0.03 inches of water is maintained throughout the asbestos abatement project (this pressure drop is affected by the air change rate). The U.S. Occupational Safety and Health Administration (OSHA) requires a pressure differential of at least 0.02 inches of water.

Use of System During Removal Operations

The exhaust units should be started before any asbestos-containing material is disturbed, after completion of the critical barriers. After removal has begun, the units should run continuously to maintain a constant negative pressure until final air clearance has been achieved. The units **should not be turned off** at the end of the work shift or when removal operations temporarily stop.

Employees should start removing the asbestos material at a location farthest from the exhaust units and work toward them. If an electric power failure occurs, removal must stop immediately and should not resume until power is restored and exhaust units are operating again.

Because airborne asbestos fibers are microscopic in size and tend to remain in suspension for a long time, the exhaust units must keep operating throughout the entire abatement project, decontamination, and final clearance processes.

Leaving the negative pressure system operating during the final cleanup and clearance process allows the suspended fibers the potential to be "cleaned" from the air. Also, until the results of final clearance air samples are known, the confining and minimizing aspects of negative pressure filtration are needed to ensure leakage of contaminated air outside the enclosure does not occur.

To ensure continuous operation (and therefore continuous negative pressure differential), a spare negative pressure exhaust unit(s) should be readily available at all times.

Filter Replacement

All filters must be accessible from the work area or "contaminated" side of the barrier. Thus, personnel responsible for changing filters while the negative pressure system is in use should wear approved respirators and other protective equipment. The operating life of a HEPA filter depends on the level of particulate contamination in the environment in which it is used. During use, filters will become loaded with dust, which increases resistance to air flow and diminishes the air-handling capacity of the unit. The difference in pressure drop across the filters between "clean" and "loaded" conditions is a convenient means of estimating the extent of air-flow resistance and determining when the filters should be replaced.

When the pressure drop across the filters (as determined by the Magnehelic gauge or manometer on the unit) exceeds the pressure specified by the manufacturer, the pre-filter should be replaced first. The pre-filter, which fan suction will generally hold in place on the intake grill, should be removed with the unit running by carefully rolling or folding in its sides. Any dust dislodged from the pre-filter during removal will be collected on the intermediate filter. The used pre-filter should be wetted and placed inside a six mil plastic bag, sealed and labeled, and disposed of as asbestos waste. A new pre-filter is then placed on the intake grill. Filters for pre-filtration applications may be purchased as individual precut panels or in a roll of specified width that must be cut to size.

If the pressure drop still exceeds the manufacturer's specified pressure after the pre-filter has been replaced, the intermediate filter is replaced. With the unit operating, the pre-filter should be removed, the intake grill or filter access opened, and the intermediate filter removed. Any dust dislodged from the intermediate filter during removal will be collected on the HEPA filter. The used intermediate filter should be wetted and placed in a sealable plastic bag (appropriately labeled) and disposed of as asbestos waste. The gasket between the filter and the housing should be inspected for any gaps or cracks. Worn gaskets should be replaced as needed. A new HEPA filter (structurally identical to the original filter) should then be installed. The intake grill and intermediate filter should be put back in place, the unit turned on, and the pre-filter positioned on the intake grill.

Whenever the HEPA filter is replaced, the pre-filter and intermediate filter should also be replaced.

When several exhaust units are used to ventilate a work area, negative pressure can be maintained during the HEPA filter replacement and the direction of air flow into the work area will be maintained. If only two exhaust units are operating on-site, a backup unit should be available and operating before an original unit is shut down for HEPA filter replacement. An abatement enclosure should <u>never</u> have only one exhaust unit operating. A failure of this sole unit for any reason would eliminate the negative pressure in the work area. Thus, the risk of asbestos fiber release to the outside environment is controlled with additional unit(s).

Any filters used in the system may be replaced more frequently than the pressure drop across the filters indicates is necessary. Experience has shown that pre-filters, for example, should be replaced two to four times a day or when accumulations of particulate matter become visible. Intermediate filters must be replaced once every day or so, and the HEPA filter may be replaced at the beginning of each new project. (Used filters must be disposed of as asbestos-containing waste). Conditions in the work area dictate the frequency of filter changes. In a work area where fiber release is effectively controlled by thorough wetting and good work practices, fewer filter changes may be required than in work areas where the removal process is not well controlled. It should also be noted that the collection efficiency of a filter generally improves as particulate accumulates on it. Thus, filters can be used effectively until resistance (as a result of excessive particulate loading) diminishes the exhaust capacity of the unit.

Dismantling the System

As gross removal nears completion, filters should be checked for loading and replaced if necessary. If a pre-filter is being used on the outside of the exhaust unit, it should be removed before final cleanup begins. When the negative air system is shut down at the end of the project, the filters should be left in the negative air filtration unit and the openings sealed with polyethylene and duct tape and/or sprayed with spray polyethylene to avoid spreading contamination when the unit is moved from the work site. **Filters in the exhaust system should not be replaced after final clearance sampling is complete in order to avoid any risk of re-contaminating the area.**

Tips For Using Negative Air Pressure Systems:

1. Check the integrity of the gasket between the HEPA filter and housing each time the filter is changed, or after the unit has been transported to a new location.

2. A general rule of thumb for filter life during "average" removal is:

    2 hours for the 1/2" pre-filter
    24 hours for the 2" pre-filter
    500 hours for the 12" HEPA filter

    Changing out the 1/2" pre-filter frequently (every 20-30 minutes) during "heavy" removal will prolong the life of the much more expensive HEPA filter.

3. Before removal begins, check the availability of a 20 amp circuit. Most negative air machines require 18 amps for startup and 15 amps during normal operation.

4. Negative air units usually pull less volume than the rating assigned by the manufacturer. For instance, a unit rated at 2,000 cfm will typically pull 1300-1500 cfm. Also, as filters load, the cfm is reduced. Note: The reduced flow volume at the maximum accepted pressure drop (see manufacturer's literature) should be the criteria used for this calculation. Adjust your calculations accordingly for the number of units necessary.

5. Start the negative air system before beginning work and check to see if it is functioning properly. Make sure there is adequate makeup air; otherwise the polyethylene may be pulled away from the walls.

6. Smoke tubes are useful for checking airflow inside the containment.

7. Use heavy duty extension cords to energize the negative air filtration units. If a series of cords are connected, take necessary precautions to avoid shock hazards. Make sure the temporary electrical system is properly grounded.

8. As a rule of thumb, the containment area should be no larger than 10,000 square feet for efficient use of a negative air filtration system.

9. The negative air system is more effective in reducing fiber concentrations when laborers start removal at the farthest point from the negative air units and work toward them.

10. When venting the negative air filtration exhaust outside a window, a good seal can be formed by placing a piece of plywood with a hole cut for the flex duct in the window and sealing it with duct tape. Another seal can be formed by placing a piece of six mil polyethylene over the plywood template and cutting a slip in it for insertion of the exhaust duct. Tape is used to seal the space around the slit in the polyethylene and the duct.

11. The use of supplied air respirators will increase the air pressure in the work area. Negative air filtration units should always be used in conjunction with Type C respirators to prevent build-up of positive pressure.

Wet Removal Techniques

EPA regulations that cover the removal of asbestos material (40 CFR, Part 61, Subparts A&M, 1973 with subsequent amendments and revisions) require wetting the material before removal begins and keeping it wet as it is removed, bagged, transported, and disposed of.

Two advantages to the use of wet methods for removing asbestos materials include a reduction in airborne fiber concentrations that are generated during removal and a reduction in the effort required to remove the material. Wet removal is based on the ability of water to lower the potential for the asbestos-containing material to release airborne asbestos fibers and increase the settling rate of fibers that are released. Airborne fiber concentrations may be reduced significantly by using wet removal techniques rather than dry.

The positive effects of wet removal can be further enhanced by adding a wetting agent to the water. The wetting agent (i.e. surfactant) is a combination of chemicals which aids in the penetration of water into the material and increases the probability of individual fiber wetting. Various wetting agents are available which have been used in the agricultural industry and fire fighting profession for many years. EPA recommends a wetting agent consisting of 50% polyoxyethylene ester and 50% polyoxyethylene ether in a ratio of 1 ounce to 5 gallons of water. This wetting agent is not as effective with materials that contain a high percentage of amosite and crocidolite asbestos because amphiboles (i.e., amosite and crocidolite) do not absorb water. Sometimes, Asbestos Project Designers will impose an efficiency for the negative air units in the contract documents.

Removal of Sprayed or Troweled Friable Surfacing Materials from Ceilings

At this point of the abatement project, the work area has been sealed off with at least two layers of six mil fire retardant polyethylene on the floors and two layers of six mil fire retardant polyethylene on the walls (see section on Preparation of Work Area). The decontamination unit and negative air filtration units are in place, and the scaffolding, ladders, various sizes of short- and long-handled scrapers and other removal equipment have been brought into the work area.

EQUIPMENT USED FOR REMOVAL OF FRIABLE INSULATION MATERIALS

The first step in the removal process is to thoroughly wet the ceiling material with a low pressure mist of amended water. The material should be misted lightly with amended water to initially wet the surface; then a saturation coat is applied. The material can be wetted using a low pressure pump system or water hose with garden sprayer attached which can mix the wetting agent with the water. A hand pump garden sprayer can be used for small projects. Application with large pump systems or airless sprayers may cause leakage behind the barrier seals resulting in contamination of the walls and floors. Also, the initial impact of water applied with high pressure may cause elevated airborne fiber concentrations, therefore the low pressure and careful technique in application should be used. Time should be allotted between spraying with amended water and removal to provide for maximum penetration into the material. If the timeframe allows, the ceiling material should be thoroughly saturated with amended water the night before removal starts. (Note: the added weight of the amended water may cause delamination of this material overnight.)

Removal of ceiling material is carried out in two stages -- gross and secondary removal. Gross removals typically are conducted with a three- or four-man team. Two men working from a mobile scaffold with rails remove the friable material using scrapers. Wide blades can be used if the material comes off easily. Workers of approximately the same height should be paired together on the scaffolds. One or two workers on the ground package the moist material in six mil plastic bags or plastic-lined fiber drums before it has time to dry out. Rubber dust pans, plastic snow shovels, push brooms, and standard house brooms should be used to collect and bag the wet material. Do not use metal shovels or dust pans that can cause inadvertent tears in the polyethylene floor barriers. The crew that bags the material also repositions the scaffold as needed, relocking the wheels after each move. If several crews are removing material, it may be more time efficient to designate a "spray" person who walks from one area to the next, keeping the material on the ceiling and the floor wet and misting the air to maintain low airborne fiber concentrations. The spray person can also check for damaged floor barriers and promptly repair them.

Bags containing the waste material are processed for waste load-out, either by wet wiping, placing in another "clean" bag, or placing into fiber drums. (See Waste Disposal Requirements Section.) All bags should be removed from the work area at least by the end of the work day. Removal of bags on a continual basis provides for easier movement (particularly if workers are wearing air-supplied respirators) in the work area.

After removing as much of the sprayed-on material as possible with scrapers, crews begin secondary removal. Depending on the type of substrate (material underneath the friable insulation), various techniques and tools may be required. Common types of ceiling construction to which friable insulation materials may be applied include concrete, 3 coat plaster system, suspended metal lath, concrete joists and beams, metal deck, corrugated steel, steel beam, or bar joist. The surface substrate may be smooth, rough, or pitted and will affect the difficulty of secondary removal. Typically, a combination of brushing and wet wiping is used to remove the remaining residue. Nylon bristled brushes should be used instead of wire brushes, which may break the small fibers into smaller fibers. The rags used for wet wiping should not leave any fabric fibers on the substrate which might be mistaken as visual contamination. High efficiency particulate air (HEPA) vacuum cleaners are also useful for removing "hard-to-get-to" residue.

While crews are working from scaffolds or ladders to remove all remaining residue from the ceilings, workers should also be cleaning material off the polyethylene wall barriers and any stationary objects in the area. Brooms, wet rags, or squeegees are good for this purpose. Secondary removal is finished when all visual contamination is removed from the ceilings. The next phase is final cleanup (discussed in detail in Chapter XIII, Cleaning Up the Work Area).

Removal of Thermal System Insulation from Pipes, Boilers, and Tanks

There is a wide variation in the types of asbestos-containing thermal system insulation used on pipes, boilers, and tanks. Pipes may be insulated with preformed fibrous wrapping, corrugated paper, a chalky mixture containing magnesia, fiber felt, and insulating cement. (Note: There are older materials labeled "magnesia" that contain asbestos and new materials also labeled "magnesia" that contain glass fiber rather than asbestos.) Usually a protective jacket, which may also contain asbestos, made of paper, tape, cloth, metal, or cement covers the insulation materials. Boilers and tanks may be insulated with asbestos "blankets" on wire lath, preformed block, or the chalky magnesia mixture which is typically covered with a finishing cement. Different approaches are typically required for removing these asbestos-containing materials than sprayed-on or troweled-on ceiling insulation; however, the same protective measures are used. Careful handling and packaging is required in many cases because of the metal jackets, bands, or wire associated with the insulation materials.

Glovebags, which can be sealed around sections of pipe to form "mini-containment areas", may be used in some situations for removing pipe insulation (see Glovebag Section). Insulated objects which are not readily accessible or are too large or hot for application of the glovebag technique, may require a full area enclosure with modified removal techniques.

Because insulation on pipes, boilers, and tanks may contain as much as 70% asbestos and, because areas where these materials are being removed are often confined, high airborne fiber concentrations may occur. Also, these materials are more difficult to saturate with water and may often contain amosite, which is not controlled as well with water as other types of asbestos. If these situations cannot be controlled by higher air flow rates and other engineering techniques, then Type C airline respirators are recommended for workers engaged in removal of asbestos from pipes and boilers.

Removal of insulation from pipes, tanks, or boilers can be accomplished by two-person teams. Cuts or slits are made in the insulation material, a spray nozzle is inserted, and the material is wetted to the extent feasible. One man cuts away the insulation and bags while the other continuously sprays the material with amended water. Any metal bands or wire that is removed should be folded or rolled and placed in polyethylene to avoid lacerating personnel.

After the gross material is removed, nylon brushes are used to thoroughly clean the pipes, tanks, or boilers. (In cases when pipes are extremely hot, nylon brushes may melt and wire brushes may be the only tool available.) Particular care must be taken to clean the fittings and joints where a cement-plaster type material has been removed. After brushing, the surfaces are wet-wiped and the final cleanup phase begins.

Dry Removal Techniques

Dry removal, which requires specific EPA approval and approval from the NYSDOL, may be appropriate for some types of asbestos-containing materials that have been previously encapsulated and will not absorb amended water. There are special conditions that preclude the use of water, such as a room containing electrical supply lines that cannot be de-energized during the removal project, hot steam pipes, crawl spaces, etc. Dry removal techniques can be used successfully, but require much skill and attention to critical details in order to minimize airborne fibers in the workplace and to adequately confine all airborne fibers to the workplace enclosure. Proven procedures include use of large vacuum systems, small area containment with localized HEPA filtered exhaust, and re-circulating HEPA units inside the work area.

The dry removal procedures selected for a given situation must be carefully matched to the existing work area conditions, the type of asbestos and the skill of the work force; adding layers of enclosure plastic, adding airlock chambers to the decontamination units, providing double or triple, rigid primary barriers (in addition to several layers of primary polyethylene), and increasing the number of negative procedures. These added confining and minimizing measures obviously add cost to the project. It is always much easier to control airborne fibers using wet techniques. It is recommended that all reasonable and safe avenues for wet removal be thoroughly explored before resorting to dry removal. It must also be noted that dry removal requires **job specific EPA NYSDOL approval**, and approval is sometimes difficult to obtain. It is very important that all personnel use maximum personal protection during dry removal because of the constant and high potential for elevated airborne fiber levels.

Special Considerations

Amended water is not totally effective in controlling fibers emitted from material containing amosite asbestos. Some contractors reportedly use ethylene glycol, removal encapsulants, and/or oils to help reduce amosite emissions. Others have an encapsulant which is diluted so that it dries slowly and does not harden before the asbestos material can be removed from the pipes or boilers. Some manufacturers are currently conducting comparative testing of these wetting methods to determine which is the most effective.

Steam or hot water distribution networks should be shut down if at all possible, when insulation is being removed. If these systems must stay on line, special consideration must be given to avoid heat stress and skin burns.

When airline respirators are being used by workers, care must be taken not to let the airlines come into contact with hot pipes which must burn a hole in the rubber line. When air lines are worn by persons working from scaffolds, care must be taken not to wrap the airlines around objects on the ground or the scaffold. See chapter on Type C respirators that address safety considerations.

bjectives: To understand the proper techniques for preparing and working including setting up a decontamination unit.

Learning Tasks: Information in this Chapter should enable participants to:

- Understand objectives of work area preparation.

- Become familiar with the sequence and methods for accomplishing tasks in work area preparation

- Know the functions of a decontamination unit.

- Become familiar with the basic construction of a decontamination unit.

- Know procedures for entering and leaving the work area using the decontamination unit.

- Become familiar with the necessary materials and equipment used for prepping the work area and building a decontamination unit.

ASBESTOS ABATEMENT EQUIPMENT AND ESTABLISHING THE DECONTAMINATION UNIT

The main purpose of properly preparing the work area (where an asbestos response action is to take place) prior to a response action is to prevent exposure to airborne concentrations of asbestos fibers to both workers and building occupants. Airborne fibers that are generated by disturbance of asbestos-containing material may remain suspended in the air for long periods of time because of their small size and aerodynamic properties. These airborne asbestos fibers can migrate via air currents to other parts of the building.

Preparation of the work area before an asbestos abatement project begins serves the primary purpose of containing fibers that are released within the work area. Good preparation techniques serve to protect interior finishes such as hardwood floors or carpets from water damage and to reduce cleanup efforts. Preventing injury through appropriate safety practices is another major consideration in work area preparation (see Chapter on Other Safety and Health Considerations).

Each project has unique requirements for effective preparation. For instance, the sequence of steps would probably be different for preparing a boiler room than preparing an area with asbestos material above a suspended ceiling. This may be attributed to the age of the building, the physical condition of materials, as well as HVAC system involvement. The following are general guidelines that can be modified to address specific problems encountered on an asbestos abatement project.

STEP 1 - Conduct Walkthrough Survey of the Work Area

The contractor, building owner, and project designer should make a walkthrough survey of the building or facility to inventory the ACM, note any special conditions, and photograph any existing damages. Information gained can be used to prepare an abatement plan and to aid in preparation of a realistic quotation. Complete documentation of existing conditions through the use of field notes, photographs, and videotape may benefit those involved, if litigation should occur at a later date.

Note: The exact sequence of work area preparation is described in 12 NYCRR Part 56.

STEP 2 - Post Warning Signs

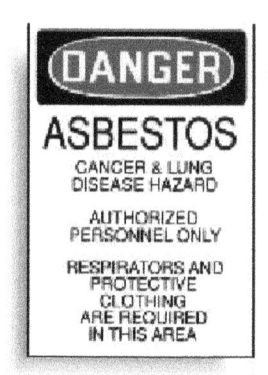

Warning signs that demarcate regulated work areas should be displayed at each location (entrances and exits) where airborne concentrations of asbestos may be in excess of the 0.1 f/cc permissible exposure limit (TWA) or the 1.0 f/cc excursion limit. Signs should be positioned such that any person would notice the warning before entering the area, and be able to take the proper necessary protective actions.

The warning signs are required to contain the following information: (1) that asbestos is a dangerous cancer and lung disease hazard, (2) that authorized personnel only are allowed in the work area, and (3) that respirators and protective clothing are required before entering the area. See 29CFR 1926.1101(k) of the OSHA Construction Industry Standard for sign specifications. These signs are available from most safety supply companies or asbestos abatement contractor suppliers.

STEP 3 - Shut Down the Heating, Ventilating, and Air Conditioning System (HVAC)

The HVAC system supplying the work area should be shut down and isolated to prevent entrainment of asbestos dust throughout the building. To avoid inadvertent activation of the HVAC system while removal operations are in progress, the control panel should be tagged and locked. Personnel need to be warned not to activate any control panels. HVAC system balancing needs to be considered to avoid over-pressurization in the occupied portions of buildings.

All vents and air ducts inside the work area should be covered and sealed with two layers of six-mil polyethylene and duct tape. The first layer of polyethylene (poly) should be left in place until the area has passed final visual inspection and clearance air monitoring.

HVAC filters, which may be contaminated with asbestos dust, should be removed and disposed of in the same manner as the other asbestos-containing materials (see Disposal of Waste). If the filters are contaminated, the inside walls of the air ducts are probably also contaminated, and the contractor should make efforts to clean or dispose of them.

STEP 4 - Clean/Remove Non-Stationary Items from the Work Area

Preparation for constructing negative-pressure enclosures, as required per 29 CFR 1926.1101(g) should begin with the cleaning of all objects in the work area. The objects should first be vacuumed with a HEPA vacuum and cleaned with amended water, unless they are made of material that will be damaged by the wetting agent. Wiping with plain water is recommended in those cases where amended water will damage the object. Non-stationary items should be removed from the work area (e.g., desks, chairs, rugs, and light fixtures) to ensure that these objects do not become contaminated with asbestos. Drapes should be removed for cleaning or disposal. Carpets contaminated with debris, or suspected of being contaminated, should be disposed of as asbestos-containing waste.

Workers involved with the cleaning and removal should at least wear a half mask HEPA filter dual cartridge respirator and disposable clothing when initial preparation work is being carried out.

STEP 5 - Cover and Seal Stationary Items with Polyethylene

Before the asbestos response action begins, objects that cannot be moved from the asbestos-contaminated work area should be HEPA vacuumed or wet-wiped and covered with six-mil fire retardant polyethylene sheeting. They should be securely taped with duct tape or plastic tape to achieve an airtight seal around the object and to ensure that they do not become contaminated during the removal project. Items not being removed may include large pieces of machinery, blackboards, water fountains, toilets, etc. Use of two layers of six-mil polyethylene is a good recommended practice and is required by Part 56. These layers of polyethylene (poly) must be left in place.

A specific outline of items to be covered and sealed is included here.

    A.   Windows and Doors

        The edges of all the windows should be sealed with 2" or 3" wide high quality duct tape. After the edges have been taped, the windows should be covered and sealed with six-mil fire retardant poly and duct tape.

        Covering windows and all other doors not being used during abatement with two separate layers of six mil fire retardant polyethylene (called critical barriers), before covering the walls provides a back-up layer of protection and saves time in installation, because it reduces the number of edges of poly that must be cut and taped. A single entrance to be used for access and egress to the work area should be selected. This would most likely be the decontamination area which is discussed later in this Chapter.

    B.   Floor

        Six mil fire retardant poly sheets should be used to cover the floor in the work area. Several sheets will need to be seamed together with spray adhesive and duct tape. To check the integrity of the seal, blue or red carpenter's chalk may be placed beneath the seam line. If a water leak occurs, the seam line will darken in color. Any leaks that occur should be promptly cleaned up. The poly floor sheets would be cut and peeled back to access the wet area. After mopping up the water and any contamination that leaked through, the area should be wet-wiped with clean rags. After the area dries, it is HEPA-vacuumed, and the peeled-back sheets are put back in place and sealed with duct tape. An additional "patch" sheet can be placed over this area and sealed with tape to provide extra protection.

        After joining the sheets of poly together, the floor covering should be cut to the proper dimensions, allowing the poly to extend twenty-four inches (minimum 12 inches) up the wall, all the way around the room. The poly should be flush with the walls at each corner to prevent damage by foot traffic.

        When the first layer of poly has been secured in place, the walls are covered with six mil fire retardant poly and a second layer should be laid on the floor with the seams of the first and second layers offset.

The second layer of six mil fire retardant poly should extend a few inches above the first layer on the wall and be secured with duct tape.

Potential slippery spots may be encountered when covering stairs or ramps and care must be taken to provide traction for foot traffic. Wet poly is very slippery and can create serious tripping hazards. To provide better footing, masking tape or thin wood strips can be placed on top of the poly to provide rough surfaces in these areas.

C. Walls

After the first layer of polyethylene has covered the floors, multiple layers of six-mil fire retardant polyethylene are used to cover the walls. The sheets of six mil fire retardant poly should be hung from the top of the wall below the ceiling and should extend to the floor/wall conjuncture. Overlapping of the vertical sheets will be necessary; the seams should be sealed with adhesive duct tape.

Duct tape alone will not support the weight of the poly after exposure to the varying environmental conditions that occur inside the work area. The sheets may be hung using a combination of nails and furring strips (small wood blocks), or adhesive and staples, and sealed with four-inch duct tape. Nails may cause some minor damage to the interior finish; however, it is usually more time efficient to touch up the nail holes than to repeatedly repair fallen barriers.

D. Light Fixtures

Light fixtures will have to be removed or detached to gain access to asbestos-containing material. Before beginning this task, the electrical supply must be shut off, locked, and tagged. The light fixtures should be wet-wiped before they are removed from the area.

STEP 6 - Locate and Secure the Electrical System

Amended water is typically used to saturate asbestos-containing, sprayed-on material prior to removal. This creates a humid environment with damp to very wet and slippery floors. To eliminate the potential for a shock hazard, the electrical supply to the work area should be de-energized, locked out, and tagged before removal operations begin. The following items need to be addressed before removal actually begins:

- Identify and de-energize electrical circuits in the work area.

- Lock the breaker box after the system has been shut down and place a warning tag on the box. The breaker box can't be locked if it contains energized circuits for non-work areas; individual breakers may have to be locked out. Custodial personnel should be consulted about electrical distribution to other areas of an occupied building.

- Make provisions for supplying the work area with electricity from outside the work area, which is equipped with a ground-fault-interrupt system.

- If the electrical supply cannot be disconnected, energized parts must be insulated or guarded from employee contact and any other conductive object.

STEP 7 - Securing the Work Area

The work area should be secured to prevent contamination from spreading beyond the work area. See Part 56-7-7. All entrances should be secured when removal operations are not in progress. Provisions must also be made to secure the decontamination station entrance when no one is on the job site. Security guards may be a reasonable precaution, depending on the nature of the project. When the work area is occupied, padlocks must be removed to permit emergency escape routes. Arrows should be taped or painted on the poly-covered walls to indicate the location of exits.

Nonessential personnel should not be permitted to enter the work area. A job log should be maintained onsite (in the clean area) for recording who enters the work area and the time each person enters and exits the work zone. The project supervisor (or designee) should be sure that the log is maintained on a daily basis.

ESTABLISHING A DECONTAMINATION UNIT

Employers involved in asbestos removal, demolition, or renovation operations must provide their employees with hygiene facilities to be used to decontaminate asbestos-exposed workers, equipment, and clothing when such employees leave the work area. The decontamination station is designed to allow passage to and from the work area during asbestos operations with minimal leakage of asbestos-containing dust to the outside. A typical decontamination unit consists of a clean change room, a shower, and an equipment room separated by airlocks. The work area will be kept under negative air pressure 24 hours a day, including weekends, until final air clearance is achieved.

Materials used to construct a typical unit include: 2-inch by 4-inch lumber for the frame, 1/4 inch to 1/2 inch plywood or six mil fire retardant poly for the walls, duct tape, staples, and nails. The floor should be covered with three layers of six-mil fire retardant polyethylene at least two of which must be reinforced.

Chapters of the decontamination unit can be built separately to allow for easy disassembly and re-use (frames only, not poly) at other areas of buildings or at other job sites. Designs of decontamination stations may vary with each project depending on the size of the crew and the physical constraints imposed by the facility.

Customized trailers that can be readily moved from one location to the next are also used as decontamination stations. The cost of these units depends on the size and features. A company conducting work at many different locations would probably recover this initial investment over time.

Whether a decontamination station is constructed on site or is in the form of a trailer, the basic design components are the same.

Clean Room

As described in the OSHA Asbestos Standard for the Construction Industry (1926.1101), the clean room is an uncontaminated room having facilities for the storage of employees' street clothing and uncontaminated materials and equipment. It is an area in which employees remove their street clothes, store them, and don their respirators and disposable protective clothing. This room is where workers dress in clean clothes after showering. Furnishings for the clean room should include: benches, lockers for clothes and valuables, and nails or hooks for hanging respirators. Extra disposable coveralls and towels can be stored in the clean change room.

Shower Room

For a large project, the shower should have on either side of it, two airlocks with both the clean and dirty change rooms on either side of the airlocks. Workers pass through the shower room on their way to the removal area, and use the showers on their way out after leaving contaminated clothing in the equipment room. Although most job specifications require only a single showerhead, installation of multiple showers may be time and cost effective if the work crew is large. OSHA requires cold and hot water with separate controls.

Shower wastewater should be drained, collected, and filtered through a system before disposal into the sanitary sewer. A system containing a series of several filters with progressively smaller pore size (100, 50, 5 micron) is recommended to avoid rapid initial clogging of the filtration system by larger particles. Wastewater may need to be retained in sealed barrels or containers and/or holding tanks for appropriate disposal. For example, Alabama, Georgia, Maryland, and New Jersey have written specifications for handling shower wastewater.

EQUIPMENT AREA
SKETCH OF TYPICAL DECONTAMINATION AREA
AND WASTE LOAD-OUT AREA

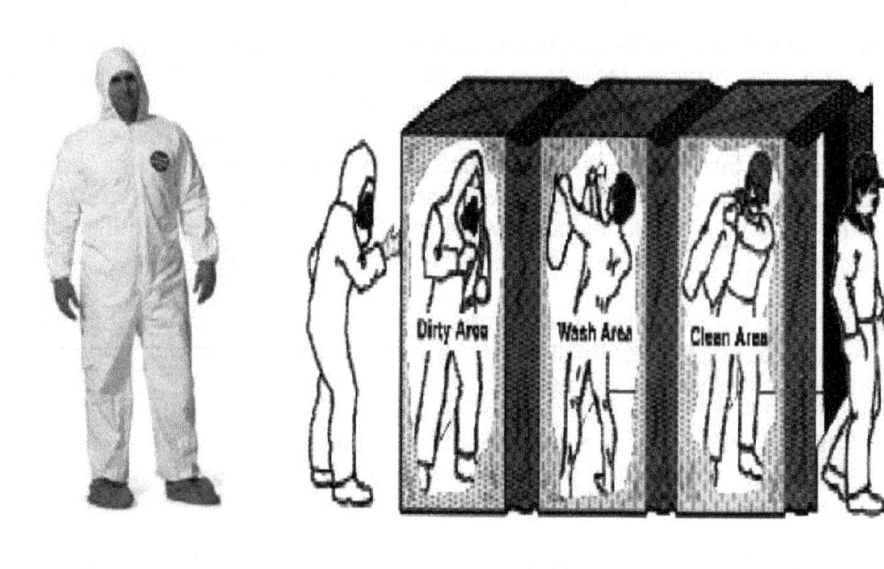

SEQUENCE OF PROCEDURES FOR
ENTERING and EXITING the WORK AREA

IN THE CLEAN ROOM, WORKER:

1. Enters clean room
2. Removes clothing, places in locker
3. Puts on nylon swim suit (optional)
4. Puts on clean coveralls
5. If separate disposable foot coverings are used, these are put on
6. Applies tape around ankles, wrists, etc.
7. Inspects respirator, puts it on, checks fit
8. Puts on hood over respirator head straps
9. Proceeds to equipment room

IN THE EQUIPMENT ROOM, WORKER:

10. Puts on any additional clothing - deck shoes, hard hat, etc.
11. Collects necessary tools and proceeds to WORK AREA

IN THE WORK AREA, WORKER:

12. Brushes off contamination

IN THE EQUIPMENT ROOM, WORKER:

13. Removes all clothing except respirator
14. Places disposable protective clothing in a bag or bin
15. Stores any other contaminated articles

16. Proceeds to shower

IN THE SHOWER, WORKER:

17. Washes respirator and soaks filters (without removing)
18. Removes respirator, washes with soap and water, disposes of contaminated filters in receptacle in shower, or reaches into dirty room to place filters into easily accessible disposal bag
19. Washes swim suit
20. Thoroughly washes body and hair

IN THE CLEAN ROOM, WORKER:

21. Dries off, dresses in clean coveralls or street clothes
22. Cleans and dries respirator, replaces filters (if applicable

Equipment Room

This area, also called the dirty change room, is the contaminated area where workers remove their protective coveralls and where equipment, boots or shoes, hardhats, goggles and any additional contaminated work clothes are stored. Workers place disposable clothing such as coveralls, booties and hoods in bins before leaving this area for the shower room. Respirators are worn into the shower and thoroughly soaked with water before they are taken off. The equipment room will probably require cleanup several times daily to prevent asbestos materials from being tracked into the shower and clean rooms.

Airlocks

Airlocks are formed by overlapping two sheets of polyethylene at the exit of one room and two sheets at the entrance to the next room with three feet of space between the barriers. There are various methods used for constructing airlocks.

Waste Load-Out Area

The waste load-out area (separate from the decontamination unit and not used for personnel egress) is used as a short-term storage area for bagged waste and as a port for transferring waste to the truck. An enclosure can be constructed to form an airlock between the exit of the load-out area and an enclosed truck.

The outside of the waste containers should be free of all contaminated material before removal from the work area. Gross contamination should be wiped or scraped off containers before they are placed in the load-out area. Any remaining contamination should be removed by wet wiping; the bagged material can be placed in a second clean bag.

Waste Decontamination Procedures

The clean room, shower, and equipment room must be sealed completely to ensure that the sole source of airflow through these areas originates from uncontaminated areas outside the asbestos removal, demolition, or renovation enclosure. After construction of the enclosure is completed, a ventilation system(s) should be installed to create a negative pressure within the enclosure with respect to the area outside the enclosure.

OBJECTIVES:

1. Recognize the need for effective respiratory protection for Project Monitors for asbestos.

2. Understand the procedures for the proper selection of respiratory protection equipment.

3. Understand the use and limitations of respirators.

4. Become familiar with the concept of protection factors and how they relate to respirator selection and use.

5. Recognize the components of an effective respiratory protection program.

6. Understand the importance of proper fit testing procedures for respirators.

7. Recognize the need for and use of protective clothing and other personal protective equipment.

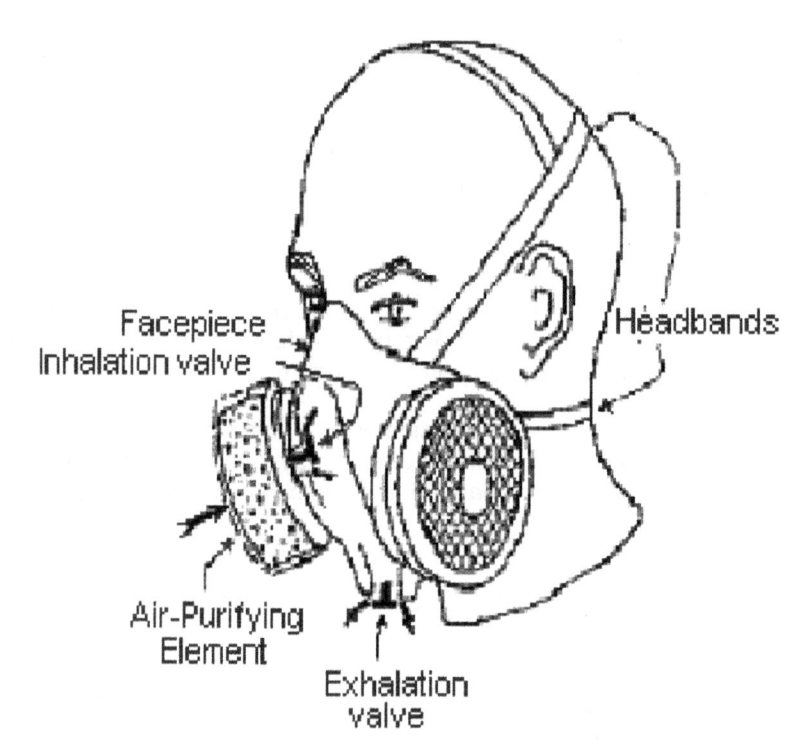

Typical Half-Mask Respirator

INTRODUCTION:

Project monitors must wear appropriate personal protective equipment for his/her own protection when performing sampling and assessment activities. This will normally include a respirator and protective clothing. Depending on the specific project, additional protective measures may be necessary for eye protection.

There are three ways that hazardous materials can enter the body: (1) through the gastrointestinal tract, usually via the mouth, (2) through the skin, and (3) through the respiratory system. Asbestos does not appear to pose a serious threat to the body through the first or second routes of entry. It can, however, cause serious diseases when it enters the body through the respiratory system.

RESPIRATORY SYSTEM

The respiratory system is a gaseous (air) pump containing a series of airways leading from the nose and mouth down into the air sacs (alveoli) where there is an exchange of oxygen and carbon dioxide. The main components of the respiratory system, from top to bottom are as follows:

- Nose and mouth
- Throat
- Larynx (voice box)
- Trachea (wind pipe)
- Bronchi (branches from trachea)
- Alveoli (air sacs in the lung)
- Diaphragm and chest muscles

The human body has certain natural defenses to protect itself against inhaling dust. The most important of these is the muco-ciliary escalator. Airways of the upper respiratory tract (trachea through bronchi) are lined with <u>cilia</u> (hair-like protrusions) covered with a layer of mucous. These cilia are constantly sweeping upward quickly, then down slowly, and thus moving the mucous and trapped materials up at a rate of approximately one-inch per minute. This is an important clearance mechanism, which prevents most large particles from reaching the alveoli in the lungs. Particulates trapped in the mucous are carried back up to the throat where they are swallowed or expectorated. Unfortunately, this natural defense mechanism does not prevent all asbestos fibers from reaching the lungs where damage can occur. Accordingly, respirators must be worn to provide further protection when asbestos exposure is likely.

RESPIRATORY HAZARDS

Respiratory hazards are generally divided into two categories; toxic contaminants and oxygen deficiency. Generally, building inspections would not pose oxygen deficiency hazards. However, since there may be projects and circumstances where it can be a problem, oxygen deficiency must always be considered. For example, there could be an oxygen deficiency problem while inspecting in steam tunnels, mechanical chases, or boilers. Failing to consider oxygen deficiency could result in a fatality on any project.

Toxic contaminants are the more common category of respiratory hazards encountered on inspections. Those toxic contaminants are generally subdivided into two categories: particulates and gaseous materials (or a combination of the two). Asbestos fibers are an example of the particulate subcategory, and carbon monoxide is an example of the gaseous subcategory. It is possible to have both of these hazardous substances, as well as others, in a work area at the same time.

The control of respiratory hazards often involves three steps:

- Assessing the hazards;
- Reducing or eliminating the hazards;
- Providing respiratory protective equipment.

Chapter 8 – Personal Protective Equipment

The asbestos detection and control industry is actually based on these first two steps. Buildings and other structures are inspected or surveyed to assess potential asbestos hazards. When a potential asbestos hazard exists, a group or contractor is called upon to reduce or eliminate the hazard through removal, encapsulation, or enclosure of the material. Thus, the third step, respirators, can be avoided to protect the building occupants.

RESPIRATOR CLASSIFICATIONS

There are two general categories of respiratory protection devices: air-purifying and supplied-air respirators. For most building inspections, air-purifying respirators will provide the needed protection. Accordingly, the discussion of the uses and limitations of supplied air respirators is limited (See Exhibit J-1 for picture of various types of respirators).

Air-Purifying Respirators

These respirators remove the hazardous contaminant from the breathing air before it is inhaled. They consist of a soft, rubber facepiece and a replaceable filter or cartridge. Two major sub-categories of air-purifying respirators are the mechanical filter type and the chemical cartridge type. The mechanical filter variety is designed to protect against particulate contaminants such as asbestos. The chemical cartridge type protects against gaseous contaminants such as solvent vapors. Each respirator assembly is approved for a particular contaminant; care must be taken in choosing the appropriate unit. High efficiency particulate air (HEPA) filters designed for asbestos are typically purple or magenta in color. These filters will remove 99.97 percent of particles 0.3 micrometers or greater in diameter.

Air-purifying respirators are further categorized based on their degree of face coverage. The half-mask respirator covers half the face - from the bridge of the nose to under the chin. A full-face respirator covers the face from the forehead to under the chin. The more extensive coverage provides a better fit and a higher degree of protection Air-purifying respirators depend upon breathing action to draw atmospheric air through the respirator filter or cartridge where it is decontaminated hence; they are referred to as negative pressure respirators.

Powered Air-Purifying Respirators (PAPR's)

A special subcategory of air-purifying respirator is the Powered Air-Purifying (PAPR) type. It uses the same types of cartridges and filters as regular air purifying respirators to clean the air. PAPR's, however, are positive-pressure devices, which employ a portable rechargeable battery pack, and blower to force contaminated air through a filter or cartridge, where it is cleaned and supplied to the wearer's breathing zone. PAPRS are available in both tight-fitting and loose-fitting styles. Because the air is being drawn from the immediate work area, they too offer no protection against oxygen deficiency. An advantage of using a powered air-purifying respirator is that it supplies air at a positive pressure within the facepiece, helmet, or hood so that any leak is usually outward.

Supplied-Air Respirators

These respirators supply uncontaminated, breathing air from a source independent of the surrounding atmosphere. Air is delivered to the facepiece through an airline (a hose). These respirators are often referred to as "air-line respirators". A second type of supplied air respirator is the self-contained breathing apparatus (SCBA). The user carries the source of breathable air, usually a tank of compressed air.

Airline respirators come in several distinct versions: demand, pressure-demand and continuous-flow. They are distinguished by their regulator and valve design. EPA and NIOSH recommend the pressure-demand type if supplied-air respirators are selected.

Supplied-air respirators also have limitations:

- The trailing airline restricts the user's mobility.
- The air supply of a SCBA respirator is limited.
- The bulk and weight of a SCBA respirator make it impractical for strenuous work or for use in confined spaces.

○ Backup units or supplemental air-purifying respirators should be available if the air supply is interrupted.

RESPIRATORY PROTECTION PROGRAM

Respirators are commonly used to help protect against inhalation hazards. However, a respiratory protection program is not simply donning a respirator and expecting to be adequately protected.

Any employer who requires or permits employees to wear a respirator must have a written respiratory protection program. This is required by OSHA in both of their asbestos standards (29 CFR 1910.1001 and 1926.1101) and respiratory protection regulations (29 CFR 1910.134). The written respirator program establishes standard operating procedures concerning the use and maintenance of respiratory equipment. In addition to having such a written program, the employer must also be able to demonstrate that the program is enforced and updated as necessary.

The OSHA regulations spell out just what must be included in a written program. Below, those items are discussed with special emphasis on applications to work performed by Project Monitors.

An effective respirator program, as adapted from A Guide to Respiratory Protection for the Asbestos Abatement IndustryUSEPA/NIOSH publication EPA-560-OPTS-8&001 (September 1986) should include:

1. A written statement of company policy, including assignment of individual responsibility, accountability, and authority for required activities of the respiratory protection program.
2. Written standard operating procedures governing the selection and use of respirators.
3. Respirator selection (from NIOSH approved and certified models) on the basis of hazards to which the worker is exposed. MSHA has not had a role in certifying respirators since 1998.
4. Medical examination of workers to determine whether or not they may be assigned an activity where respiratory protection is required.
5. User training in the proper use and limitations of respirators (as well as a way to evaluate the skill and knowledge obtained by the worker through training).
6. Respirator fit testing.
7. Regular cleaning and disinfecting of respirators.
8. Routine inspection of respirators during cleaning, and at least once a month and after each use for those respirators designated for emergency use.
9. Storage of respirators in convenient, clean, and sanitary locations.
10. Surveillance of work area conditions and degree of employee exposure (e.g., through air monitoring).
11. Regular inspection and evaluation of the continued effectiveness of the program.

All of the above items are required by OSHA, if employees wear respirators during work, or if the OSHA permissible exposure limit (PEL) or excursion limit (EL) is exceeded. Although not required, one additional program element is recommended:

12. Recognition and resolution of special problems as they affect respirator use (e.g., facial hair, eye glasses, etc.)

Establishing a Policy

Every employer should prepare a clear concise policy regarding the use of respirators by their employees when performing building inspection activities for asbestos. This policy should serve as the guiding principal for the preparation, implementation, and enforcement of an effective respiratory protection program.

Designation of a Program Administrator

A program administrator must be designated by name. This person is responsible for implementation of, and adherence to, the provisions of the respiratory protection program. It is usually a good idea to also designate a person who is responsible for enforcement of the procedures at each job site. This may apply to a Project Monitor. Procedures should also be outlined for enforcement of the program. Enforcement procedures and the development of the program as a whole should be done in conjunction with and input from the employees and/or their representative(s).

Selection and Use of Respiratory Protection Equipment

The selection of appropriate respiratory equipment generally involves three steps:

1. Identifying the hazards,
2. Evaluating the hazards,
3. Providing proper respiratory protection equipment to suit the conditions and the individual.

The purpose of inspecting buildings and structures is to determine the presence (or absence) of ACM and to identify conditions which are potentially hazardous. Until the level of hazard is evaluated, Project Monitors should assume that fiber levels could be high enough to be of concern.

The respirator selected, and the respiratory program established must conform to Occupational Safety and Health Administration (OSHA) standards, and guidelines published by respirator manufacturers. The OSHA respirator standard (29 CFR 1910.134) requires that only approved respirators are used. In addition, the respirator must be approved for protection specifically against asbestos fibers.

The National Institute for Occupational Safety and Health (NIOSH) is the official respirator testing and approval agency for respirators. If the entire respirator assembly including cartridges, filters, and hoses, passes NIOSH test criteria, then NIOSH issues an approval number. The specific number is preceded by the letters "TC", which indicates the respirator assembly was "Tested and Certified".

In addition to an assigned identification number associated with each unit, a label identifying the type of hazard the respirator is designed to protect against accompanies a NIOSH approved respirator. Additional information on the label, indicates limitations and identifies the component parts approved for use with the basic unit.

Although some single-use disposable dust masks were at one time "approved" by NIOSH for use with asbestos, they should not be used during asbestos inspections. NIOSH has stated that these respirators do not provide adequate protection against asbestos. As a rule of thumb, negative pressure, air-purifying respirators with HEPA filters may be used during building inspections.

Protection Factors

Respirators offer varying degrees of protection against asbestos fibers. The key to understanding the differences between types of respirators (air-purifying, powered-air purifying, air-supplied) is the amount of protection afforded the wearer. To compare these, one must understand the concept of a <u>protection factor</u> (PF).

A protection factor is a number obtained when the concentration of a contaminant outside the mask is divided by the concentration found inside the mask. This simple formula is illustrated below.

Protection Factor (PF) = $\dfrac{\textbf{Concentration outside mask}}{\textbf{Concentration inside mask}}$

The protection factor depends greatly on the fit of the mask to the wearer's face. Accordingly, the protection offered by any one respirator will be different for each individual person. Further, the protection constantly changes depending upon the worker's activities and even shaving habits. When a worker laughs or coughs inside a respirator, the protection factor will decrease since it will not "fit" as well during laughing or coughing. Similarly, a worker who forgot to shave one morning will not receive as much protection that day since the mask will not fit as well to the face. The importance of properly fitting the mask should now be obvious.

It is virtually impossible to measure the concentration inside the mask (where the worker is breathing) for each worker, all the time, during the various activities he or she may be conducting. Accordingly, protection factors, based on extensive research, have been developed for different categories of respirators. Using these protection factors, it is easy to determine what type of respirator is appropriate to maintain the concentration of asbestos inside the mask below a certain level. (A level of 0.01 fibers per cubic centimeter (f/cc) is often cited as the desired level inside the mask) Using established protection factors, the Project Monitor may select the appropriate respirator to maintain the concentration inside the respirator below 0.01 f/cc. It should be noted that the protection factors for powered-air purifying respirators are estimated on the most recent data available. (Supplied-air respirators are not included since they are unlikely to be needed by Project Monitors.)

SUGGESTED RESPIRATOR SELECTION FOR PROTECTION AGAINST ASBESTOS WHEN PROPERLY FITTED FOR USE AND PROPERLY MAINTAINED

Maximum airborne fiber concentration outside the respirator to maintain exposure inside the

Respirator Selection	PF	Maximum Use Concentration
High efficiency air-purifying type (half mask)	10	1.0 f/cc
High efficiency air-purifying type (full face mask)	50	5.0 f/cc
Powered air-purifying (PAPR) helmet type	1000	100 f/cc
Powered-air purifying (PAPR) tight-fitting mask	1000	100 f/cc

Medical Surveillance

Only those individuals who are medically capable to wear respiratory protection equipment shall be issued one. Before being issued a respirator, an employee will receive pertinent tests for medical and physical conditions. Medical tests to be conducted by a physician often include: pulmonary function tests (at least an initial), a chest X-ray, electrocardiogram and any other tests deemed appropriate by the examining physician. A medical history in the form of a questionnaire is collected as well for each individual. Other factors to be considered by a physician may include: emphysema, asthma, chronic bronchitis, heart disease, anemia, hemophilia, poor eyesight, poor hearing, hernia, lack of use of fingers or hands, epileptic seizures, and other factors which might inhibit the ability of an employee to wear respiratory equipment.

Employee Training Program

Each employee designated to wear a respirator must receive adequate training. The training session (initial and periodic training) should be conducted by a qualified individual to ensure that employees understand the limitations, use, and maintenance of respiratory equipment. The OSHA Asbestos Standards require that employee training be repeated at least annually.

Respirator Fitting

One of the most important elements of an effective respirator program is fitting. The OSHA Asbestos Standards (29 CFR 1910.1001 and 1926.1101) and the OSHA Respirator Standard (29 CFR 1910.134) require that the fit of respirators be tested when the respirator is issued, and every 12 months thereafter for all tight-fitting respirators. The fit of the respirator should also be checked each time that it is worn. Procedures for fit-testing and fit-checking should be addressed in the written respirator program.

Once the appropriate respirator has been selected for the contaminant, and conditions to which an individual is exposed, the respirator must be fit-tested. A respirator will not provide protection unless the air passes through the filter or canister, or unless all of the air comes from the supply system. If the face seal is not tight or the connections are loose an individual may think he or she is breathing through the purifying system, but may actually be breathing around it.

Several different respirators may have to be tried before one is found that fits properly. For any tight-fitting type respirator, beards and bushy sideburns may have to be shaved. Respirator face pieces generally will not seal over them. Similarly, gum and tobacco chewing cannot be permitted since excess facial movement can break the face seal. If a person wears prescription glasses, a respirator facepiece, which will accommodate the glasses should be considered. Contact lenses should not be worn while wearing a respirator.

There are two types of fit-checks, positive and negative-pressure, and there are two categories of fit-testing, qualitative (pass/fail) and quantitative (measures levels within the mask). Only those tests applicable to asbestos work are discussed below.

Negative Pressure Fit Check

For this test, the wearer closes off the inlet of the filters or cartridges by covering them with the palms of the hands or by squeezing the breathing tube so that air cannot pass through. Then inhale so that the facepiece collapses slightly, and hold his/her breath for about 10 seconds. If the facepiece remains slightly collapsed and no inward leakage of air is detected, the respirator passes the test. This test can only be used on respirators with tight fitting face pieces. Its potential drawback is that hand pressure can modify the facepiece seal and cause false results.

Positive Pressure Fit Check

This test is similar in principle to the negative pressure test. It is conducted by closing off the exhalation valve of the respirator and gently exhaling into the facepiece. The respirator fit is considered passing if positive pressure can be built up inside the facepiece without evidence of outward air leakage around the facepiece. Remember that these two fit-checks should also be done every time a respirator is put on.

If the respirator selected fails to pass these simple tests, the fit-testing should not proceed further. Instead, another size or another brand should be donned and these tests repeated. Alternatively, it may only be necessary to adjust the straps on the respirator and repeat the tests. Once the wearer has successfully passed the negative and positive pressure fit-checks, the actual fit-test may be conducted. The OSHA standards permit qualitative fit-testing for half-mask, air-purifying respirators. Quantitative fit-testing is required for powered air-purifying respirators, and supplied-air respirators.

Qualitative Fit-Testing

During fit testing, the respirator straps must be properly located, in accordance with the manufacturers direction, and must be as comfortable as possible. Over-tightening the straps will sometimes reduce facepiece leakage, but the wearer may be unable to tolerate the respirator for any length of time. The facepiece should not press into the face and shut off blood circulation or cause major discomfort. At the time of respirator selection, a visual inspection of the fit should always be made by a second person.

Once the respirator has been selected, and no visual leaks are evident, a negative pressure check and positive pressure check are performed by the wearer. These simple procedures are described above.

The actual qualitative fit-test method chosen is at the discretion of the employer, as long as it is one of four specified in Appendix A of the OSHA Respiratory Protection Standard (29 CFR 1910.134.) The procedures used must follow those in this appendix whether irritant smoke, isoamyl acetate, Bitrex, or saccharin is chosen as the test agent. The irritant smoke test is summarized below.

Irritant Smoke Test

If the positive- and negative-pressure fit-checks were successful, the irritant smoke test is administered. It can be used for both air-purifying and supplied air respirators. However, an air-purifying respirator must have high efficiency filters. The test substance is an irritant smoke (stannic chloride). Sealed glass and plastic tubes with substances to generate this smoke are available from safety supply companies. When the tube ends are broken and air passed through them with a squeeze bulb, a dense, irritating smoke is emitted.

The irritant smoke is sprayed/squeezed into a small hole punched in the bag near the respirator wearer's head. If the wearer detects the irritant smoke inside the respirator, it indicates a defective fit: the qualitative fit test is failed. The advantage to this test is that the wearer usually reacts involuntarily to leakage by coughing or sneezing. The likelihood of pretending to pass this test is low.

Note: This test must be performed with caution, because the irritant smoke is highly irritating to the eyes, skin, and mucous membranes. When testing a half face mask respirator, the eyes must be kept tightly closed or protected with vapor-tight goggles.

Quantitative Fit-Testing

Quantitative fit testing is requires a detectable test substance, which can be generated into the air, specialized equipment to measure the airborne concentration of the substance, and a trained tester. A sodium chloride solution or corn oil may be used to perform these tests. The person to be tested puts on a probed version of the respirator and enters a chamber, which contains the test substance in the air. The airborne concentration of the substance is measured outside the respirator and inside the respirator while the tester mimics several typical work related activities. The specific degree of protection - fit factor - can be determined for the wearer and respirator.

In the past, quantitative fit testing was usually performed in a laboratory. However, portable fit testing units are available and some companies offer on-site testing.

Cleaning and Disinfection of Respirators

Whenever possible, a respirator should be reserved for the exclusive use of a single individual. Following each use, the respirator should be cleaned and disinfected. The following procedures can be used to clean a respirator

- Wash with a detergent or a combination detergent and disinfectant, in warm water using a brush.

- Rinse in clean water, or rinse once with a disinfectant and once with clean water. The clean water rinse is particularly important because traces of detergent or disinfectant left on the mask can cause skin irritation and/or damage respirator components.

- Air dry on a rack or hang; position the respirator so that the facepiece elastomer will not be deformed during drying.

Routine Inspection of Respirators

Inspection of the respirator is an important, routine task. It should be done before and after each use. The respirator should be checked for the following defects:

a. Air-Purifying Respirators (half-mask and full facepiece)

Elastomeric facepiece should be checked for:

1. Excessive dirt
2. Cracks, tears, or holes
3. Distortion from improper storage
4. Cracked, scratched or loose fitting lens
5. Broken or missing mounting clips

Head straps should be checked for:

1. Breaks or tears
2. Loss of elasticity
3. Broken or malfunctioning buckles or attachments
4. Excessively worn serration of the head harness, which might allow the facepiece to slip

Inhalation valve, exhalation valve, should be checked for:

1. Detergent residue, dust particles or dirt on valve seal
2. Cracks, tears, or distortion in the valve material or valve seat.
3. Missing or defective valve cover

Filter elements should be checked for:

1. Proper filter for the hazard
2. Approval designation (TC #)
3. Missing or worn gaskets
4. Worn threads
5. Cracks or dents in filter housing

b. Powered Air Purifying Respirators

Check facepiece, head straps, valve, and breathing tube, as for regular air purifying respirators.

Hood or helmet, if applicable - check for:

1. Headgear suspension (adjust properly for wearer)
2. Cracks or breaks in face shield (replace face shield)

c. Supplied Air Respirators

Facepiece, head strap and valves should be checked as specified above. In addition the following checks should be performed:

Breathing tube should be checked for:

1. Cracks
2. Missing or loose hose clamps
3. Broken or missing connectors

Hood, helmet or suit should be checked for:

1. Head gear suspension
2. Cracks or breaks in face shield.

Air supply system should be checked for:

1. Breaks or kinks in air supply hoses and end fitting attachments
2. Tightness of connections
3. Rips and setting of regulators and valves (consult manufacturer's recommendations)
4. Correct operation of air purifying elements and carbon monoxide or high temperature alarms

Repair

At some point any respirator will need replacement parts or some other repair. OSHA requires that the person who repairs respirators be trained and qualified. It is important to realize that respirator parts from different manufacturers are not interchangeable. NIOSH approval is invalidated if parts are substituted.

Respirator Storage

Proper storage is very important. OSHA requires that respirators be protected from dust, sunlight, heat, extreme cold, excessive moisture, and damaging or contaminating chemicals. When not in use, the respirator should be placed in a closed plastic bag and stored in a clean, convenient, sanitary location.

Surveillance of Working Conditions

An employer must provide adequate surveillance of the employee's working conditions to be certain the respirator selected provides adequate protection. In the case of Project Monitors, this includes a determination if other hazardous airborne contaminants might be encountered for which the respirator chosen is not adequate. It may also include periodic air monitoring to estimate the asbestos exposure. This provides the needed information to determine if the respirator chosen affords sufficient protection to the individual.

Respirator Program Evaluation and Recordkeeping

The respirator program shall be evaluated at least annually with program adjustments, as appropriate, made to reflect air sampling or other evaluation results. Compliance with the aforementioned points of the program should be reviewed; respirator selection, purchase of approved equipment, medical screening of employees, fit testing, issuance of equipment and associated maintenance, storage, repair and inspection, and appropriate surveillance of work area conditions.

Attention should be given to proper recordkeeping. Records which should be kept include: names of employees trained in respirator use, documentation of the care and maintenance of respirators, medical reports of each respirator user, possible airborne concentrations of asbestos fibers during work, and any problems encountered during projects with regards to respiratory equipment. A checklist for self-evaluation of a respiratory protection program follows in this chapter

PROTECTIVE CLOTHING

It is important to understand why protective clothing may need to be worn. The primary reason is to keep gross amounts of suspected asbestos-containing debris off the body, hair, etc. The use of protective clothing will minimize the chance of bringing asbestos out of a facility and into the home. Protective clothing for air sampling purposes may consist of disposable body coveralls, foot covering, and head covering. The foot and head covering should be attached to the coveralls. This eliminates the need to tape openings between garments. For air sampling purposes, protective clothing may be worn over street clothes. The disposable coveralls, foot, and head coverings are available from many sources and constructed of several materials. Coveralls, with foot and head covering attached usually cost about $_____ each when purchased in quantity. Separately, the coveralls cost approximately $_____, head covering about $_____ and foot covering about $_____ per pair. It is important to realize that many "bargain" prices may not be a bargain at all. The less expensive coveralls often use less material. Accordingly, coveralls marked "XL" may be too small for many persons. Be sure to check the construction of the coveralls as well. Double stitching on seams will last longer, but cost more. When leaving the site, the Project Monitor should exercise care in removing protective clothing:

1. HEPA vacuum off any debris accumulated on the Project Monitor's garments.

2. Remove all protective garments and equipment (except respirator) in an isolated area

3. All disposable clothing should be placed in plastic bags and labeled as asbestos-containing waste.

4. Non-disposable clothing should be sealed in a plastic bag and labeled as asbestos contaminated clothing. Procedures for the handling and laundering of asbestos-contained clothing must be in compliance with the OSHA asbestos standard 29 CFR 1926.1101.

5. Once the plastic bag is properly sealed, respirators may be taken off.

OTHER PERSONAL PROTECTIVE EQUIPMENT

Additional protective equipment may be necessary depending on the specific project. The most common other protective equipment will include eye protection. This is especially important when collecting air samples. Goggles or safety glasses (with side shields) are often adequate. Hard hats, safety shoes, and hearing protection may also be necessary on certain projects.

RESPIRATOR PROGRAM CHECKLIST

In general, the respirator program should be evaluated at least annually with program adjustments, as appropriate, and renamed to reflect the evaluation results. Program function can be separated into administration and operation.

A. Program Administration

(1) Is there a written policy, which acknowledges employer responsibility for providing a safe and healthful workplace, and assigns program responsibility, accountability, and authority?

(2) Is program responsibility vested in one individual who is knowledgeable and who can coordinate all aspects of the program at the job site?

(3) Can feasible engineering controls or work practices eliminate the need for respirators?

_____ (4) Are there written procedures/statements covering the various aspects of the respirator program, including:

_____ designation of an administrator;

_____ respirator selection;

_____ purchase of approved equipment;
_____ medical aspects of respirator usage;
_____ issuance of equipment;
_____ fitting;
_____ training;
_____ maintenance, storage, and repair;
_____ inspection;
_____ use under special conditions; and
_____ work area under surveillance?

B. Program Operation

(1) Respiratory protective equipment selection and assignment

_____ Are work area conditions and employee exposures properly surveyed?

_____ Are respirators selected on the basis of hazards to which the employee is exposed?

_____ Are selections made by individuals knowledgeable of proper selection procedures?

_____ Are only approved respirators purchased and used; do they provide adequate protection for the specific hazard and concentration of the contaminant?

_____ Has a medical evaluation of the prospective user been made to determine physical and psychological ability to wear the selected respiratory protective equipment?

_____ Where practical, have respirators been issued to the users for their exclusive use, and are there records covering issuance?

(2)   Respiratory protective equipment fitting

_____ Are the users given the opportunity to try on several respirators to determine whether the respirator they will subsequently be wearing is the best fitting one?

_____ Is the fit tested at appropriate intervals?

_____ Are those users who require corrective lenses properly fitted?

_____ Are users prohibited from wearing contact lenses when using respirators?

_____ Is the facepiece-to-face seal tested in a test atmosphere?

_____ Are workers prohibited from entering contaminated work areas when they have facial hair or other characteristics which prohibit the use of tight-fitting face pieces?

(3)   Respirator use

_____ Are respirators being worn correctly (i.e., head covering over respirator straps)?

_____ Are workers keeping respirators on all the time when necessary?

(4)   Maintenance of respiratory protective equipment

(a)   Cleaning and Disinfecting

_____ Are respirators cleaned and disinfected after each use?

_____ Are proper methods of cleaning and disinfecting utilized?

(b)   Storage

_____ Are respirators stored in a manner so as to protect them from dust, sunlight, heat, excessive cold or moisture, or damaging chemicals?

_____ Are respirators stored properly in a storage facility so as to prevent them from deforming?

_____ Is storage in lockers and tool boxes permitted only if the respirator is in a carrying case or carton?

(c)Inspection

_____Are respirators inspected before and after each use and during cleaning?

_____Are qualified individuals/users instructed in inspection techniques?

_____Is respiratory protective equipment designated as "emergency use" inspected at least monthly (in addition to after each use)?

_____Is a record kept of the inspection of "emergency use" respiratory protective equipment?

(d) Repair

_____Are replacement parts used in repair, those of the manufacturer of the respirator?

(5)   Special use conditions

_____Is a procedure developed for respiratory protective equipment usage in atmospheres immediately dangerous to life or health?

_____Is a procedure developed for equipment usage for entry into confined spaces?

(6)   Training

_____Are users trained in proper respirator use, cleaning, and inspection? Are users trained in the basis for selection of respirators?

_____Are users evaluated, using competency-based evaluation, before and after training?

Detailed procedure for Asbestos Sampling and Analysis
Non-Mandatory –
29 CFR 29 CFR 1910.1001 App B

- **Part Number:** 1910
- **Part Title:** Occupational Safety and Health Standards
- **Subpart:** Z
- **Subpart Title:** Toxic and Hazardous Substances
- **Standard Number:** 1910.1001 App B
- **Title:** Detailed procedure for Asbestos Sampling and Analysis Non-Mandatory

Appendix B to §1910.1001 – Detailed Procedures for Asbestos Sampling and Analysis -- Non-Mandatory

Matrix:
OSHA Permissible Exposure Limits:
Time Weighted Average.......................... 0.1 fiber/cc
Excursion Level (30 minutes)................. 1.0 fiber/cc

Collection Procedure:
A known volume of air is drawn through a 25-mm diameter cassette containing a mixed-cellulose ester filter. The cassette must be equipped with an electrically conductive 50-mm extension cowl. The sampling time and rate are chosen to give a fiber density of between 100 to 1,300 fibers/mm(2) on the filter.

Recommended Sampling Rate .... 0.5 to 5.0 liters/ minute (L/min)
Recommended Air Volumes:
Minimum.. 25 L
Maximum.. 2,400 L

Analytical Procedure: A portion of the sample filter is cleared and prepared for asbestos fiber counting by Phase Contrast Microscopy (PCM) at 400X.

Commercial manufacturers and products mentioned in this method are for descriptive use only and do not constitute endorsements by USDOL-OSHA. Similar products from other sources can be substituted.

1. Introduction

This method describes the collection of airborne asbestos fibers using calibrated sampling pumps with mixed-cellulose ester (MCE) filters and analysis by phase contrast microscopy (PCM). Some terms used are unique to this method and are defined below:

Asbestos: A term for naturally occurring fibrous minerals. Asbestos includes chrysotile, crocidolite, amosite (cummingtonite-grunerite asbestos), tremolite asbestos, actinolite asbestos, anthophyllite asbestos, and any of these minerals that have been chemically treated and/or altered. The precise chemical formulation of each species will vary with the location from which it was mined. Nominal compositions are listed:

Chrysotile .... $Mg_3Si_2O_5(OH)_4$
Crocidolite .... $Na_2Fe_2^{3+}Fe_3^{2+}Si_8O_{22}(OH)_2$
Amosite .... $(Mg,Fe)_7Si_8O_{22}(OH)_2$
Tremolite-actinolite.. $Ca_2(Mg,Fe)_5Si_8O_{22}(OH)_2$
Anthophyllite .... $(Mg,Fe)_7Si_8O_{22}(OH)_2$

Asbestos Fiber: A fiber of asbestos which meets the criteria specified below for a fiber.

Aspect Ratio: The ratio of the length of a fiber to its diameter (e.g. 3:1, 5:1 aspect ratios).

Cleavage Fragments: Mineral particles formed by comminution of minerals, especially those characterized by parallel sides and a moderate aspect ratio (usually less than 20:1).

Detection Limit: The number of fibers necessary to be 95% certain that the result is greater than zero.

Differential Counting: The term applied to the practice of excluding certain kinds of fibers from the fiber count because they do not appear to be asbestos.

Fiber: A particle that is 5 um or longer, with a length-to-width ratio of 3 to 1 or longer.

Field: The area within the graticule circle that is superimposed on the microscope image.

Set: The samples which are taken, submitted to the laboratory, analyzed, and for which, interim or final result reports are generated.

Tremolite, Anthophyllite, and Actinolite: The non-asbestos form of these minerals which meet the definition of a fiber. It includes any of these minerals that have been chemically treated and/or altered.

Walton-Beckett Graticule: An eyepiece graticule specifically designed for asbestos fiber counting. It consists of a circle with a projected diameter of 100 + or - 2 um (area of about 0.00785 mm^2) with a crosshair having tic-marks at 3-um intervals in one direction and 5-um in the orthogonal direction. There are marks around the periphery of the circle to demonstrate the proper sizes and shapes of fibers. This design is reproduced in Figure 1. The disk is placed in one of the microscope eyepieces so that the design is superimposed on the field of view.

1.1. History

Early surveys to determine asbestos exposures were conducted using impinger counts of total dust with the counts expressed as million particles per cubic foot. The British Asbestos Research Council recommended filter membrane counting in 1969. In July 1969, the Bureau of Occupational Safety and Health published a filter membrane method for counting asbestos fibers in the United States. This method was refined by NIOSH and published as P & CAM 239. On May 29, 1971, OSHA specified filter membrane sampling with phase contrast counting for evaluation of asbestos exposures at work sites in the United States. The use of this technique was again required by OSHA in 1986. Phase contrast microscopy has continued to be the method of choice for the measurement of occupational exposure to asbestos.

1.2. Principle

Air is drawn through an MCE filter to capture airborne asbestos fibers. A wedge shaped portion of the filter is removed, placed on a glass microscope slide and made transparent. A measured area (field) is viewed by PCM. All the fibers meeting defined criteria for asbestos are counted and considered a measure of the airborne asbestos concentration.

1.3. Advantages and Disadvantages

There are four main advantages of PCM over other methods:

(1) The technique is specific for fibers. Phase contrast is a fiber counting technique which excludes non-fibrous particles from the analysis.

(2) The technique is inexpensive and does not require specialized knowledge to carry out the analysis for total fiber counts.

(3) The analysis is quick and can be performed on-site for rapid determination of air concentrations of asbestos fibers.

(4) The technique has continuity with historical epidemiological studies, so that estimates of expected disease can be inferred from long-term determinations of asbestos exposures.

The main disadvantage of PCM is that it does not positively identify asbestos fibers. Other fibers which are not asbestos may be included in the count unless differential counting is performed. This requires a great deal of experience to adequately differentiate asbestos from non-asbestos fibers. Positive identification of asbestos must be performed by polarized light or electron microscopy techniques. A further disadvantage of PCM is that the smallest visible fibers are about 0.2 um in diameter, while the finest asbestos fibers may be as small as 0.02 um in diameter. For some exposures, substantially more fibers may be present than are actually counted.

1.4. Workplace Exposure

Asbestos is used by the construction industry in such products as shingles, floor tiles, asbestos cement, roofing felts, insulation and acoustical products. Non-construction uses include brakes, clutch facings, paper, paints, plastics, and fabrics. One of the most significant exposures in the workplace is the removal and encapsulation of asbestos in schools, public buildings, and homes. Many workers have the potential to be exposed to asbestos during these operations.

About 95% of the asbestos in commercial use in the United States is chrysotile. Crocidolite and amosite make up most of the remainder. Anthophyllite and tremolite or actinolite are likely to be encountered as contaminants in various industrial products.

1.5. Physical Properties

Asbestos fiber possesses a high tensile strength along its axis, is chemically inert, non-combustible, and heat resistant. It has a high electrical resistance and good, sound absorbing properties. It can be weaved into cables, fabrics or other textiles, and also matted into asbestos papers, felts, or mats.

2. Range and Detection Limit

2.1. The ideal counting range on the filter is 100 to 1,300 fibers/mm(2). With a Walton-Beckett graticule this range is equivalent to 0.8 to 10 fibers/field. Using NIOSH counting statistics, a count of 0.8 fibers/field would give an approximate coefficient of variation (CV) of 0.13.

2.2. The detection limit for this method is 4.0 fibers per 100 fields or 5.5 fibers/mm(2). This was determined using an equation to estimate the maximum CV possible at a specific concentration (95% confidence) and a Lower Control Limit of zero. The CV value was then used to determine a corresponding concentration from historical CV vs fiber relationships. As an example:

Lower Control Limit (95% Confidence) = AC - 1.645(CV)(AC)

Where:

AC = Estimate of the airborne fiber concentration (fibers/cc)
   Setting the Lower Control Limit = 0 and solving for CV:
0 = AC - 1.645(CV)(AC)
CV = 0.61

This value was compared with CV vs. count curves. The count at which CV = 0.61 for Leidel-Busch counting statistics or for an OSHA Salt Lake Technical Center (OSHA-SLTC) CV curve (see Appendix A for further

information) was 4.4 fibers or 3.9 fibers per 100 fields, respectively. Although a lower detection limit of 4 fibers per 100 fields is supported by the OSHA-SLTC data, both data sets support the 4.5 fibers per 100 fields value.

3. Method Performance -- Precision and Accuracy

Precision is dependent upon the total number of fibers counted and the uniformity of the fiber distribution on the filter. A general rule is to count at least 20 and not more than 100 fields. The count is discontinued when 100 fibers are counted, provided that 20 fields have already been counted. Counting more than 100 fibers results in only a small gain in precision. As the total count drops below 10 fibers, an accelerated loss of precision is noted. At this time, there is no known method to determine the absolute accuracy of the asbestos analysis. Results of samples prepared through the Proficiency Analytical Testing (PAT) Program and analyzed by the OSHA-SLTC showed no significant bias when compared to PAT reference values. The PAT samples were analyzed from 1987 to 1989 (N = 36) and the concentration range was from 120 to 1,300 fibers/mm^2[2].

4. Interferences

Fibrous substances, if present, may interfere with asbestos analysis.

Some common fibers are:

Fiberglass
Anhydrite
Plant Fibers
Perlite Veins
Gypsum
Some Synthetic Fibers
Membrane Structures
Sponge Spicules
Diatoms
Microorganisms
Wollastonite

The use of electron microscopy, or optical tests such as polarized light, and dispersion staining, may be used to differentiate these materials from asbestos when necessary.

5. Sampling

5.1. Equipment

5.1.1. Sample assembly (The assembly is shown in Figure 3). Conductive filter holder consisting of a 25-mm diameter, 3-piece cassette having a 50-mm long electrically conductive extension cowl. Backup pad, 25-mm, cellulose. Membrane filter, mixed-cellulose ester (MCE), 25-mm, plain, white, 0.4 to 1.2-um pore size.

Notes:

1. Do not re-use cassettes.
2. Fully conductive cassettes are required to reduce fiber loss to the sides of the cassette due to electrostatic attraction.
3. Purchase filters which have been selected by the manufacturer for asbestos counting, or analyze representative filters for fiber background before use. Discard the filter lot if more than 4 fibers/100 fields are found.
4. To decrease the possibility of contamination, the sampling system (filter-backup pad-cassette) for asbestos is usually preassembled by the manufacturer.
5. Other cassettes, such as the Bell-mouth, may be used within the limits of their validation.

5.1.2. Gel bands for sealing cassettes.

5.1.3. Sampling pump.

Each pump must be a battery operated, self-contained unit small enough to be placed on the monitored employee and not interfere with the work being performed. The pump must be capable of sampling at the collection rate for the required sampling time.

5.1.4. Flexible tubing, 6-mm bore.

5.1.5. Pump calibration.

Stopwatch and bubble tube/burette or electronic meter.

5.2. Sampling Procedure

5.2.1. Seal the point where the base and cowl of each cassette meet with a gel band or tape.

5.2.2. Charge the pumps completely before beginning.

5.2.3. Connect each pump to a calibration cassette with an appropriate length of 6-mm bore plastic tubing. Do not use luer connectors -- the type of cassette specified above has built-in adapters.

5.2.4. Select an appropriate flow rate for the situation being monitored. The sampling flow rate must be between 0.5 and 5.0 L/min for personal sampling and is commonly set between 1 and 2 L/min. Always choose a flow rate that will not produce overloaded filters.

5.2.5. Calibrate each sampling pump before and after sampling with a calibration cassette in-line (Note: This calibration cassette should be from the same lot of cassettes used for sampling). Use a primary standard (e.g. bubble burette) to calibrate each pump. If possible, calibrate at the sampling site.

Note: If sampling site calibration is not possible, environmental influences may affect the flow rate. The extent is dependent on the type of pump used. Consult with the pump manufacturer to determine dependence on environmental influences. If the pump is affected by temperature and pressure changes, correct the flow rate using the formula shown in the section "Sampling Pump Flow Rate Corrections" at the end of this appendix.

5.2.6. Connect each pump to the base of each sampling cassette with flexible tubing. Remove the end cap of each cassette and take each air sample open face. Assure that each sample cassette is held open side down in the employee's breathing zone during sampling. The distance from the nose/mouth of the employee to the cassette should be about 10 cm. Secure the cassette on the collar or lapel of the employee using spring clips or other similar devices.

5.2.7. A suggested minimum air volume when sampling to determine TWA compliance is 25 L. For Excursion Limit (30 min sampling time) evaluations, a minimum air volume of 48 L is recommended.

5.2.8. The most significant problem when sampling for asbestos is overloading the filter with non-asbestos dust. Suggested maximum air sample volumes for specific environments are:

Environment	Air vol. (L)
Asbestos removal operations (visible dust)	100
Asbestos removal operations (little dust)	240
Office environments	400 to 2,400

Caution: Do not overload the filter with dust. High levels of non-fibrous dust particles may obscure fibers on the filter and lower the count or make counting impossible. If more than about 25 to 30% of the field area is obscured with dust, the result may be biased low. Smaller air volumes may be necessary when there is excessive non-asbestos dust in the air.

While sampling, observe the filter with a small flashlight. If there is a visible layer of dust on the filter, stop sampling, remove and seal the cassette, and replace with a new sampling assembly. The total dust loading should not exceed 1 mg.

5.2.9. Blank samples are used to determine if any contamination has occurred during sample handling. Prepare two blanks for the first 1 to 20 samples. For sets containing greater than 20 samples, prepare blanks as 10% of the samples. Handle blank samples in the same manner as air samples with one exception: Do not draw any air through the blank samples. Open the blank cassette in the place where the sample cassettes are mounted on the employee. Hold it open for about 30 seconds. Close and seal the cassette appropriately. Store blanks for shipment with the sample cassettes.

5.2.10. Immediately after sampling, close and seal each cassette with the base and plastic plugs. Do not touch or puncture the filter membrane as this will invalidate the analysis.

5.2.11. Attach and secure a sample seal around each sample cassette in such a way as to assure that the end cap and base plugs cannot be removed without destroying the seal. Tape the ends of the seal together, since the seal is not long enough to be wrapped end-to-end. Also, wrap tape around the cassette at each joint to keep the seal secure.

5.3. Sample Shipment

5.3.1. Send the samples to the laboratory with paperwork requesting asbestos analysis. List any known fibrous interferences present during sampling on the paperwork. Also, note the workplace operation(s) sampled.

5.3.2. Secure and handle the samples in such that they will not rattle during shipment, nor be exposed to static electricity. Do not ship samples in expanded polystyrene peanuts, vermiculite, paper shreds, or excelsior. Tape sample cassettes to sheet bubbles, and place in a container that will cushion the samples in such a manner that they will not rattle.

5.3.3. To avoid the possibility of sample contamination, always ship bulk samples in separate mailing containers.

6. Analysis

6.1. Safety Precautions

6.1.1. Acetone is extremely flammable and precautions must be taken not to ignite it. Avoid using large containers or quantities of acetone. Transfer the solvent in a ventilated laboratory hood. Do not use acetone near any open flame. For generation of acetone vapor, use a spark free heat source.

6.1.2. Any asbestos spills should be cleaned up immediately to prevent dispersal of fibers. Prudence should be exercised to avoid contamination of laboratory facilities or exposure of personnel to asbestos. Asbestos spills should be cleaned up with wet methods and! or a High Efficiency Particulate-Air (HEPA) filtered vacuum.

Caution: Do not use a vacuum without a HEPA filter -- It will disperse fine asbestos fibers in the air.

6.2. Equipment

6.2.1. Phase contrast microscope with binocular or trinocular head.

6.2.2. Widefield or Huygenian 10X eyepieces (Note: The eyepiece containing the graticule must be a focusing eyepiece. Use a 40X phase objective with a numerical aperture of 0.65 to 0.75).

6.2.3. Kohler illumination (if possible) with green or blue filter.

6.2.4. Walton-Beckett Graticule, type G-22 with 100 plus or minus 2 um projected diameter.

6.2.5. Mechanical stage.

A rotating mechanical stage is convenient for use with polarized light.

6.2.6. Phase telescope.

6.2.7. Stage micrometer with 0.01-mm subdivisions.

6.2.8. Phase-shift test slide, mark II (Available from PTR optics Ltd., and also McCrone).

6.2.9. Pre-cleaned glass slides, 25 mm X 75 mm. One end can be frosted for convenience in writing sample numbers, etc., or paste-on labels can be used.

6.2.10. Cover glass #1 1!2.

6.2.11. Scalpel (#10, curved blade).

6.2.12. Fine tipped forceps.

6.2.13. Aluminum block for clearing filter (see Appendix D and Figure 4).

6.2.14. Automatic adjustable pipette, 100- to 500-uL.

6.2.15. Micropipette, 5 uL.

6.3. Reagents

6.3.1. Acetone (HPLC grade).

6.3.2. Triacetin (glycerol triacetate).

6.3.3. Lacquer or nail polish.

6.4. Standard Preparation

A way to prepare standard asbestos samples of known concentration has not been developed. It is possible to prepare replicate samples of nearly equal concentration. This has been performed through the PAT program. These asbestos samples are distributed by the AIHA to participating laboratories.

Since only about one-fourth of a 25-mm sample membrane is required for an asbestos count, any PAT sample can serve as a "standard" for replicate counting.

6.5. Sample Mounting

Note: See Safety Precautions in Section 6.1. before proceeding. The objective is to produce samples with a smooth (non-grainy) background in a medium with a refractive index of approximately 1.46. The technique below collapses the filter for easier focusing, and produces permanent mounts which are useful for quality control and inter-laboratory comparison.

An aluminum block or similar device is required for sample preparation.

6.5.1. Heat the aluminum block to about 70 deg. C. The hot block should not be used on any surface that can be damaged by either the heat or from exposure to acetone.

6.5.2. Ensure that the glass slides and cover glasses are free of dust and fibers.

6.5.3. Remove the top plug to prevent a vacuum when the cassette is opened. Clean the outside of the cassette if necessary. Cut the seal and/or tape on the cassette with a razor blade. Very carefully separate the base from the extension cowl, leaving the filter and backup pad in the base.

6.5.4. With a rocking motion cut a triangular wedge from the filter using the scalpel. This wedge should be one-sixth to one-fourth of the filter. Grasp the filter wedge with the forceps on the perimeter of the filter, which was clamped between the cassette pieces. DO NOT TOUCH the filter with your finger. Place the filter on the glass slide sample side up. Static electricity will usually keep the filter on the slide until it is cleared.

6.5.5. Place the tip of the micropipette containing about 200 uL acetone into the aluminum block. Insert the glass slide into the receiving slot in the aluminum block. Inject the acetone into the block with slow, steady pressure on the plunger while holding the pipette firmly in place. Wait 3 to 5 seconds for the filter to clear, remove the pipette and slide from the aluminum block.

6.5.6. Immediately (less than 30 seconds), place 2.5 to 3.5 uL of triacetin on the filter (Note: Waiting longer than 30 seconds will result in increased index of refraction and decreased contrast between the fibers and the preparation. This may also lead to separation of the cover slip from the slide).

6.5.7. Lower a cover slip gently onto the filter at a slight angle to reduce the possibility of forming air bubbles. If more than 30 seconds have elapsed between acetone exposure and triacetin application, glue the edges of the cover slip to the slide with lacquer or nail polish.

6.5.8. If clearing is slow, warm the slide for 15 min on a hot plate having a surface temperature of about 50 deg. C to hasten clearing. The top of the hot block can be used if the slide is not heated too long.

6.5.9. Counting may proceed immediately after clearing and mounting are completed.

6.6. Sample Analysis

Completely align the microscope according to the manufacturer's instructions. Then, align the microscope using the following general alignment routine at the beginning of every counting session and more often if necessary.

6.6.1. Alignment

(1) Clean all optical surfaces. Even a small amount of dirt can significantly degrade the image.

(2) Rough focus the objective on a sample.

(3) Close down the field iris so that it is visible in the field of view. Focus the image of the iris with the condenser focus. Center the image of the iris in the field of view.

(4) Install the phase telescope and focus on the phase rings. Critically center the rings. Misalignment of the rings results in

astigmatism which will degrade the image.

(5) Place the phase-shift test slide on the microscope stage and focus on the lines. The analyst must see line set 3 and should see at least parts of 4 and 5 but, not see line set 6 or 6. A microscope/microscopist combination which does not pass this test may not be used.

6.6.2. Counting Fibers

(1) Place the prepared sample slide on the mechanical stage of the microscope. Position the center of the wedge under the objective lens and focus upon the sample.

(2) Start counting from one end of the wedge and progress along a radial line to the other end (count in either direction from perimeter to wedge tip). Select fields randomly, without looking into the eyepieces, by slightly advancing the slide in one direction with the mechanical stage control.

(3) Continually scan over a range of focal planes (generally the upper 10 to 15 um of the filter surface) with the fine focus control during each field count. Spend at least 5 to 15 seconds per field.

(4) Most samples will contain asbestos fibers with fiber diameters less than 1 um. Look carefully for faint fiber images. The small diameter fibers will be very hard to see. However, they are an important contribution to the total count.

(5) Count only fibers equal to or longer than 5 um. Measure the length of curved fibers along the curve.

(6) Count fibers which have a length to width ratio of 3:1 or greater.

(7) Count all the fibers in at least 20 fields. Continue counting until either 100 fibers are counted or 100 fields have been viewed; whichever occurs first. Count all the fibers in the final field.

(8) Fibers lying entirely within the boundary of the Walton-Beckett graticule field shall receive a count of 1. Fibers crossing the boundary once, having one end within the circle, shall receive a count of 1/2. Do not count any fiber that crosses the graticule boundary more than once. Reject and do not count any other fibers even though they may be visible outside the graticule area. If a fiber touches the circle, it is considered to cross the line.

(9) Count bundles of fibers as one fiber unless individual fibers can be clearly identified and each individual fiber is clearly not connected to another counted fiber. See Figure 1 for counting conventions.

(10) Record the number of fibers in each field in a consistent way such that filter non-uniformity can be assessed.

(11) Regularly check phase ring alignment.

(12) When an agglomerate (mass of material) covers more than 25% of the field of view, reject the field and select another. Do not include it in the number of fields counted.

(13) Perform a "blind recount" of 1 in every 10 filter wedges (slides). Re-label the slides using a person other than the

original counter.

6.7. Fiber Identification

As previously mentioned in Section 1.3., PCM does not provide positive confirmation of asbestos fibers. Alternate differential counting techniques should be used if discrimination is desirable. Differential counting may include primary discrimination based on morphology, polarized light analysis of fibers, or modification of PCM data by Scanning Electron or Transmission Electron Microscopy.

A great deal of experience is required to routinely and correctly perform differential counting. It is discouraged unless it is legally necessary. Then, only if a fiber is obviously not asbestos should it be excluded from the count. Further discussion of this technique can be found in reference 8.10.

If there is a question whether a fiber is asbestos or not, follow the rule:

"WHEN IN DOUBT, COUNT."

6.8. Analytical Recommendations -- Quality Control System

6.8.1. All individuals performing asbestos analysis must have taken the NIOSH course for sampling and evaluating airborne asbestos or an equivalent course.

6.8.2. Each laboratory engaged in asbestos counting shall set up a slide trading arrangement with at least two other laboratories in order to compare performance and eliminate inbreeding of error. The slide exchange occurs at least semiannually. The round robin results shall be posted where all analysts can view individual analyst's results.

6.8.3. Each laboratory engaged in asbestos counting shall participate in the Proficiency Analytical Testing Program, the Asbestos Analyst Registry or equivalent.

6.8.4. Each analyst shall select and count prepared slides from a "slide bank". These are quality assurance counts. The slide bank shall be prepared using uniformly distributed samples taken from the workload. Fiber densities should cover the entire range routinely analyzed by the laboratory. These slides are counted blind by all counters to establish an original standard deviation. This historical distribution is compared with the quality assurance counts. A counter must have 95% of all quality control samples counted within three standard deviations of the historical mean. This count is then integrated into a new historical mean and standard deviation for the slide.

The analyses done by the counters to establish the slide bank may be used for an interim quality control program if the data are treated in a proper statistical fashion.

7. CALCULATIONS

7.1. Calculate the estimated airborne asbestos fiber concentration on the filter sample using the following formula:

Where:

AC = Airborne fiber concentration

(For Equation A)

FB = Total number of fibers greater than 5 um counted
FL = Total number of fields counted on the filter
BFB = Total number of fibers greater than 5 um counted in the blank

BFL = Total number of fields counted on the blank
ECA= Effective collecting area of filter (385 mm(2) nominal for a
    25-mm filter.)

FR = Pump flow rate (L/min)
MFA = Microscope count field area (mm(2)). This is 0.00785 mm(2) for a
    Walton-Beckett Graticule.
T = Sample collection time (min)
1,000 = Conversion of L to cc

Note: The collection area of a filter is seldom equal to 385 mm(2). It is appropriate for laboratories to routinely monitor the exact diameter using an inside micrometer. The collection area is calculated according to the formula:

Area = pi(d/2)(2)

7.2. Short-cut Calculation

Since a given analyst always has the same inter-pupillary distance, the number of fields per filter for a particular analyst will remain constant for a given size filter. The field size for that analyst is constant (i.e. the analyst is using an assigned microscope and is not changing the reticle).

For example, if the exposed area of the filter is always 385 mm(2) and the size of the field is always 0.00785 mm(2), the number of fields per filter will always be 49,000. In addition it is necessary to convert liters of air to cc. These three constants can then be combined such that ECA/(1,000 X MFA) = 49. The previous equation simplifies to:

7.3. Recount Calculations

As mentioned in step 13 of Section 6.6.2., a "blind recount" of 10% of the slides is performed. In all cases, differences will be observed between the first and second counts of the same filter wedge. Most of these differences will be due to chance alone, that is, due to the random variability (precision) of the count method. Statistical recount criteria enables one to decide whether observed differences can be explained due to chance alone, or are probably due to systematic differences between analysts, microscopes, or other biasing factors.

The following recount criterion is for a pair of counts that estimate AC in fibers/cc. The criterion is given at the type-I error level. That is, there is 5% maximum risk that we will reject a pair of counts for the reason that one might be biased, when the large observed difference is really due to chance.

Reject a pair of counts if:
Where:

AC1 = lower estimated airborne fiber concentration
AC2 = higher estimated airborne fiber concentration
ACavg = average of the two concentration estimates
CV(FB) = CV for the average of the two concentration estimates

If a pair of counts are rejected by this criterion then, recount the rest of the filters in the submitted set. Apply the test and reject any other pairs failing the test. Rejection shall include a memo to the industrial hygienist stating that the sample failed a statistical test for homogeneity, and the true air concentration may be significantly different than the reported value.

7.4. Reporting Results

Report results to the industrial hygienist as fibers/cc. Use two significant figures. If multiple analyses are performed on a sample, an average of the results is to be reported unless any of the results can be rejected for cause.

Quality Control

The OSHA asbestos regulations require each laboratory to establish a quality control program. The following is presented as an example of how the OSHA-SLTC constructed its internal CV curve as part of meeting this requirement. Data is from

395 samples collected during OSHA compliance inspections and analyzed from October 1980 through April 1986.

Each sample was counted by 2 to 5 different counters independently of one another. The standard deviation and the CV statistic were calculated for each sample. This data was then plotted on a graph of CV vs. fibers/mm(2). A "least squares regression" was performed using the following equation:

CV = antilog1(10)[A(log(10)(x))(2)+B(log(10)(x))+C]

where:
 x = the number of fibers/mm(2)

Application of least squares gave:

 A = 0.182205
 B = -0.973343
 C = 0.327499

Using these values, the equation becomes:

CV = antilog(10)[0.182205(log(10)(x))(2)-0.973343(log(10)(x))+0.327499]

Sampling Pump Flow Rate Corrections

This correction is used if a difference greater than 5% in ambient temperature, and/or pressure, is noted between calibration and sampling sites and the pump does not compensate for the differences.

Where:

Q(act) = actual flow rate
Q(cal) = calibrated flow rate (if a rotameter was used, the rotameter
     value)
P(cal) = uncorrected air pressure at calibration
P(act) = uncorrected air pressure at sampling site
T(act) = temperature at sampling site (K)
T(cal) = temperature at calibration (K)

Walton-Beckett Graticule

When ordering the Graticule for asbestos counting, specify the exact disc diameter needed to fit the ocular of the microscope and the diameter (mm) of the circular counting area. Instructions for measuring the dimensions necessary are listed:

(1) Insert any available graticule into the focusing eyepiece and focus so that the graticule lines are sharp and clear.

(2) Align the microscope.

(3) Place a stage micrometer on the microscope object stage and focus the microscope on the graduated lines.

(4) Measure the magnified grid length, PL (um), using the stage micrometer.

(5) Remove the graticule from the microscope and measure its actual grid length, AL (mm). This can be accomplished by using a mechanical stage fitted with verniers, or a jeweler's loupe with a direct reading scale.

(6) Let D = 100 um. Calculate the circle diameter, d(c)(mm), for the Walton-Beckett graticule and specify the diameter

when making a purchase:

$$d(c) = \frac{AL \times D}{PL}$$

Example: If PL = 108 um, AL = 2.93 mm and D = 100 um, then,

$$d(c) = \frac{2.93 \times 100}{108} = 2.71 mm$$

(7) Each eyepiece-objective-reticle combination on the microscope must be calibrated. Should any of the three be changed (by zoom adjustment, disassembly, replacement, etc.), the combination must be recalibrated. Calibration may change if interpupillary distance is changed. Measure the field diameter, D (acceptable range: 100 plus or minus 2 um) with a stage micrometer upon receipt of the graticule from the manufacturer. Determine the field area (mm(2)).

Field Area = pi(D/2)(2)
If D = 100 um = 0.1 mm, then
Field Area = pi(0.1 mm/2)(2) = 0.00785 mm(2)

The Graticule is available from: Graticules Ltd., Morley Road, Tonbridge TN9 IRN, Kent, England (Telephone 011-44-732-359061) also available from PTR Optics Ltd., 145 Newton Street, Waltham, MA 02154 [telephone (617) 891-6000] or McCrone Accessories and Components, 2506 S. Michigan Ave., Chicago, IL 60616 [phone (312)-842-7100]. The graticule is custom made for each microscope.

Counts for the Fibers in the Figure

Structure No.	Count	Explanation
1 to 6	1	Single fibers all contained within the circle.
7	1/2	Fiber crosses circle once.
8	0	Fiber too short.
9	2	Two crossing fibers.
10	0	Fiber outside graticule.
11	0	Fiber crosses graticule twice.
12	1/2	Although split, fiber only crosses once.

SAMPLING LOG FORM

Sample Number	Location of Sample	Pump. I.D.	Start Time	Middle Time	End time	Flow Rate

EXAMPLE LABORATORY
[............ FILTER MEDIA DATA ....]

Laboratory ID	Client ID	Type	Diameter mm	Effective Area, mm2	Pore Size, tm	Analyzed Area, mm2	Sample Volume, cc

INDIVIDUAL ANALYTICAL RESULTS
CONCENTRATION

Laboratory I.D.	Client I.D.	# Asbestos Structures	Analytical Sensitivity, s/cc	Structures/mm^2	Structures/cc

The analysis was carried out to the approved TEM method. This laboratory is in compliance with the quality specified by the method.

_____   _____
Date   Authorized Signature

INTRODUCTION

Effective safety management begins in the planning stages of the abatement project. Asbestos Project Monitors must be knowledgeable with these specifications. Experience indicates that it is less costly and more efficient to prevent hazards rather than react to accidents or incidents. Though the abatement contractor is directly responsible for the safety and health of the worker, the Project Monitor can incorporate many safety features into their daily work functions that will assure a smoother and safer project.

The Project Monitor must first be aware of the potential hazards that are associated with an asbestos removal project. Once the hazards are identified, then measures can be specified where possible to eliminate the hazards by redesign or substitution of equipment or procedures that are unsafe. If the hazard cannot be eliminated, the next approach is to reduce it by isolating it, guarding against it, or diluting it. To protect against hazards that cannot be eliminated or reduced, the design specifications must then require the use of specific protective equipment, work practices, and/or related safety training.

The procedures used in a typical abatement project, such as sealing the work area, using wet methods, working at heights on ladders and scaffolding, and shutting down building systems, add new dimensions to the task of providing a safe working environment. This section will identify and address various hazards associated with these tasks including electrical shock, falls from scaffolding, ladders, walking and working surfaces, fire, emergency procedures, heat-related disorders, carbon monoxide poisoning, and the need for body protection and hazard communication. The effort spent to incorporate these safety considerations into the project design is as important to the success of the project as the effort spent in designing engineering controls to confine and minimize fibers in the work site.

The Project Monitor should include a clause in the specification requiring the contractor to notify the building owner's representative when a hazard is identified. The contractor is required to take appropriate corrective actions to protect the asbestos abatement workers. Contractors should also be required to comply with the OSHA general construction safety regulations, specifically requiring a "competent person" [29 CFR 1926.32(d)] be on site, and the need for an accident prevention program [29 CFR 1026.20(b)(2)].

ELECTRICAL SAFETY

Electrical shock is one of the most common hazards, and one that gives the least warning. Incorrect wiring, improper grounding, and lack of proper shielding results in over 1,000 workers each year being electrocuted nationwide. Many of these fatalities result from contact with just 120 volts alternating current (AC).

Three factors determine the severity of electrical shock. These are:

- The amount of current flowing through the body,
- The path of the current flowing through the body,
- The time the current is allowed to flow through the body.

These factors vary greatly. The path of the current depends upon the points of contact. Most often the path is from the hands, through the body, and out the feet. The amount of electrical resistance determines, in part, the amount of current flow. Moist skin or damp conditions greatly reduce electrical resistance, and significantly increase a person's risk of serious injury if he comes in contact with a current source. In addition to the obvious shock potential, many deaths result from falls after a nonfatal electrical shock. During the design phase, potential electrical hazards to the workers should be identified and, where possible, eliminated or, at a minimum, guarded or isolated. The more common hazards are discussed below.

Identification of Wiring Faults in the Building

Wiring faults in the building include open ground paths, reverse wiring polarity, and hot neutral wires. These common faults can easily be identified with a volt/ohm meter or with plug-in type circuit testers and should be corrected prior to project start-up. This is particularly important if these circuits will be used to provide power inside the work area. Any wiring faults identified should be corrected by a qualified electrician prior to their use.

Uninsulated or Exposed Energized Wiring or Equipment

Asbestos removal projects are often part of renovation or remodeling projects. Overhead lighting is usually removed for cleaning. Equipment or machinery may have been moved out of the area before the removal job with wiring left in place. Damaged equipment or electrical fixtures may need to be repaired. All of these things create potential sources of contact with the energized electrical circuits. When possible, the Project Monitor should require that circuits that will not be used during removal efforts be turned off and locked out. **Wiring and electrical connections should always be considered energized until tested and proven otherwise.** Unenclosed wiring junctions in overhead areas should be addressed by the Project Monitor since they are a particularly likely point of contact for removal workers.

Asbestos Abatement Project Where the Building Remains Occupied

Electrical circuits or service panels that are located inside the removal area and that service other parts of the building ,can present a challenge to the Project Monitor. Sealing transformers or control boxes may not be possible due to heat build-up. If this situation is encountered, an alternative design will need to be developed that will allow for air circulation around these units. Dry removal may be necessary to avoid a potential serious shock exposure. Additionally, where this situation is encountered, all breakers and switches must be clearly labeled in case power must be secured to other areas of the building during the removal project. When a dry removal is necessary, approval by local EPA NESHAP authorities and by NYSDOL is necessary to avoid citation for failure to use wet methods. An alternative written plan must be submitted by the Project Monitor to NESHAP authorities and to NYSDOL (in the form of a site specific variance).

Providing Power to the Work Area

Providing power to the work area can create hazards not normally associated with building systems. Since OSHA considers abatement projects subject to the construction industry safety and health standard (29 CFR 1926), there are special requirements for supplying temporary power to extension cords, portable electrical tools, electric air sampling pumps, electric equipment, and portable electrical appliances. This must be done by supplying power through ground fault circuit interrupters (GFCI).

An assured equipment grounding conductor program requires regular inspection (usually monthly or more often if needed) of all tools, cords, and electrical devices with written documentation maintained [29 CFR 1926.404(b)]. Since it is very difficult to document compliance with an assured equipment grounding conductor program, it is best to require the use of GFCIs. The use of GFCIs is required to protect circuits and provides the safest and most feasible power source available, since any significant current leakage will trip the circuit (see Figure VIII-1). These devices prove most effective when placed as near as possible to the "load" and kept out of areas of high humidity. However, high-quality commercially available GFCI's are now on the market and can work in both high- and low-humidity environments.

Hazards on Abatement Projects

Common electrical devices on abatement projects that present potential hazards and need to be addressed in the project specifications are lights, HEPA vacuum cleaners, negative air systems, drills, saws, heaters, sump pumps and, often, radios. All of these should be inspected regularly for damage, proper grounding, and integrity of insulation.

Chapter 10 Safety and Health Issues other than Asbestos

When possible, nonmetallic tools should be specified for vacuuming or scraping to prevent a possible shock if wiring is cut or contact is made with energized equipment. Specifying insulated handles on metal scrapers is another option. Hard rubber or plastic scrapers, while more difficult to find, perform well for removal. Fiberglass ladders reduce or eliminate a ground path if a worker contacts an energized circuit.

TWO BASIC FORMS OF GFCI DEVICES

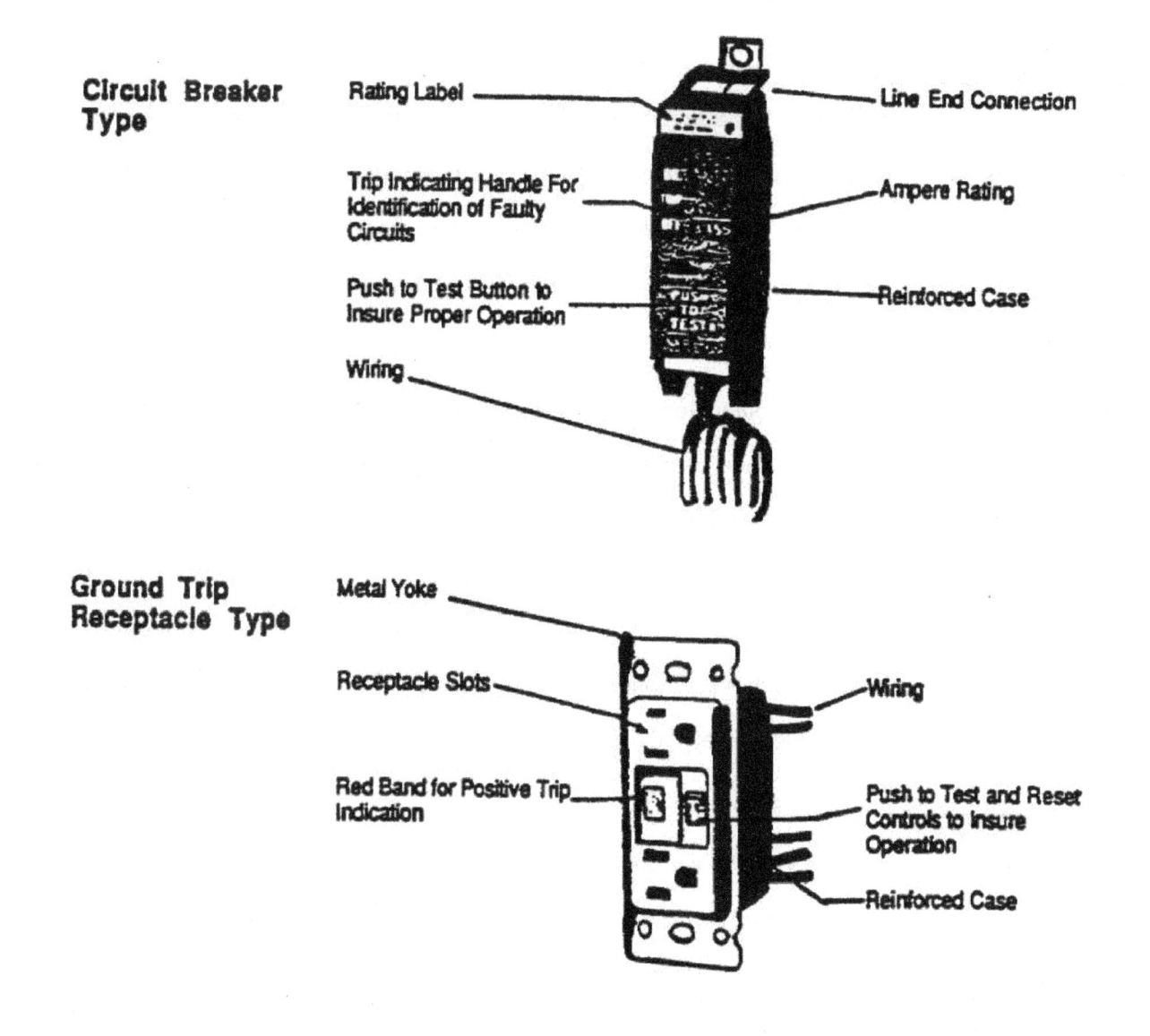

Circuit Breaker Type
- Rating Label
- Line End Connection
- Trip Indicating Handle For Identification of Faulty Circuits
- Ampere Rating
- Push to Test Button to Insure Proper Operation
- Reinforced Case
- Wiring

Ground Trip Receptacle Type
- Metal Yoke
- Receptacle Slots
- Wiring
- Red Band for Positive Trip Indication
- Push to Test and Reset Controls to Insure Operation
- Reinforced Case

Wiring should be elevated, when feasible, to keep it away from water on the floor, to avoid damage from foot traffic and scaffolds, and to keep it from being a trip hazard.

When designing plans to reduce or eliminate electrical hazards, the Project Monitor needs to make sure that the plan complies with OSHA's lockout/tagout standard (29 CFR 1910.147). This standard requires that all potential sources of energy, whether liquid, gas, electrical, chemical thermal, or mechanical operations, be locked by the person performing the work, and that person is the only one with the keys to unlock the device. Additionally, a tag must be attached to serve as a warning sign or label to other workers in the area. If energy sources are required to be disconnected by the contractor, the project specifications must require the contractor to follow proper lockout/tagout procedures.

SCAFFOLDING SAFETY

$$(B)(f) = (W)(A)$$

Where:
- B = height from floor to ceiling
- f = force required to upset scaffold
- W = weight of scaffold and worker
- A = half the width of the scaffold

Example:
- B = 14 feet
- f = X
- W = 199 lb. (scaffold) + 175 lb. (worker) = 374 lbs.
- A = 1 foot

Force to upset = 26.7 lbs.

$(14)(X) = (374)(1)$

$X = (374 \times 1) / (14)$

$X = 26.7$ lbs.

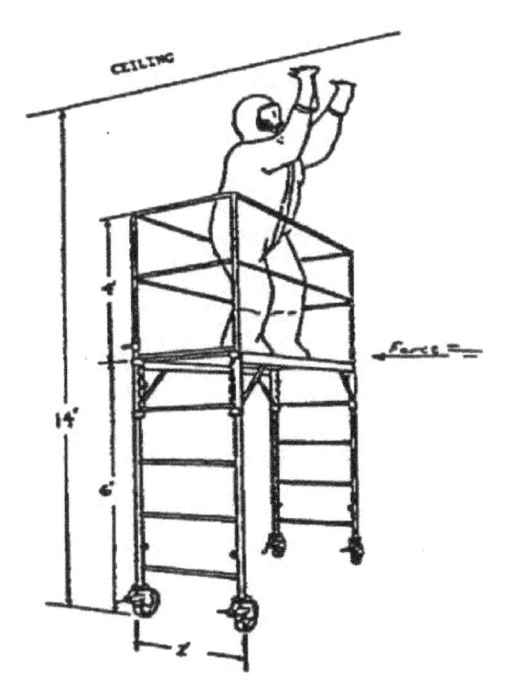

Most asbestos abatement projects will involve the use of scaffolding. Proper set-up, regular inspection, and basic maintenance should not be overlooked. In many removal projects, manually-propelled mobile scaffolding provides a convenient and efficient work platform. OSHA standard 29 CFR 1926.451 requires that, when free-standing mobile scaffolding is used, the height shall not exceed four times the minimum base dimension (usually the width). This requirement is based on the fact that scaffolding easily tips. This illustration shows a simple method to estimate a reasonable amount of force necessary to tip a scaffold.

Since relatively little force is required to tip a scaffold, it becomes important to make sure that wheels on mobile scaffolds move freely, are lubricated and are in good repair. If rented scaffolding is used, all components must be inspected prior to accepting it.

(**NOTE:** This formula is an estimated way to obtain a reasonable idea of the force needed to upset scaffolding. Many variables need to be considered in addition to those illustrated.)

All components such as cross bracing, railings, pin connectors, planking or scaffold-grade lumber must be available before the units are assembled. Workers should be careful to keep debris bagged and obstacles off the floor where mobile scaffolds will be used. If a wheel catches debris on the floor when the unit is moved, additional force will be required to move it. This additional force may be all that is needed to tip the unit. Caution should be used when using mobile scaffolding on sloping floors, such as an auditorium.

Guard rails (42 inches in height) should always be installed on scaffolding used for abatement projects. Workers are usually looking up while working and can easily step off the edge of an unprotected scaffold. OSHA requires that guard rails be used when scaffolding is over 4 feet tall and is less than 45 inches wide. Any time scaffolding is 10 feet or higher, toe boards must also be in place. No guard rails are required when scaffolding is less than 4 feet tall, although it is a good recommendation.

Additionally, scaffolding must, at a minimum, meet the following requirements:
- When guard rails are required, mid rails (21 inches high) are also necessary.
- Upright supports should be positioned at intervals no greater than 6-8 feet apart.
- If, due to the configuration of the work area, people must routinely pass underneath the scaffolding, then a screen (number 18 gauge wire one-half inch mesh or equivalent) is required from toe board to mid rail.
- The scaffolding must be designed to support four times the maximum load that will be placed on the scaffolding.
- Planking used on scaffolding must be scaffold-grade lumber and extend past the sides by at least 6 inches, but less than 12 inches, unless it is secured to the frame.
- Scaffolding must be equipped with a ladder to reach the working platform.

As with the other areas of hazard identification and accident prevention, when there is a need for scaffolding, the project design should specify the use of required devices and do so in the safest manner possible.

LADDER SAFETY

Ladders, as well as scaffolding, are some of the most commonly used pieces of equipment on an asbestos removal site. To assist the Project Monitor, the following list of ladder safety rules or hazard-elimination ideas are presented. These ideas should be considered when developing plans to incorporate safety into the project design.

- Ladders with broken, missing, or defective parts are prohibited.
- Ladder feet must be on a substantial base.
- Work area at top and bottom of ladder must be kept clear.
- No job-made ladders are allowed.
- Metal ladders are prohibited near electrical equipment and lines (within 10 feet). Fiberglass ladders should be selected to avoid electrical hazards.
- Ladders shall be used at pitch of 4 to 1 (1 foot out of every 4 feet of elevation) or secured to prevent displacement during use.
- Ladders shall not be used in a horizontal position as scaffolding, platform, or walkboard.
- Only one person per ladder is allowed and the person must always face the ladder when going up or down.
- An attendant should be used in high-traffic areas.
- A worker must not climb higher than the third rung from the top on a straight ladder or the second step from the top of stepladders.
- Wood ladders shall not be painted.
- Ladders must always be inspected before use.
- Stepladders should only be used when fully open.

WALKING AND WORKING SURFACES

The National Safety Council estimates that there are over 250,000 disabling injuries in work-related falls each year. Over 40 percent of the injured workers are employed in the construction industry. Reducing the potential for slips, trips, and falls is a challenge in the work areas that are sealed with polyethylene and kept damp to reduce airborne fibers. This results in very slick surfaces. Disposable booties are a potential trip hazard; air and electrical cables also create trip hazards. All of these conditions create potential worker hazards even before removal begins.

Some of these walking and working surface hazards can be eliminated by using the following **guidelines:**

- When designing a project, consider the height of the work to be done, equipment to be used, and possible trip hazards. Inspect the walking and working surfaces.

- The use of disposable booties may be impractical in many removal situations. They may come apart and create a serious trip hazard. Seamless rubber boots, slip-on shoes or safety shoes with nonskid soles may be worn over the booties, or in place of the booties.

- Require the contractor to minimize water on floors. Wet polyethylene is very slick and water increases the risk of electrical shock.

- Develop designs calling for placement of airlines and electrical cords in positions that do not cause them to run across travelways. When possible, have these lines and cords suspended off the walking and working surfaces.

- Require that debris be minimized on floors by continuous cleaning.

- Require the contractor to keep equipment, tools, and associated items clear of main travelways.

FIRE SAFETY

Fire prevention must be given a high priority during the design phase. The wood and polyethylene materials used on asbestos removal sites increase the potential for fires and risk to human life. The Project Monitor will need to be concerned with fire safety features such as fire alarm systems, travel distances, exits, and emergency lighting.

A pre-design survey of the project site should first be conducted to determine potential fire hazards, sources of ignition, hot spots, location of fire suppression systems, and locations of current exits. The survey data is then correlated to the number of workers that will be in the area, the square footage of the containment area, and the types of combustible or flammable materials that will remain in the project area. This information will allow the Project Monitor to include fire safety procedures that will reduce or eliminate the chance of fire in the containment area.

Untreated polyethylene has a combustion temperature of approximately 150 degrees to 170 degrees. Polyethylene will start to burn slowly and pick up speed as more heat is generated. It gives off heavy black smoke as a combustion by-product. The flame spread is slow and steady as the combustion process continues. As an additional concern, thermal decomposition may produce toxic gases. The respirators worn by asbestos removal workers generally will not adequately protect them from the smoke and toxic gases produced. Because of this combustion threat, designs should require polyethylene sheeting to be kept away from heat sources such as transformers, steam pipes, boilers, and equipment that will be heated during the removal phase. **It is required to specify the use of fire-retardant polyethylene.**

The Project Monitor should consult OSHA, the National Fire Protection Association (NFPA), and local fire code requirements before sealing off an area and blocking entrances and exits. For example, a poorly-written contract specification might require "one means of egress through a properly designed decontamination system;" however, a better and more correct design would require alternative emergency exits and all on-site personnel entering the work area to be familiar with these exits.

Some additional fire safety procedures that may need to be incorporated into the Project Design are outlined below:

- Specifications must require all sources of ignition to be removed. Gas and other fuel sources must be cut off and pilot lights in boilers, hot water tanks, and compressors extinguished.

- Specifications should identify "hot spots." Quite often design specifications may require draping equipment instead of sealing it off to prevent overheating (i.e., computers, terminal boards, switch panels, transformers).

- Require the cut-off of supply to steam lines, electric and steam heaters, and radiators. Do not permit the polyethylene to be against hot surfaces.

- Specifications must require the marking of exits from work area and posting directional arrows when exits are not visible from remote work areas. This can easily be done using duct tape or indelible marker on polyethylene walls and barriers. It is recommended that half of these directional arrows be placed close to the ground to assist workers who may be crawling in smoky conditions to escape a fire.

- Specifications should require that trash and debris be kept to a minimum (e.g., tape, polyethylene, bags, lumber).

- If the work area is large and many workers are present, several emergency exits may need to be included in the project design. Choose exits that are locked from the outside, but can be opened from the inside. A daily inspection must be conducted to ensure secondary exits are not blocked. Many local codes address these issues.

- Lighting of exits and exit routes should be included in the project design.

Chapter 10 Safety and Health Issues other than Asbestos Issues

Project Address: 5555 Any Industrial Drive, Any Suburb, GA
Project Phone #: 333-3333

```
                    ┌─────────────┬──────────────┐
                    │    LAB      │   OFFICES    │
                    │             │              │
                    ├──┬──────────┤              │
                    │  │ SHIPPING │   RECEIVING  │
EMERGENCY ←─────────┤  │          │              │
EXIT                │  └──────────┤              │
                    │ BOILER ROOM │  ○  ○   °°   │
                    │ ▭  ▭        │  ▭    ▭      │
                    ├──┬──────────┤              │
                    │  │ LOAD-OUT │              │
                    └──┘          └──┬────┬──────┘
                                     │DECON│
                                     │     │
                                     └──┬──┘
                                        ↓
                                     PRIMARY
                                      EXIT
```

Emergency Phone Numbers

Ambulance:	333-9999	Suburb General Hospital
Fire:	911 or 303-5555	Suburb County Fire Dept.
Police:	911 or 303-6666	Suburb Police Dept.

The Project Monitor must be alert to the potential flammable vapors in industrial areas (solvents such as naphtha, toluene, xylene, etc., during the design phase). This is especially critical in industrial vacuuming operations where vacuum motors are not explosion proof. Compressed air vacuums may be required.

Specifications should require a nearby telephone be available at all times for notification of authorities in an emergency. A retractable blade knife should be readily available at each emergency exit for use in cutting polyethylene sheeting.

EMERGENCY PROCEDURES

OSHA 29 CFR 1926.24 requires that every job site have a fire protection and prevention program. This program must cover procedures to be used in case of fire, which includes heavy smoke conditions, power failure, air supplied respirator compressor failure, accidents, and worker injury.

The Project Monitor and contractor will need to establish a system for alerting workers of an emergency that will require evacuation of the asbestos containment and work area. A compressed air horn provides an effective alarm that can be heard and does not rely on a power source. All persons entering the containment and work area must be familiar with the evacuation alarm signal and all primary and secondary exits. A simple floor plan of the work area must be posted near the work area entrance to familiarize persons entering the site with the location of exits, fire suppression equipment, and emergency telephone numbers

FLOOR PLAN OF WORK AREA SHOWING EXITS, EMERGENCY TELEPHONE NUMBERS, PROJECT ADDRESS

Additional considerations in the development of an emergency plan include:

- A description of the manner in which emergencies will be announced.
- Emergency escape procedures and emergency escape routes.
- Procedures for workers who must remain to operate critical operations that may take time to shut down.
- Procedures to account for all workers after evacuation.
- Rescue and medical duties and responsibilities.
- Before beginning the project, provisions should be made for prompt medical attention in case of serious injury or other medical emergency.
- Some local codes may require that the Project Monitor or contractor notify local emergency services of the type of operations (i.e., asbestos removal) that are on site.
- Names and/or job titles of people to be contacted for additional emergency information.
- A list of the major job-site fire hazards.
- Names and/or job titles of people responsible for maintenance of fire prevention and fire suppression equipment.
- Names and/or job titles of people responsible for the control of fuel source hazards.
- Posting local fire department and rescue squad telephone numbers.
- The contractor needs to make sure that workers understand that the emergency hazard becomes more immediate than the asbestos hazard, and workers may need to violate polyethylene barriers. This can be covered in the written and posted emergency action plan.
- Specifications should require that a monitor be outside at all times and trained in fire watch and emergency procedures. This person should also be trained in first aid and in the treatment of heat stress.

HEAT-RELATED DISORDERS

As explained in the section covering personal protection, the OSHA asbestos standard for the construction industry requires that all workers who are exposed to asbestos at or above the PEL's, or who are required to wear a respirator, be given medical screening. The main objective of the medical screening is to determine whether the employee is medically qualified to wear a respirator while performing abatement activities. The examining physician or clinic must additionally be aware that respirators may be worn under hot, adverse conditions. During warm months, or in hot environments, heat exhaustion and heat stroke are serious hazards faced by workers, particularly those not acclimated to the heat.

For projects conducted in hot environments, design specifications should require the contractor to develop and submit a plan that will reduce or eliminate heat-related disorders. Each of the disorders and techniques for prevention are discussed below.

Heat Exhaustion

Symptoms:

- Fatigue, weakness, profuse sweating, normal temperature, pale clammy skin, headache, cramps, vomiting, fainting

Treatment:

- Medical alert
- Remove worker from hot area
- Have worker lay down and raise feet
- Apply cool wet cloths
- Loosen or remove clothing (remove disposal suit)
- Allow small sips of water or salt replenishment beverage, if victim is not vomiting

Heat Stroke

Symptoms:

- Dizziness, nausea, severe headache, hot dry skin, confusion, collapse, delirium, coma, and death

Treatment:

- Medical emergency
- Remove worker from hot area
- Remove clothing
- Have worker lay down
- Cool the body (shower, cool wet cloths)
- Do not give stimulants

NOTE: The major difference in symptoms between heat exhaustion and heat stroke is that with heat exhaustion the person is pale and sweating profusely; and with heat stroke, the person is very hot, red, and has dry skin due to lack of sweating.

The prevention and causes of both heat-related disorders are as follows:

Prevention:
- Frequent breaks away from the heat
- Increase fluid intake
- Allow worker to become acclimatized to heat
- External cooling (vortex cooling, ice vests)
- Reduce caffeine intake
- No alcohol
- Breathable protective clothing
- Increased air movement

Causes:
- High temperature
- High humidity
- Low air movement
- Hard work
- Not enough breaks away from the heat
- Insufficient fluid intake
- Full-body clothing

- Worker not acclimated to head

Other measures that can be implemented to reduce heat-related disorders include the use of air-supplied cooling vests (available with high-pressure supplied air systems), an increase in number of HEPA filtration units to increase air flow, and scheduling work at night when temperatures are cooler.

CARBON MONOXIDE HAZARDS

When supplied-air respirators are in use, it is important that an outside monitor who is familiar with the airline system remains close by to correct problems associated with the breathing air. <u>Carbon monoxide</u> poisoning is perhaps the most important of these problems. Carbon monoxide exposure problems could develop if an outside source of carbon monoxide such as a truck exhaust is drawn into the air intake of the compressor supplying breathing air, or if it contaminates the make-up air being drawn into the containment area. Both of these problems should be taken care of during the design phase by requiring the compressor intake to be elevated 10-15 feet, and/or prohibiting vehicles from idling near the decontamination unit.

It is important to note that the symptoms of carbon monoxide poisoning are similar and may be confused with those of heat-related disorders. The symptoms, common sources, and allowable limits for carbon monoxide are outlined below:

Symptoms:

- Dizziness, nausea, headache, drowsiness, vomiting, collapse, coma, and death (note similarity of symptoms to heat-related disorders)

Sources:

- Oil lubricated compressor
- Internal combustion engine
- Open flame and fire
- Unvented gas
- Kerosene heaters

Description of Carbon Monoxide:

- Colorless, odorless, and tasteless

Limits:

☐ 10 parts per million (ppm) (Grade D breathing air for airline respirators, maximum allowable concentration)

☐ 50 ppm (OSHA permissible exposure limit time-weighted average over eight hours)

PERSONAL PROTECTIVE EQUIPMENT

While the enforcement of proper use and wearing of <u>personal protective equipment (PPE)</u> is the direct responsibility of the employer, the Project Monitor may need to recommend certain types of PPE on particular projects. When the Project Monitor recommends or requires that PPE be used, it should also be required to be maintained in sanitary and reliable condition necessary to protect workers from hazards which could cause injury or illness.

When addressing personal protective equipment for asbestos removal personnel, the following guidance should be used;

- Recommend work gloves as part of PPE to workers exposed to asbestos. This is particularly important when metal lath, suspended ceiling grids, and other materials are being removed. The OSHA asbestos standard requires full body covering.

- Scrapers, retractable knives, wire cutters, chisels, and other sorts of bladed tools are frequently used and can cause injuries. Recommend tools with insulated handles.

- Many puncture and cut wounds occur when removing metal lath or cutting duct work. Recommend the use of good work practices and PPE and have a first aid kit available.

- OSHA requires that protective hard hats be worn on a job site where there is exposure to falling objects, electric shock, or burn.

- Recommend the wearing of non-fogging face shields or goggles for operations involving potential eye injury. Full-face respirators are most effective (if non-fogging).

- Where possible, design work so workers do not have to reach extensively overhead. Get them up to the job.

- Recommend that workers use proper lifting methods.

- Recommend the use of the "buddy system" for lifting and moving heavy objects.

- Recommend the use of hand carts or rolling pallets when possible. Keep manual material handling to a minimum.

- Recommend proper footwear for the hazards that are present on the job site, including steel toed shoes, if necessary.

HAZARD COMMUNICATION STANDARD

The hazard communication standard, also known as the right-to-know rule, covers both general industry and the construction industry. It was promulgated by OSHA in August 199\87 as 29 CFR 1926.59 and 29 CFR 1910.1200. The purpose of this standard is to ensure that the hazards of chemicals or materials used in the workplace are identified and that this information, along with information on protective measures and procedures, is passed on from manufacturer to employer to employee. Elements required under this standard include a comprehensive written hazard communication program, labeling of hazardous materials, employee training, and maintaining <u>material safety data sheets (MSDS).</u>

Employers are required to inform affected workers about hazardous chemicals or materials to which they are exposed on the job site. This notification is done through a written program, maintaining material safety data sheets, maintaining labels, and conducting worker training on these lines.

The Project Monitor must be aware that exposure to hazardous materials can occur in a number of tasks associated with asbestos removal work. Examples include spray adhesives, surfactants, encapsulants, paints, products used for lockdown of fibers, mastic removers, materials left in the work area by the building owner and, of course, the asbestos. The Project Monitor should require the contractor to document that there is a program in place, that workers have received training on possible hazards and precautions, and that the correct MSDS have been obtained for hazardous chemicals being used on site.

All hazardous chemicals used on the job site must have material safety data sheets available which include all health hazard exposures as well as physical hazards and emergency procedures. The material safety data sheets must be accessible to all workers during any working time which includes all three shifts as applicable. Material safety data sheets are available from manufacturers, suppliers of products, and from owners of buildings where hazardous materials are handled in the removal area. The Project Monitor should coordinate with the contractor, since the contractor may fall under the umbrella of hazard communication programs of the building owner who works with the on-site hazardous chemicals or materials.

MATERIAL SAFETY DATA SHEET

I. PRODUCT IDENTIFICATION

Trade Name:
Spray Poly

Manufacturer's Name:
MPT Products Company
350 Main Street
Atlanta, Georgia 30303

Date Prepared
February 2, 2007

Emergency Telephone Number:
1-800-555-1212

II. HAZARDOUS INGREDIENTS INFORMATION

Ingredient:	CAS Number:	Percent:	TWA:	STEL
Ammonium Hydroxide	1336-21-6	0.2	50 ppm	35 ppm

III. PHYSICAL/CHEMICAL CHARACTERISTICS

Boiling Point:
100°C

Specific Gravity (H2O+1):
1.09

Vapor Pressure (mm Hg.):
760 @ 100°C

Melting Point:
0°C

Vapor Density (Air=1):
.63

Evaporation Rate (Butyl Acetate):
1

Solubility in Water:
Dispersible

Appearance and Odor:
Milky white liquid, mild ammonia odor, Ph 8.5 - 9.5

MATERIAL SAFETY DATA SHEET

IV.　FIRE AND EXPLOSION DATA

Flash Point (Method used):
N/A

Flammable Limits
LEL: **N/A**　　UEL: **N/A**

Extinguishing Media:
Water or Foam

Special Fire Fighting Procedures:
None

Unusual Fire and Explosion Hazards:
Combustible by-products - oxides of carbon.

V. HEALTH HAZARD DATA

Route(s) of Entry　　Inhalation: **X**　　Skin:　　Ingestion:

Health Hazards (Acute and Chronic):
Irritation of the respiratory tract. Testing completed by the MPT Consulting Company, Marietta, Georgia, States and exposure level of greater than 11ppm of ammonia during product application without air movement.

Carcinogenicity　　NTP:
No
IARC Monographs:
No
OSHA Regulations:
No

Signs and Symptoms of Exposures: **Ammonia - burning eyes, runny nose, coughing and possible chest pain.**

Medical Conditions Generally Aggravated by Exposure: **Impaired pulmonary function.**

First Aid Procedures:
Eye contact: **Wash eyes immediately with large amounts of water and seek medical attention.**
Skin Contact: **Wash with soap and water all areas of body contacted by product.**
Inhalation: **Remove to fresh air and seek medical attention if symptoms persist.**
Ingestion: **Seek medical attention.**

MATERIAL SAFETY DATA SHEET

VI. REACTIVITY DATA

Stability:
Stable

Conditions to Avoid:
None

Incompatibility (Materials to Avoid):
None

Hazardous Polymerization:
Will not Occur

Conditions to Avoid:
None

VII. SPILL OR LEAK PROCEDURES

Precautions in case of spill or leak:

No special requirements. Spills or release should be diked to prevent spreading. Allow material to dry then strip film. Flush with water, larger spills can be coagulated with 0.3% calcium chloride or spills should be absorbed with sand or porous inorganic material and then collected for disposal.

Waste Disposal:
In accordance with local regulations for disposal of non-hazardous waste.

VIII. SPECIAL PROTECTION INFORMATION

Protective Equipment:
Ammonia or HEPA/Ammonia piggyback respiratory equipment depending on regulations.
Goggles or face shield if splashing.
At end of work period, and before eating, wash with soap and water all areas of body in contact with this product.

Ventilation:
If TWA or STEL is exceeded.

MATERIAL SAFETY DATA SHEET

IX. SPECIAL PRECAUTIONS

Waste Disposal Method:

In accordance with local regulations for disposal of non-hazardous waste.

Shipping, Handling and Storage:

No special requirements.

Note: These MSDS are for example and educational purpose only and should not be used as a specific MSDS on any asbestos abatement project. The sole purpose is for general guidance in what may be contained in a MSDS.

AIR SAMPLING PROTOCOLS, REQUIREMENTS AND DATA INTERPRETATION

INTRODUCTION

Design specifications should contain specific air monitoring requirements for the asbestos removal project. **The sampling and analytical methods used during various project phases, and the acceptable fiber levels associated with each activity, must be clearly stated in the specifications**. This section covers the application of air monitoring for abatement projects, regulatory requirements, and procedures for good practice, how air samples are collected, the various analytical techniques, and interpretation of laboratory data. Qualifications for the Air Monitor and the analytical laboratory are also discussed.

PURPOSES OF AIR MONITORING AND REGULATORY REQUIREMENTS

Air sampling involves drawing a known volume of air through a filter and analyzing that filter for the presence of asbestos fibers. The filter is housed in a plastic cassette which is attached to a sampling pump with flexible tubing. The sampling pump can be either electric (plug-in) or battery powered and is calibrated to draw a known volume of air through the filter material over a given period of time, usually expressed in liters of air per minute (lpm).

Two basic air sampling methodologies are area and personal monitoring. Area samples are collected with a pump, tubing and filter cassette (called the sampling train) at a stationary location four to six feet above floor level. Personal samples are collected in the same manner as area samples, except the pump is hung from a belt around the worker's waist and the filter cassette is attached, pointing downward, to the worker's lapel or collar. The samples are collected from within the breathing zone (as close to the nose and mouth as possible) of an individual, but outside the respirator.

In relation to asbestos hazard identification and control during removal projects, air monitoring can be used for:
1. **occupational exposure measurement**
2. **abatement surveillance**
3. **abatement clearance testing**

Before the removal project begins, air sampling may be conducted to determine background concentrations. This is particularly important if there are locations outside the contained work area, but within the building, where there are suspected or known asbestos-containing material ,or other fibrous materials which may be interpreted as asbestos.

During the project, air monitoring is used as a quality assurance tool to determine if engineering controls are effective to assess worker exposures and to document whether fibers are being contained in the work area. At the completion of the removal project, air monitoring is used in conjunction with a thorough visual inspection to determine if the standards for re-occupancy have been met.

Occupational Exposure Measurement

The Occupational Safety and Health Administration (OSHA) and the NYSDOL require the asbestos abatement contractor to conduct personal air monitoring for workers. Since this is the responsibility of the employer, specific requirements for personal air monitoring are usually not included in the contract documents between the abatement contractor and building owner. The contractor may have a trained employee who collects the personal samples and submits them to a laboratory, or an air monitoring firm may be retained to conduct personal monitoring. Exposure levels are measured by sampling the air in the breathing zone of workers who are conducting various types of activities such as scraping, bagging, and spraying. **For OSHA compliance the samples are analyzed by a phase contrast microscope.** Phase contrast microscopy (PCM) will be discussed in more detail later in this section. The analytical results are compared to the following OSHA limits.

OSHA Limit	Fiber Concentration	Exposure Duration
Permissible Exposure Limit (PEL)	0.1 fibers/cubic centimeter (cc)	8 hours
Action Level (AL)	0.1 fibers/cubic centimeter (cc)	8 hours
Excursion Limit (EL)	1.0 fibers/cubic centimeter (cc)	30 minutes

Each limit has associated worker protection requirements that must be invoked if it is exceeded. The key limit for asbestos abatement work from a regulatory standpoint is the permissible exposure limit (PEL). Workers must be provided respirators with a high enough protection factor to keep their exposures below 0.1 fibers/cc inside the respirator.

However, it is recognized as good practice and has been taught in EPA curricula for a number of years that 0.01 fibers/cc, not 0.2 fibers/cc, should be the limit for the level inside the worker's respirator. The requirements triggered by the PEL/TWA and the excursion limit include continued air monitoring, a medical surveillance program, worker training, and documentation. Since all of these are performed in association with an abatement project anyway, these limits are more pertinent to the maintenance personnel and various tradesmen who are also covered by the OSHA

Standard for the Construction Industry (29 CFR 1926.1101) or the EPA Worker Protection Rule (40 CFR Part 763 Subpart G).

The employer must conduct initial, representative monitoring at the start-up of each abatement project. This has generally been interpreted as sampling at least 25 percent of the workers that are conducting various removal tasks -- i.e., scraping, wetting, bagging. Personal monitoring must be conducted on a daily basis unless the workers are wearing supplied air respirators; or unless the contractor submits data (for OSHA approval) from a previous job which is nearly identical to the current project, and the data indicates fiber concentrations did not exceed the PEL's. If the daily air monitoring results indicate by statistically reliable measurements that exposures are below the PEL level, the contractor can stop daily monitoring. Monitoring must resume if a different type of ACM is encountered or if work conditions change in any way. The employer must notify affected employees of the monitoring results as soon as they are received from the laboratory.

While the collection and interpretation of personal air sample results is not the regulatory or legal responsibility of the building owner or the owner's representative, some designers may elect to require the contractor to submit personal sampling results to the Project Monitor. The Monitor can then compare the airborne fiber levels to the protection afforded by the respirators being used to determine if the contractor is in compliance with the regulations or the project specifications. Additionally, personal monitoring of the Project Monitor can be performed by the owner's representative to evaluate fiber control effectiveness, and results can be shared with the contractor.

Abatement Surveillance

To check for potential fiber leaks during the removal phase, stationary area air samples are usually collected from strategic locations around the outside perimeter of the containment area. Potential leakage points where sampling should be conducted include the clean side of the containment barriers separating the work area from occupied parts of the building, and just outside the clean room of the decontamination unit. If the removal project is being conducted in a multi-story building, area samples should generally be collected from floors above and below the abatement activity. The results of these area samples are compared to the background and previous shift concentrations that were measured in the same locations before the project began. Usually this concentration is below 0.1 fibers/cc by PCM. PCM is used for abatement surveillance because sample results can be obtained quickly, and sudden increases in fiber concentration would indicate a potential problem.

There is currently a requirement for conducting abatement surveillance monitoring outside the containment area--(NYSDOH ELAP). It is considered good practice and is usually specified to be conducted by an air monitoring firm representing the building owner. The contractor may elect to conduct abatement surveillance monitoring if the specifications do not designate this activity. The specifications should indicate what action will be taken if concentrations that exceed background levels or some other decision criterion, such as 0.01 f/cc, are detected outside the containment barrier. In order to use outside air monitoring data as an effective surveillance tool, the data must be available within a few hours after sample collection. Ideally, a field microscope is set up on-site and the building owner's representative collects and analyzes the samples. A percentage of the fibers that are read in the field (typically 10 percent) are then sent to a laboratory that participates in a nationally recognized QA/QC program for a quality control check. Refer to the discussion of laboratory and microscopes' qualifications at the end of this section.

Area air samples must also be placed outside the building during the abatement project to detect leakage of fibers from the work site. Typically, pumps are placed at doors or windows near the exhaust of the negative air filtration units, and at the waste loadout area. Care must be exercised to ensure that outside samples are not overloaded with dust or other debris. Also, filter cassettes placed too close to the exhaust stream of the negative air filtration units will not give a meaningful indication of fiber leakage from these units. Samples should either be collected isokinetically, which demands special sampling equipment and a greater degree of expertise, or placed about 6-10 exhaust duct diameters downstream from the exhaust unit where fibers are more likely to be captured by the sampling apparatus.

In addition to outside perimeter samples, specifications may stipulate the collection of area samples inside the containment area during abatement. This is typically done when there are building occupants elsewhere in the building. Two to three samples, with a minimum 600 liters of air each day, are usually adequate to index airborne fiber concentrations inside the work area. A radical increase in area concentrations would signal that work practices need to be adjusted from one day to the next. **The design specifications may contain a "stop work" clause if a certain fiber concentration is exceeded in the work area**. For example, 0.5 f/cc by PCM may be defined by the Designer as the level which cannot be exceeded inside the work area for a particular type of project. If area air sampling indicates fibers are being generated at concentrations above this level, then the contractor may be required to stop work and review wetting procedures, number of air changes per hour, and housekeeping procedures in an effort to lower fiber counts. This serves as an additional safeguard for preventing contamination outside the containment barrier. **It is important to note that the "stop work"**

decision criteria will vary greatly depending on the type and percent of asbestos present, the friability of the material, the ability of the material to absorb water, and nature of the project.

Abatement Clearance Testing

The regulations promulgated by EPA for schools, in accordance with the Asbestos Hazard Emergency Response Act of 1986 (40 CFR 763, Subpart E), outline specific requirements for clearance testing of abatement projects. Currently, there are no federal regulations which require clearance testing in public and commercial buildings. Many Project Designers elect to apply the protocol outlined by regulations for clearance in non-school and commercial buildings, because it is considered as the current industry standard and there is published guidance for using the procedures.

Visual Clearance Inspection

The project specifications should clearly require a thorough visual inspection of the work area by the building owner's representative prior to final clearance air sampling. Generally, the owner's representative (i.e.-Project Monitor) and the contractor's representative conduct a walk-through to closely check for evidence of visible debris on surfaces, in corners, and difficult-to-access places.

There is a procedure for performing a visual inspection published by the American Society for Testing and Materials (ASTM) entitled Standard E 1368, Standard Practice for Visual Inspection of Asbestos Abatement Projects. The specifications should indicate this procedure will be used, outline an alternate procedure, or have the inspector submit the visual inspection procedures that will be used in writing to the contractor prior to project set-up.

Reference the section on lockdown and replacement materials.

AHERA Protocol for Clearance Testing--Once the work area has passed visual inspection criteria clearance air sampling can be performed to estimate the concentration of residual fibers. The AHERA procedures for final clearance air sampling, analytical sequence and clearance level requirements for asbestos abatement projects conducted in school buildings

AHERA SAMPLING PROTOCOL

SAMPLING ORGANIZATION
    Must have written quality control procedures and documents which verify compliance.

- Sampling must be performed by qualified individuals completely independent of the abatement contractor.

SAMPLING EQUIPMENT

- Commercially available cassettes must be used.
- Loaded cassettes must be prescreened to assure they do not contain elevated background levels.
- Filter media must be mixed cellulose ester having a pore size less than or equal to 0.45 um or polycarbonate having a pore size less than or equal to 0.4 um.
- The collection filter is placed in series with a 5.0 um back-up filter and support pad.
- Reloading of cassettes is not permitted.

SAMPLE COLLECTION

- Conduct thorough visual inspection prior to sampling.
- Critical workplace barriers over windows, doors, vents, etc. remain in place.
- Perform leak check on sampling train.
- Calibrate pumps before and after each use.
- Pump flow rate of 1 to less than 10 liters per minute for 25 mm cassettes (proportionally higher for large diameter filters).
- Isolate pump vibration from filter cassette.
- Orient cassette 45° downward from horizontal.
- Clearly label all samples
- Maintain log of all pertinent sampling data.
- Use aggressive sampling techniques.
- Collect a recommended minimum of 1.199 liters:
  - 5 per abatement area
  - 5 per ambient area (where "make-up air comes from")
  - 2 field blanks (1 near entrance to work area; 1 at ambient site)
  - 1 sealed blank
  - Collect a minimum of 1,199 liters with a 25 mm cassette or 2,799 liters with a 37 mm cassette.
  - Turn sample cassette upright before turning pump off.

SEQUENCE FOR ANALYZING CLEARANCE SAMPLES IN ACCORDANCE WITH AHERA PROTOCOL

SEQUENCING

Collect at least 13 Samples.

Analyze at least 5 inside samples.

If greater than or equal to 1,199 liters of air sampled for 25 mm cassettes, or 2,799 liters of air for 37 mm cassettes, area passes if arithmetic mean is less than or equal to 70 asbestos structures per square millimeter of filter area.

If less than 1,199 liters (2,799 liters for 37 mm cassette) of air sampled, or if greater than 70 s/mm^2, analyze 3 blanks.

If arithmetic mean of blanks is greater than 70 s/mm^2, terminate analysis, identify and eliminate source of contamination, collect new samples.

If arithmetic mean of blanks is less than 70 s/mm^2, analyze outside samples and compare with Z-test on the logarithms of the inside and outside levels.

> If Z-test results are less than or equal to 1.65, response action is complete.

> If Z-test results are greater than 1.65, re-clean and re-sample.

The AHERA protocol requires that analyses be performed with the transmission electron microscope, unless the project involves less than 160 square feet or 260 linear feet of asbestos-containing material. Phase contrast microscopy can be used to analyze clearance samples from the smaller projects.

For TEM analysis, a minimum of thirteen samples are collected with at least five from the abatement area, five from where the make-up air comes from, two field blanks, and one sealed blank. Samples are collected by aggressive air sampling techniques which involve physically or mechanically agitating the air in the work area during the sampling process. There is a non-mandatory aggressive sampling protocol provided in Appendix A of the AHERA regulations. This procedure provides for using the exhaust of a one-horsepower leaf blower to sweep floors, ceilings, walls and other surfaces in the work area to dislodge any residual fibers.

Stationary fans are placed in locations which will not interfere with air monitoring equipment. Fan air is directed toward the ceilings to keep any dislodged fibers airborne, and at least one fan is used for each 10,000 cubic feet of work site.

The purpose of final clearance air sampling using aggressive techniques is to produce a "worst case" scenario. The procedure is designed to sample asbestos in the air and on surfaces through re-entrainment. If the work area passes the final clearance level in this "worst case" environment, then the likelihood of airborne asbestos fiber levels above the clearance level when the area is reoccupied is remote.

The AHERA protocol for the large removal projects is designed so that samples can be analyzed in stages in order to possibly avoid the expense of analyzing all thirteen. The sequencing of analyses is outlined in Table X-2. In order to utilize the phased analyses, at least 1,199 liters of air must be sampled with 25 mm cassettes, or 2,799 liters of air must be sampled when 37 mm cassettes are used. Initially, the five samples (minimum) collected from inside the removal area are analyzed by TEM. **If the arithmetic mean of the five samples is less than or equal to 70 asbestos structures per square millimeter (<70 s/mm^2) of the filter area, the area passes and can be opened for re-occupancy by unprotected personnel.** The <70 s/mm^2 criterion is considered to be the filter background level--the concentration of structures per square millimeter of filter then is considered statistically indistinguishable from the concentration measured on the blanks (filters through which no air has been drawn).

If the arithmetic mean of the five inside samples exceeds <70 s/mm^2, then the next step is to analyze the two field blanks and the sealed blank to determine if the blanks are contaminated, or if there is some contamination being introduced in the sample preparation. If the blanks are contaminated, then the source of contamination must be eliminated and re-sampling must be conducted.

If the blanks are not contaminated, then the next step is to analyze the five samples collected outside the work area and perform a statistical procedure termed the Z-test on the logarithms of the inside and outside sample concentrations to determine if there is a significant difference between the inside and outside concentration. If the Z-test indicates there is no significant difference, then the area passes the clearance criteria and can be reoccupied. If the Z-test indicates the ambient area samples are significantly less contaminated with asbestos fibers than the samples from inside the removal area, then the contractor must re-clean the work area and re-sampling must be conducted. Additional information regarding the Z-test is provided in the EFP publication "Guidelines for Conducting the AHERA TEM Clearance Test to Determine Completion of an Asbestos Abatement Project" (EPA 560/ 5-89-001).

The purpose of the Z-test is to make an allowance for projects that are conducted in areas that may have elevated concentrations of asbestos in the ambient or make-up air that is being pulled inside the removal area. An example of this might be the illegal demolition of a nearby building which contains ACM, or the concurrent performance of an activity with PCM clearance controls (e.g., operations and maintenance work).

Experience in using this protocol since 1987 indicates that most of the time if the inside samples fail the initial screening test of 70 s/mm^2, the Z-test is usually failed also. For this reason, many contractors and designers prefer to re-clean the work area if the first round of testing indicates levels are above 70 s/mm^2. It is common for the Project Designer to specify that the contractor will bear the cost for additional testing, if final clearance is not achieved during the first round of testing.

As mentioned previously, the AHERA protocol allows PCM to be used for clearance testing of small removal projects (less than 260 linear feet or 160 square feet). The procedure for small projects involves collecting only five samples from the inside of the removal area. Samples are collected using aggressive sampling techniques and approximately 3,000 liters of air should be collected for each sample. If any one of these five samples exceeds 0.01 fibers per cubic centimeter by PCM (NIOSH Method 7400), then the work area must be re-cleaned and re-sampled. This concentration is generally considered the limit of detection of PCM area samples in an abatement project and is, therefore, issued as a clearance level.

Other Sampling and Analytical Protocol -- While the AHERA protocol must be used for abatement projects in schools, and it is generally recommended for use in commercial and public buildings, there are some situations in which the Designer may need to consider other options. Some examples are provided here to illustrate the point. The Designer may want to further consult with an industrial hygienist when developing specifications for these types of projects.

Two examples of removal projects that may have different clearance criteria are: a building that is going to be demolished (never reoccupied) after the ACM has been removed, and a building in an industrial complex that is older and large amounts of ACM have been used throughout the complex.

For non-school buildings that are not going to be reoccupied, a clearance criteria of 0.01 f/cc by PCM is commonly used. The logic for using PCM instead of the more stringent TEM analysis is that the building will not be reoccupied, and the 0.01 f/cc by PCM is not likely to significantly contribute to ambient air contamination when the building is demolished.

In an older industrial setting that contains large quantities of damaged ACM, it may not be feasible to achieve <70 s/mm^2 by TEM if only portions of the ACM are going to be removed at one time. The Designer may need to collect data on background levels in areas adjacent to the planned project to assist in selecting the clearance criteria.

AIR SAMPLING EQUIPMENT

A brief overview is presented here to familiarize the Project Designer with the types of air sampling equipment used on abatement projects.

Sampling Pumps

Pumps used for collecting asbestos fibers are typically categorized as either high-volume pumps which are generally electric (plug in), or low-volume (personal) pumps which are battery powered. High-volume pumps are usually calibrated to draw up to ten liters or more of air per minute through the filter and are used for area air sampling. Since being able to detect low concentrations of airborne asbestos fibers relies, in part, on sampling large volume of air, high-volume pumps are useful for sampling in environments where low levels of airborne asbestos are expected (e.g., following the clean-up of an abatement project).

Battery powered or personal sampling pumps are small, light-weight pumps encased in a hard plastic shell. These pumps are usually calibrated to draw 1.0 to 2.5 liters per minute through the filter when used to index worker exposure (or potential exposure, when wearing a respirator) to airborne asbestos fibers. The pumps are worn on the worker's belt and the cassette filter, which is connected to the pump with flexible tubing, is placed in the breathing zone of the worker.

Filters

Mixed cellulose ester (MCE) is the primary type of filter material used to sample airborne asbestos fibers. MCE filters consist of cellulose strands bound together in a web called "tortuous pore" and display a very irregular surface when observed under magnification. The MCE filter media is available in various pore sizes and diameters. For personal sampling a 25 mm diameter filter with a 0.8 m to 1.2 m pore size may be used. For clearance testing in accordance with the AHERA protocol, a 25 mm or 35 mm diameter filter may be used but the pore size must be 0.45 m for an MCE filter.

All filters are housed in a sampling cassette which includes a cap with a plug extension cowl or retainer ring, the filter, the MCE diffuser, a support pad, and a cassette base. Figure X-1 details a typical sampling cassette figuration. The entire cap is removed when sampling for asbestos fibers.

Pump Calibration

The calculation of air sampling results are dependent, in part, on the total volume of air sampled. The volume of air sampled is the flow rate of the sampling pump (liters of air per minute, or lpm) multiplied by the time (in minutes) the pump ran. Accurate calibration of the pump flow rate, then, is very important in the calculation of sample results.

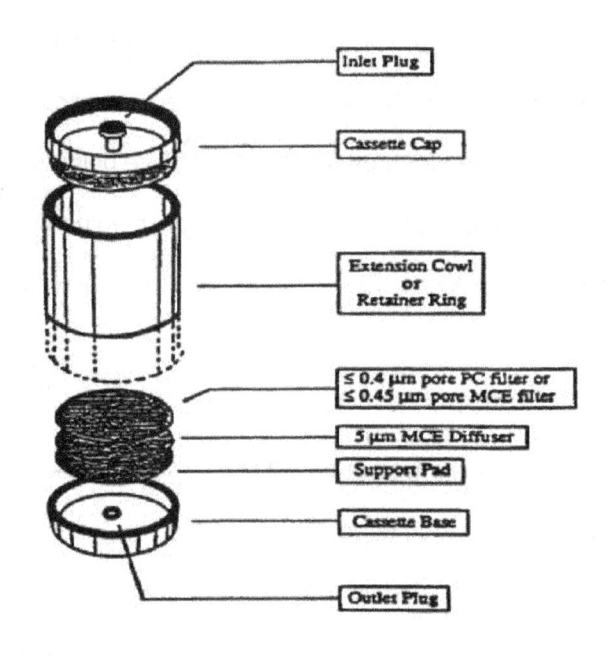

The EPA, OSHA, and NYSDOL require that sampling pumps be calibrated before and after each use, and it is good practice to maintain these calibration records together with other sampling data.

TYPICAL SAMPLING TEM CASSETTE CONFIGURATION

Although not always practical, a primary calibration standard is the best way to determine the flow rate of a sampling pump. A primary calibration standard is one that is known to have the highest degree of accuracy and repeatability when determining a pump's flow rate.

Typically, a one liter flow bubble burette or automated soap bubble meter is used as a primary calibration standard for air sampling pumps. From this, a rotameter can be calibrated and taken into the field to calibrate each sampling pump before and after use.

It is important to ensure that persons performing air monitoring are routinely calibrating their sampling pumps. Regular requests for calibration data, or requiring this data to be included in reports of sample results, are two ways to help maintain the technical and legal validity of sampling data. The Designer may want to specify that pump calibration records be submitted as part of the project documentation.

(Note: On-site analysis is NOT allowed by NYSDOL ELAP.)

ANALYTICAL ALTERNATIVES

The primary analytical techniques used for analyzing airborne fibers collected on a filter are: phase contrast microscopy (PCM), scanning electron microscopy (SEM), and transmission electron microscopy (TEM). The fibrous aerosol monitor (FAM) is an instrument which can be used in the field to obtain an index of airborne fiber levels. Applications of each of these methods (PCM, SEM, TEM, and FAM) in the analysis of air samples for asbestos are discussed below.

Phase Contrast Microscopy

Phase contrast microscopy (PCM) is a technique using a light microscope equipped to provide enhanced contrast between the fibers collected and the background filter material. Samples for analysis by PCM are collected on either a 25 mm or 37 mm mixed cellulose ester (MCE) filter with a 0.8 to 1.2 micrometer pore size. Filters are then prepared by either a liquid chemical solution or an acetone vapor that renders the filter material optically transparent. The filter is then examined under a positive phase contrast microscope at a magnification of approximately 400 times. Fibers are sized and counted using a calibrated reticule fitting into the microscope eyepiece. PCM is inexpensive ($15 to $25 per sample) and can be performed on the job site in a few hours.

Phase contrast microscopy is frequently referred to as a light microscopy method, the filter membrane method, or the NIOSH method. PCM is the analytical method specified in the Occupational Safety and Health Administration (OSHA) asbestos standards. PCM was first used to monitor asbestos workers' exposure in asbestos product manufacturing or milling operations. **Using this method, the analyst does not identify what materials the fibers are composed of, and only counts those fibers longer than five micrometers and wider than about 1.6 micrometers**. Because of these limitations, analysis by PCM typically provides only an index of total concentration of airborne fibers in the environment monitored. As the proportion of the airborne fibers which are less than 0.25 micrometers in diameter increases (e.g., nonindustrial settings such as asbestos abatement projects), PCM becomes a less reliable analytical tool.

There are three primary fiber counting methods for phase contrast microscopy. NIOSH P&CAM 239 is the original method which was implemented for estimating airborne fiber concentrations. The NIOSH 7400 method is an improved version of P&CAM 239 which provides for a more reliable limit of detection. P&CAM 239 is no longer used for compliance monitoring. The OSHA reference method (ORM) is specified in OSHA Asbestos Standards, and contains modifications to the procedures outlined in the NIOSH 7400 method for use in determining personal exposures.

Transmission Electron Microscopy

Transmission electron microscopy (TEM) is a technique which focuses an electron beam onto a thin sample mounted in the microscope column (under a vacuum). As the beam transmits through the sample, an image resulting from varying density of the sample is projected onto a fluorescent screen. Air samples for TEM analysis can be collected on either mixed cellulose ester or polycarbonate filters. Filters may be prepared using the direct transfer technique which allows for the transfer of a carbon-coated replica of the filter material (with embedded fibers and particulates, etc.) onto a copper grid suitable for TEM analysis. Alternatively, the indirect preparation technique may be employed. The uses and limitations of each technique are more fully described in the EPA publication, "Comparison of Airborne Asbestos Levels Determined by Transmission Electron Microscopy (TEM) Using Direct and Indirect Transfer Techniques," EPA publication 560/5-89-004, Washington, DC, 1990.

Several methods exist for the preparation and analysis of air samples by electron microscopy. Most significant are the mandatory and non-mandatory TEM methods set forth as appendices to 40 CFR 763, Subpart E (AHERA regulations). These methods are to be used, with restrictions, for analysis of final clearance air samples on school abatement projects. Other methods include the NIOSH 7402, and the EPA Level I, II, and III (Yamate method). Depending on the method used, preparation of the sample can take as long as 24 hours (or more) and analysis can take several hours to a day or more. However, standard preparation and analysis time for AHERA clearance samples is now in the range of 12 hours or less. As the number of laboratories with TEM capability continues to increase, the cost and turnaround time has gone down.

Scanning Electron Microscopy

Scanning electron microscopy (SEM) is a technique which uses a finely focused electron beam on the sample surface to generate an image of the surface shape. A magnified image is produced on a viewing screen. Air samples for SEM filter counting are collected on a mixed cellulose ester or a polycarbonate filter with a 0.45 micrometer pore size.

SEM can identify large fibers by morphology (physical appearance) and elemental analyses when equipped with an energy dispersive X-ray analysis system. Fibers which are 0.05 micrometers in diameter are about the smallest that can be detected using SEM under optimal conditions. This method has fiber identification problems with thin fibers and flat, platy particles that display poor contrast. Also, there is no standard protocol for this method. **Currently, SEM provides somewhat better information than PCM analysis, but the method cannot be used to conclusively identify or quantify asbestos**. SEM is not routinely used for air monitoring associated with asbestos removal projects.

Fibrous Aerosol Monitor

The fibrous aerosol monitor (FAM) is an instrument which uses laser light and electrical field technologies for a near real-time analysis of the fiber content of the air. The instrument provides a continuous measurement, with direct readout of the number or concentration of airborne fibers. It has a flow rate of about 2 liters per minute. The FAM can be used in conjunction with a strip chart recorder to provide a record of air quality conditions. **Typically used as an indicator of airborne fiber levels rather than a precision testing device, the FAM's more useful function is to alert personnel to any sudden elevation of the air fiber count.** If the FAM is used on a project, it should be used in conjunction with other traditional air sampling techniques and not in place of them.

This instrument does not distinguish fiber types and cannot discriminate between fibers and certain particles that have sufficient shape irregularities to possess fiber characteristics. The FAM does not detect fibers less than 0.5 micrometers in diameter. Laboratory tests indicate FAM concentration readings are generally within + 25 percent of the optical membrane filter count. Also, in order to obtain accurate low level (0.01 fibers/cc) readings it is necessary to operate the FAM for long periods (1000 minutes); even though the FAM will register these levels after one minute.

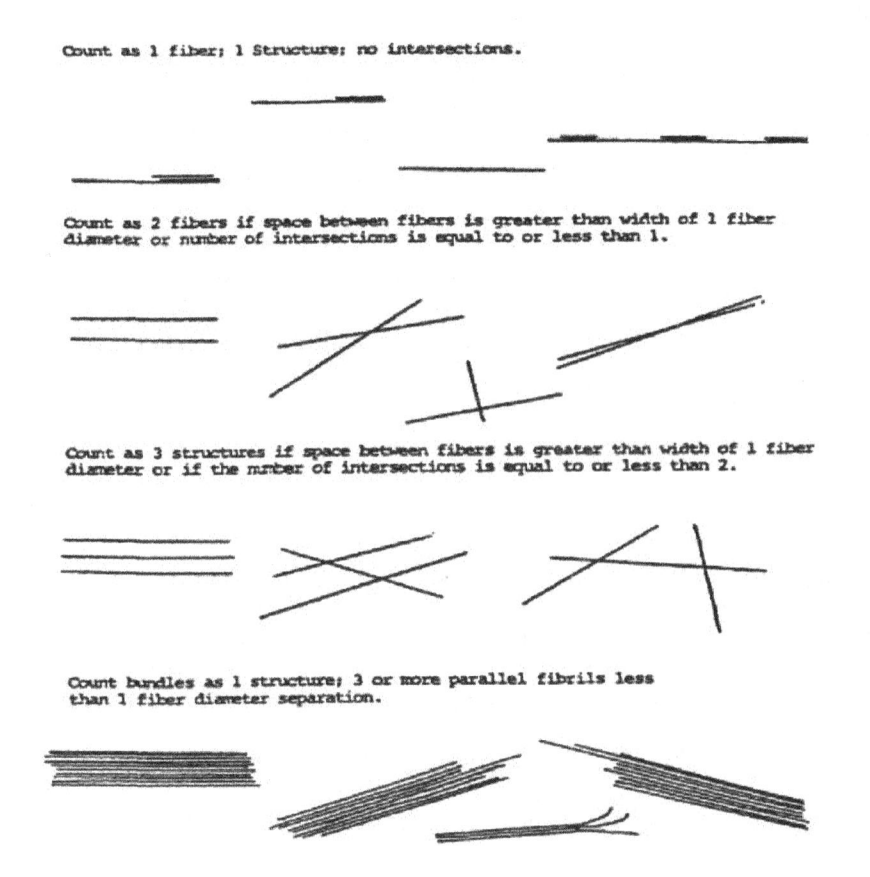

DATA INTERPRETATION

With the use of various analytical methods for asbestos sample analysis which have different counting protocol and different analytical reporting units, it can be difficult to understand what the results mean. No attempt is made here to interpret air monitoring data with respect to health effects because many more years of medical and epidemiological research will probably be required before this is clearly understood. However, a discussion of the reporting units and the definitions of the fiber as used in the different counting protocols should help the designer better understand the limitations and the usefulness of the data.

As discussed earlier, the OSHA standard which covers worker exposure monitoring requires analyses of these personal samples to be conducted by phase contrast microscopy. The counting protocol requires the analyst to only count those fibers that are at least three times longer than they are wide, and that are at least five micrometers long (approximately 1/5000 of an inch). The OSHA permissible exposure limit PEL (TWA) of 0.1 fibers/cc is somewhat difficult to visualize. It can also be expressed as 100,000 fibers per cubic meter of air. Another way to understand the 0.2 fiber/cc PEL is to visualize the size of a 10' x 10' room with a 10' ceiling. If this room had an asbestos fiber concentration of 0.2 fibers/cc, there could be over 2,500,000 fibers in the room. The AHERA protocol defines a fiber differently than the OSHA protocol. The analyst is required, using transmission electron microscopy, to count asbestos structures that have a length to width ratio of at least 5:1, and to count any asbestos structures that are longer than 0.5 microns. Structures are classified as fibers, bundles, clusters or matrices as further illustrated. Another difference is that the AHERA clearance level of 70 s/mm^2 is based on the number of fibers per filter area. The OSHA PEL is expressed as an airborne fiber concentration (fibers/cc).

While an entire course could be devoted to understanding analytical techniques and data interpretation, this short overview has been presented to help illustrate the complexity of data interpretation and the need to exercise caution. It should be apparent that PCM data cannot be interchanged with TEM data and that the counting protocol has a direct effect on the analytical result.

QUALIFICATIONS OF THE AIR MONITOR AND PROJECT MONITOR

The terms Air Monitor and Project Monitor have commonly been used interchangeably. For the purposes of the discussion on qualifications, the Air Monitor will be defined as the individual who collects air samples and reports the analytical results. The Project Monitor has a greater responsibility which may include acting as the building owner's representative to perform quality assurance on the contractor's work, construction management, and visual clearance prior to clearance sampling.

The Project Monitor may also serve as the Air Monitor or may interact with the Air Monitor.

COUNTING GUIDELINES USED IN DETERMINING ASBESTOS STRUCTURES

Count clusters as 1 structure; fibers having greater than or equal to 3 intersections.

Count matrix as 1 structure.

DO NOT COUNT AS STRUCTURES:

Fiber protrusion <5:1 Aspect Ratio

No fiber protrusion

Fiber protrusion <0.5 micrometer

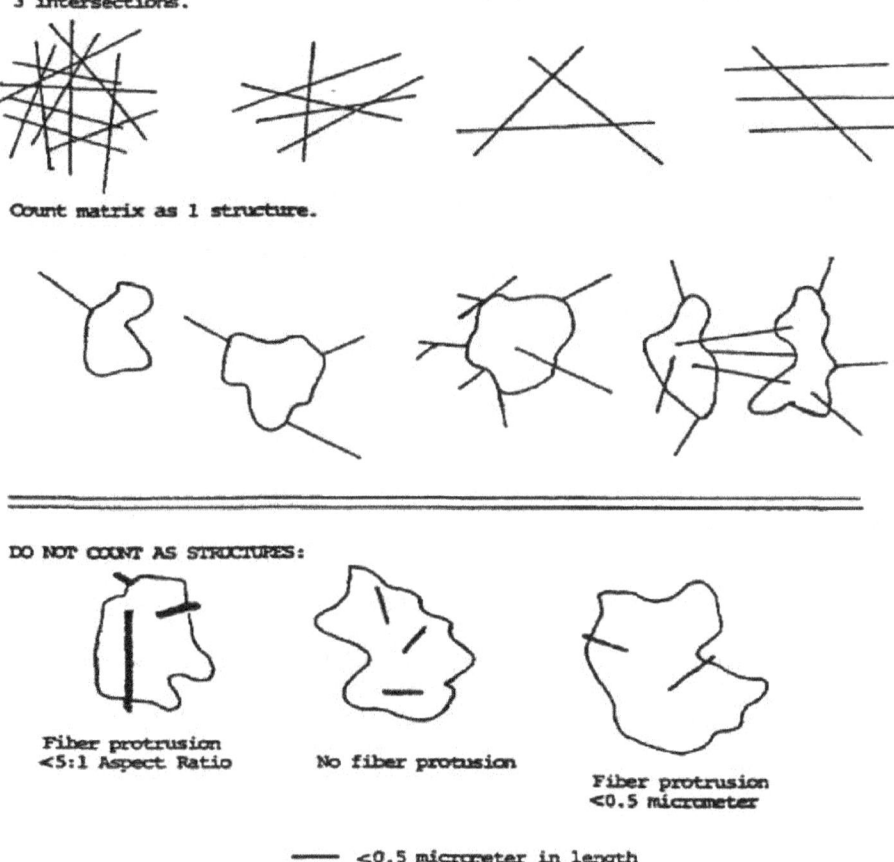

— <0.5 micrometer in length
▬ <5:1 Aspect Ratio

Reprinted from Federal Register, Vol. 52, No. 210, Friday, October 30, 1987, p. 41867.

Interpretation

There are currently no federal requirements for certification or licensing of individuals or firms that conduct air monitoring or project monitoring on asbestos abatement projects. A few states do have requirements for training and experience. The following are provided as minimum guidelines for Designers who are developing specifications for projects in states that do not have provisions for air monitoring or project monitoring personnel.

Air Monitoring Personnel

- Should have current training certificate from a NYSDOH accredit course for Asbestos Project Air Sampling Technical or Asbestos Project Monitor (with the air sampling technician credential.)

- Should have attended and passed exam in the National Institute for Occupational Safety and Health (NIOSH) 582 course for Air Sampling and Analytical Techniques (or equivalent).

- Should have on-the-job training under the supervision of an experienced Air Monitor.

Project Monitoring Personnel

- Should have current training certificate from an EPA Model Accreditation Course for Asbestos Abatement Project Supervisors or Designers.

- Should have on-the-job training under the supervision of an experienced Air Monitor.

QUALIFICATIONS FOR ANALYTICAL LABORATORY

The AHERA regulations outline qualify assurance/quality control procedures for laboratories that perform TEM analysis of clearance samples collected on school abatement projects. It is recommended that design specifications for non-school building also impose these requirements on the laboratory performing analyses. They include:

Participation in the National Voluntary Laboratory Accreditation Program (NVLAP) administered by the National Institute of Standards and Technology (NIST).

The National Institute of Standards and Technology (NIST) administers the National Voluntary Laboratory Accreditation Program (NVLAP). NVLAP is comprised of laboratory accreditation programs (LAPs) which are established on the basis of requests and demonstrated need. Each LAP includes specific calibration and/or test standards and related methods and protocols assembled to satisfy the unique needs for accreditation in a field of testing or calibration. NVLAP accredits public and private laboratories based on evaluation of their technical qualifications and competence to carry out specific calibrations or tests.

Accreditation criteria are established in accordance with the U.S. Code of Federal Regulations (CFR, Title 15, Part 285), NVLAP Procedures and General Requirements, and encompass the requirements of ISO/IEC 17025. Accreditation is granted following successful completion of a process which includes submission of an application and payment of fees bythe laboratory, an on-site assessment, resolution of any nonconformities identified during the on-site assessment, participation in proficiency testing, and technical evaluation. The accreditation is formalized through issuance of a Certificate of Accreditation and Scope of Accreditation, and publicized by announcement in various government and private media.

NVLAP accreditation is available to commercial laboratories; manufacturers' in-house laboratories; university laboratories; and federal, state, and local government laboratories. Laboratories located outside the United States may also be accredited if they meet the same requirements as domestic laboratories and pay any additional fees required for travel expenses.

NVLAP provides an unbiased third-party evaluation and recognition of performance, as well as expert technical guidance to upgrade laboratory performance. NVLAP accreditation signifies that a laboratory has demonstrated that it operates in accordance with NVLAP management and technical requirements pertaining to quality systems; personnel; accommodation and environment; test and calibration methods; equipment; measurement traceability; sampling; handling of test and calibration items; and test and calibration reports. NVLAP accreditation does not imply any guarantee (certification) of laboratory performance or test/calibration data; it is solely a finding of laboratory competence. A laboratory may cite its accredited status and use the NVLAP term and symbol on reports, stationery, and in business and trade publications provided that this use does not imply product certification.

For laboratories performing phase contrast microscopy (PCM), qualifications of **each analyst** should include:

- Participation in the Environmental Laboratory Approval Program (ELAP) Administered by NYSDOH.

- Satisfactory performance in the Proficiency Analytical Testing (PAT) Program sponsored by the National Institute of Occupational Safety and Health (NIOSH) **and/or**

- Satisfactory performance in the Asbestos Analyst Professional Registry Program sponsored by the American Industrial Hygiene Association (AIHA).

- Successful completion of a 40-hour training course in Air Sampling and Analysis (NIOSH 582 or equivalent).

In addition to these quality assurance/quality control programs, laboratories may also be accepted by the AIHA Laboratory Accreditation Program. This provides additional assurance that the laboratory exercises good general laboratory practices and record keeping procedures.

SUMMARY OF LABORATORY DATA QUALITY OBJECTIVES

Unit Operation	Quality Control Check	Frequency	Conformance Expectation
Sample receiving	Review of receiving report	Each sample	95% complete
Sample custody	Review of chain-of-custody record	Each sample	95% complete
Sample Preparation	Supplies and reagents	On receipt	Meet specs or reject
	Grid opening size	20 openings/20 grids/lot of 1000 or 1 opening/sample	100%
	Special clean area monitoring	After cleaning or service	Meet specs or reject
	Laboratory blank	1 per pre series or 10%	Meet specs or reanalyze series
	Plasma etch blank	1 per 20 samples	75%

		Multiple preps (3 per sample)	Each sample	One with cover of 15 complete grid squares
Sample analysis		System check	Each day	Each day
Performance check		Alignment check	Each day	Each day
		Magnification calibration with low and high standards	Each month or after service	95%
		ED calibration by gold standard	Weekly	95%
		EDS calibration by copper line	Daily	95%
		Laboratory blank (measure of cleanliness)	Prep 1 per series or 10% read 1 per 25 samples	Meet specs or reanalyze series
		Replicate counting (measure of cleanliness)	1 per 100 samples	1.5 x Poisson Std. Dev.
		Duplicate analysis (measure of reproducibility)	1 per 100 samples	2 x Poisson Std. Dev.
		Known samples of typical materials (working standards)	Training and for comparison with unknowns	100%
		Analysis of NBS SRM 1876 and/or RM 8410 (measure of accuracy and comparability	1 per analyst per year	1.5 x Poisson Std. Dev.
		Data entry review (data validation and measure of completeness)	Each sample	95%
Calculations and data reduction		Record and verify ID election diffraction pattern of structure	1 per 5 samples	80% accuracy
		Hand calculation of automated data reduction procedure or independent recalculation of hand-calculated data	1 per 100 samples	85%

SUMMARY

Sampling and analytical techniques provide one quantifiable method of determining if the design specifications are being executed properly. There are a variety of sampling and analytical techniques, and the appropriate ones must be selected to collect data that is representative of the environment being sampled. Project Designers and Project Monitors must have a general understanding of the various sampling and analytical techniques employed. They should also understand the limitations of the data that is generated by each procedure to recognize potential weaknesses and strengths in the design specifications.

OBJECTIVES:

1. To understand the legal liabilities and responsibilities of professionals involved in asbestos project monitoring.

2. To understand the purpose, limitations, and availability of insurance for professionals engaged in asbestos-related work.

3. To understand the purpose, limitations, and availability of bonding in asbestos-related work.

LEGAL LIABILITIES OF PROJECT MONITORS

INTRODUCTION

Project Monitors are exposed to liability due to the critical role they play in the asbestos abatement process. The air-monitoring report will be the basis for all subsequent actions taken by a facility manager to control asbestos-containing materials. The assessment report provides guidance for the development of operations and maintenance strategies, the determination of response actions, and it is an integral part of any management plan.

LIABILITY OF PROJECT MONITORS

The Project Monitor faces three areas of potential liability: regulatory, criminal, and civil.

REGULATORY LIABILITY

A Project Monitor can be held liable for non-compliance with federal, state or local regulations. Consistent with the hazardous nature of asbestos, any assessment for the presence of asbestos is understood to be a critical task. Therefore, regulatory agencies on all levels have adopted diverse and explicit regulations concerning the performance of asbestos assessments.

A primary area is the compliance with Project Monitor certification requirements. Not only must the Project Monitor take an EPA approved course and pass an examination as required by the federal government, he or she must also often comply with state, county and local regulations for certification. Other regulations that the Project Monitor must comply with relate to the use of respirators and protective clothing while conducting an inspection.

The failure to comply with regulations can result in both fines and revocation of certifications. These actions are taken by an administrative agency, such as the Environmental Protection Agency (EPA). Any arguments made by a Project Monitor against the administrative penalty must first be argued before a hearing officer. It is very difficult to successfully overturn an administrative penalty in an administrative hearing. Only after "exhausting administrative remedies" could a Project Monitor obtain relief from an administrative action by going to court.

Simply stated, failure by a Project Monitor to follow regulations can lead directly to administrative sanctions from a variety of government agencies. Once the sanctions are assessed, it is difficult for a Project Monitor to successfully overturn any administrative penalties.

CRIMINAL LIABILITY

Although remote, it is possible for a Project Monitor to be held criminally liable. In the criminal context, it is the government that is prosecuting the action. Importantly, a criminal conviction is very serious and may involve both fines and incarceration. A criminal conviction will also result in a record.

To be held criminally responsible, the Project Monitor must meet two elements. First, the Project Monitor must **know** his actions are wrong. Second, the Project Monitor must perform a **guilty act**. An example would be the Project Monitor who consciously failed to define the asbestos content of a material, was aware that the material was suspect, and was aware that his action would lead directly to extensive contamination and exposure. In this context, a District Attorney may choose to prosecute a criminal action.

CIVIL LIABILITY

Civil actions involve a suit by a private party against a private party. In contrast, both the Administrative and Criminal contexts involve employees of a government initiating a legal action. By far, civil liability is the greatest source of potential liability to the Project Monitor.

Civil liability includes actions based on contractual and tort theories.

Contractual Liability

The Project Monitor is liable for breach of contract if the services are not performed in accordance with the explicit and implicit meaning of the agreement. A contract need not be written to be enforceable; contracts can be oral as well as implied by a court from the behavior of the parties. If a court finds that there was mutuality of obligation, a meeting of the minds, and that the agreement is not against public policy, the court will attempt to strictly enforce a contract. In a contract action, the court will look to the agreement to determine the intent of the parties. The court will then enforce a contract in order to avoid unjust enrichment and in an attempt to place the parties in the position they would have been in had the agreement been performed faithfully. In terms of remedies, the court will assess financial awards; it is very rare that the court will order the parties to specifically perform the agreement.

When a contract is written, the court will first decide if the written agreement was intended to embody the entire agreement. If the court decides that the contract integrates the entire agreement between the parties, the court will focus only on the language of the contract to determine the rights of the parties. In this context, any attempt by a party to contradict the explicit terms of the contract with testimony regarding oral promises or representations will fail. The court will strictly interpret the written agreement.

Contractual liability is one of the greatest sources of liability facing a Project Monitor. The number of contract actions is a direct result of poor drafting of both proposals and contracts. Reliance on "boilerplate" language in proposals and contracts is the single most common reason for arguments, which lead to lawsuits alleging breach of contract. The failure to ensure a "meeting of the minds" by drafting a specific contract that defines the agreement is a recipe for legal actions.

The second most common cause of contract suits is the fact that more emphasis is placed on the price of the contract rather than the scope-of-work. By definition, a contract to perform an asbestos assessment is a contract to define an unknown: in other words, how much asbestos is present in a building. A properly performed asbestos survey will allow the conditions on-site, (i.e., the number, types and locations of suspect asbestos containing materials) to determine the scope-of-work (i.e., survey duration and number of samples). However, emphasis is placed on the price of the assessment. Many breach of contract suits result from a Project Monitor not being able to perform both professionally and profitably.

Perhaps the best example comes from the public bidding process, where selection on the basis of price is required by procurement regulations. In schools, most inspection contracts are bid on a competitive, fixed-fee basis after the school system has presented the building plans as a basis of the bids. In this context, the price of the contract, not the number of samples necessary to professionally define all suspect materials, becomes the focus. The only way to ensure profitability is to perform the assessment with haste and limit the number of samples. Low bid leads directly to low quality. Low quality is often the basis of a breach of contract action.

Clarity in contract language is the best means of avoiding disputes. If the Project Monitor contracted to inspect a given number of square feet based on information provided by the building owner, the owner would pay an additional amount if the square footage estimates are inaccurate. If the Project Monitor were to win a bid to inspect "all the buildings," the Project Monitor would be liable for the inspection of all areas without a square footage limitation. Does this contract include roofing materials?

The timing of the completion of an inspection can be of great concern to the school and the subject of breach of contract action. If the school officials have a timetable by which they must solicit bids from contractors, the completion of the inspection becomes an important contractual consideration. Liquidated damages are often defined in the contract and are claimed against the Project Monitor for failure to complete on time.

The extent of sampling and documentation of results are other areas in which the building owner and Project Monitor should have a clear contractual understanding. The Project Monitor should not enter into a contract in which an insufficient number of samples are specified so that the presence of asbestos may not be detected. The appropriate type of laboratory analysis at a certified laboratory should be specified in the contract. The building owner may save money in the short run by economizing on sampling, however, such practices could cause legal problems for both the building owner and the Project Monitor later.

Furthermore, if the contract calls for "best practices" or state-of-the-art protocols for area air sampling, then provides insufficient funds for sampling, the Project Monitor would be caught in a situation in which he could be open to (1) later litigation if there is asbestos-related damage and, (2) breach of contract action by the school or building owner.

The records turned over to the school or building owner by the inspector are the end product of the contracts. Not only should the nature and form of these records be specified, but also any special procedures to be followed in developing the set of records. Assuring the chain-of-custody of samples between the Project Monitor and laboratory is an example of where the Project Monitor might be personally liable to re-sample all areas of the school if proper custody procedures are not followed.

Tort Liability

A "tort" is a generic legal term for a class of theories advanced in civil litigation. Common tort theories include negligence, fraud, misrepresentation, assault and battery.

The most common tort theory advanced against a Project Monitor would be negligence. A negligence claim alleges that the Project Monitor failed to perform his/her work in accordance with the skills of the profession. To win a negligence suit, the plaintiff must prove that the Project Monitor failed to perform the services in a professional manner, using that degree of care and skill ordinarily exercised by and consistent with the standards of competent consultants practicing in the same or a similar locality. The plaintiff must prove each of the following items:

- **Duty**
- The Project Monitor had a duty to the plaintiff that is recognized in a court of law.

- **Breach of Duty**
- The Project Monitor's actions constituted a breach of the duty owed to the Plaintiff.

- **Unreasonable**
- The Project Monitor's actions were not objectively reasonable: In other words, a "reasonable Project Monitor" would not have performed as the Project Monitor did. As elements of proof, state-of-the-art practices, regulatory guidance documents and industry standards would be offered to show that the Project Monitor's actions were unreasonable.

- **Injury**
- The plaintiff must show that he/she was "injured" by the Project Monitor's actions. Fear of future consequences usually does not suffice. The plaintiff must show real-time injury such as clinical medical tests or the loss of a sale of real estate.

- **Proximate Cause**
- The Plaintiff must prove that the Project Monitor's action was the direct cause of the injury. The two events should be connected closely in time and space.

- **Damages**
- The court will award damages, in the form of monetary awards, to compensate for the injury. Some jurisdictions also allow punitive damages in addition to compensatory damages.

Negligence can arise from the Project Monitor failing to document air sampling or improperly taking area air samples. One of the great difficulties in defining a potential liability due to negligence is the lack of universally accepted performance standards for asbestos inspection activities.

LEGAL CONSIDERATIONS OF INSURANCE

Obtaining professional liability insurance is the normal method for a professional, such as an Asbestos Project Monitor, to secure protection from litigation arising from his professional activities. These policies are often referred to as Errors and Omission (E&O) Policies.

Many owners require that all professionals involved in asbestos-related work have liability insurance in order to have some financial security for significant claims that may arise. In addition, under certain state and local laws, general liability insurance in specified amounts is often required.

A related aspect of this issue is the necessity for indemnification clauses in the contract, whereby the professional is obligated to indemnify and defend the owner against claims brought against the owner arising out of the Project Monitor's work. At the same time, Project Monitors need such insurance to protect themselves against claims which can be financially ruinous, and to provide for legal defense costs against claims. While work done in accordance with specifications and applicable regulations may ultimately shield the Project Monitor from liability, the assumption of defense of a legal action by the insurance carrier, or the client building owner who indemnifies the Project Monitor, is a significant benefit.

It is obvious that insurance adds to the Project Monitor's cost of performance and thus is eventually paid by the owner. Complicating the asbestos management issue is the difficulty most professionals involved in asbestos are having-- obtaining meaningful insurance at any price. Due to the current relative unavailability of insurance, and the expense of substantive E&O policies, many owners have considered dropping or reducing insurance requirements, and sometimes are forced to do so to obtain professional services.

The relative unavailability of insurance has forced asbestos professionals in some cases to purchase any insurance available, without paying adequate attention to whether risks are covered, or the strength or credibility of the carrier. Similarly, owners are accepting insurance certificates without analyzing the coverage being offered. Changes in the type and scope of coverage offered by the insurance industry must therefore be analyzed carefully to accomplish the goal of insurance. Rather than protection against liability, insurance for some has become a "license to work" in the asbestos industry.

Those asbestos professionals who purchase insurance, regardless of the cost or quality of coverage, can obtain work. Others are forced to attempt to negotiate alternatives with owners to providing such insurance. However, unless the insured understands what coverage is being purchased, the insured may be left unprotected by merely buying a "license to work."

TYPES OF INSURANCE COVERAGE

Errors and Omissions

Asbestos Project Monitors will normally look for "Errors and Omissions" insurance to protect them against misjudgments made during project monitoring. The mistake may take the form of an inadvertent error or an unintentional omission of some nature. Errors and Omissions (E&O) coverage is written for specific professions. Many professionals (architect, Project Monitor, engineer, designer, etc.) have E&O coverage to protect them; however, asbestos related professionals may have difficulty obtaining full coverage due to the great exposure for loss in their activities. Errors and Omissions insurance is very expensive.

General Liability Insurance

Another type of coverage that Project Monitors might pursue, general liability insurance, is available and may serve as protection for events that occur during building inspections. As the name implies, general liability coverage is suitable for situations arising in the normal course of business and not related to the Project Monitor's delivery of professional opinions. The drawback to this type of insurance is that it could contain a pollution or asbestos exclusion, rendering the policy essentially ineffective for asbestos-related claims.

Occurrence Insurance

In the past, liability insurance has been written on an "occurrence" basis. Under such a policy, if an incident "occurs" while the policy is in force, coverage is afforded even if the actual claim is made some years later and even if the insured is no longer insured by the same carrier. As a result of this type of coverage, insurance carriers must defend claims brought years after the carrier no longer insures companies. With the long latency period of asbestos related disease, occurrence coverage can result in great losses to carriers who have not received premiums over a period of time. As a result, the carriers have been adding exclusions to existing policies for asbestos related third-party claims, and generally have changed the coverage from occurrence to "claims made."

Claims Made Insurance

Under a "claims made" policy, coverage exists if a claim is made while the policy is in force. In certain situations, a claim may be made during an extended reporting period ("tail") which may require an additional premium. For many risks, the difference between occurrence and claims made coverage is not significant since the liability-causing event is obvious and claims are generally asserted shortly after the event occurs. However, the release of asbestos fibers from an asbestos abatement project may not be obvious, and injury may not be detected for twenty years. Thus, if claims made coverage is obtained, it may not be of value in some cases. If (1) the insured changes insurance carriers before a claim is made, (2) the carrier terminates coverage under a policy, or (3) the carrier withdraws from the market before a claim is filed.

There is no single definition of what "claims made" means; it is mandatory that the insured read and understand the coverage provided under its policy. All exclusions, conditions, and definitions must be carefully analyzed. For example, a general liability policy written for an asbestos contractor often includes a "pollution exclusion." This excludes coverage for any personal injury or property damage caused by a broad list of substances. Generally, asbestos is included on the list and consequently the policy provides no coverage for asbestos risks.

There are several important considerations in making an analysis of available insurance coverage or in specifying same:

1. True "occurrence" coverage is rare. The terms of the policy must be reviewed carefully. Some "occurrence" policies have conditions or exclusions that negate coverage. The name of the policy makes no difference. Claims made policies may, in some situations, cover claims which arose in prior years, similar to "occurrence" policies.

2. The insurance certificate provides little or no information of benefit to an owner or Project Monitor.

3. The insurance carrier must be very carefully evaluated. Does the carrier understand the industry, and is it committed to writing proper coverage? Again, the policy terms are important.

BONDING

Traditionally, two types of bonds have been required in the construction industry to protect the owner or lender against the contractor's financial default:

- Payment bonds, under which a surety company agrees to pay for labor and materials supplied to a project in the event the contractor fails to do so; and

- Performance bonds, under which a surety agrees to complete performance of a project if the contractor fails to do so.

Abatement contractors who have had their insurance canceled or not renewed may experience difficulties in obtaining bonding. Bonding companies rely on the financial ability of the principal (the contractor) to respond to claims under payment and performance bonds. If a company is not insured against catastrophic liability, the financial underpinnings of the company are weakened, and the bonding company becomes apprehensive over issuing bonds. In a similar vein, lenders are reacting adversely to the no insurance bonding problems of such companies. Lenders are advising companies who find themselves in such positions that lines of credit will not be renewed, for the same reasons given by the bonding companies.

The difficulty being encountered by asbestos abatement contractors in obtaining bonding is severe. For reasons similar to those which caused the asbestos abatement insurance crisis, many contractors are unable to obtain sufficient bonding and, in some cases, any bonding. In addition to the general underwriting concerns about the contractor's ability to perform the work, another reason some bonding companies are unwilling to write bonds for asbestos abatement work relates directly to liability insurance problems. Because the bonding contract often has requirements for the contractor to obtain and maintain certain liability insurance coverage on the project, the bonding companies fear that if the contractor has insurance problems, such as improper coverage or cancellation during the policy period, the potential loss that may otherwise be covered by liability insurance might be covered by the contractor's performance bond.

While the traditional concepts of bond underwriting may not be applicable to abatement contractors, it is nevertheless useful to understand them. The primary considerations of the bonding company in determining whether to bond a contractor are the ability of the contractor to perform the work and the contractor's financial ability. A proven track record of successfully completed projects, without ensuing litigation, is very helpful to the contractor in demonstrating to the bonding company its ability to perform the work. Financial stability is important not only with respect to the contractor's ability to perform the work, but also its ability to satisfy its indemnity obligation to the bonding company in the event a loss is suffered under the bonds. Unlike insurance, a payment or performance bond gives the bonding company the right to recover back against the contract for any losses sustained by it under the bond. A somewhat more intangible, yet important, factor is the contractor's good character. Despite satisfactorily proving all of these items, a contractor may still not be able to obtain sufficient bonding in today's market. In such events, an owner may waive or revise bonding requirements, or arrange other contractual mechanisms to assure payment or performance.

There are numerous legal considerations involved in the evaluation of insurance and bonding coverage. The cost of insurance for asbestos abatement is significant, and if such expense is going to be undertaken, the coverage obtained should be satisfactory. While there are no easy solutions in this decision-making process, it is mandatory that contractors, Project Monitors, consultants, and owners undertake to become knowledgeable purchasers of insurance.

The shift in the types of coverage written for the contracting industry from occurrence to claims made, and the difficulty in obtaining bonds have placed greater emphasis on the contractor's commitment to the performance of work in a quality manner, the carrier's commitment to continuing to insure asbestos abatement contractors, and the quality of the carrier's coverage and insurance program in general. This makes the process of purchasing insurance more complicated, but a thorough review of the considerations outlined above will greatly assist the contractor, consultant, or owner in making a knowledgeable choice.

Chapter 13 - Recordkeeping & Report Writing CFR 763.94

(a) Records required under this section shall be maintained in a centralized location in the administrative office of both the school and the local education agency as part of the management plan. For each homogeneous area where all ACBM has been removed, the local education agency shall ensure that such records are retained for 3 years after the next Pre-inspection required under 763.85(b)(1), or for an equivalent period.

(b) For each preventive measure and response action taken for friable and nonfriable ACBM and friable and nonfriable suspected ACBM assumed to be ACM, the local education agency shall provide:

(1) A detailed written description of the measure or action, including methods used, the location where the measure or action was taken, reasons for selecting the measure or action, start and completion dates of the work, names and addresses of all contractors involved, and if applicable, their State of accreditation, and accreditation numbers, and if ACBM is removed, the name and location of storage or disposal site of the ACM.

(2) The name and signature of any person collecting any air sample required to be collected at the completion of certain response actions specified by 763.90(i), the locations where samples were collected, date of collection, the name and address of the laboratory analyzing the samples, the date of analysis, the results of the analysis, the method of analysis, the name and signature of the person performing the analysis, and a statement that the laboratory meets the applicable requirements of 763.90(i)(2)(ii).

(c) For each person required to be trained under 763.92(a) (1) and (2), the local education agency shall provide the person's name and job title, the date that training was completed by that person, the location of the training, and the number of hours completed in such training.

(d) For each time that periodic surveillance under 763.92(b) is performed, the local education agency shall record the name of each person performing the surveillance, the date of the surveillance, and any changes in the conditions of the materials.

(e) For each time that cleaning under 763.91(c) is performed, the local education agency shall record the name of each person performing the cleaning, the date of such cleaning, the locations cleaned, and the methods used to perform such cleaning.

(f) For each time that operations and maintenance activities under 763.91(d) are performed, the local education agency shall record the name of each person performing the activity, the start and completion dates of the activity, the locations where such activity occurred, a description of the activity including preventive measures used, and if ACBM is removed, the name and location of storage or disposal site of the ACM.

(g) For each time that major asbestos activity under 763.91(e) is performed, the local education agency shall provide the name and signature, State of accreditation, and if applicable, the accreditation number of each person performing the activity, the start and completion dates of the activity, the locations where such activity occurred, a description of the activity including preventive measures used, and if ACBM is removed, the name and location of storage or disposal site of the ACM.

(h) For each fiber release episode under 763.91(f), the local education agency shall provide the date and location of the episode, the method of repair, preventive measures or response action taken, the name of each person performing the work, and if ACBM is removed, the name and location of storage or disposal site of the ACM.

MED-TOX NORTHWEST ASBESTOS AIR SAMPLING DATA SHEET

SAFE ENVIRONMENT OF AMERICA, INC.

Sheet _____ of _____

Project: _____
Activity #: _____
Sample Date: _____
Abatement Contractor: _____
Competent Person: _____

Sample No.	Sample type	Pump Model	Name/Worker cert #/Soc. Sec #/tasks	# emp. rep.	PPE worn	Time (24hr)	Flow Rate (lpm)	Sample vol. (liters)	LOD (F/cc)	Results (F/field)	Results (F/cc)
		Pump No.	Location/Description/Interferences		Controls	On / Off / Total min	Pre / Post / Avg				
		Pump Model	Name/Worker cert #/Soc. Sec #/tasks	# emp. rep.	PPE worn	Time (24hr)	Flow Rate (lpm)	Sample vol. (liters)	LOD (F/cc)	Results (F/field)	Results (F/cc)
		Pump No.	Location/Description/Interferences		Controls	On / Off / Total min	Pre / Post / Avg				
		Pump Model	Name/Worker cert #/Soc. Sec #/tasks	# emp. rep.	PPE worn	Time (24hr)	Flow Rate (lpm)	Sample vol. (liters)	LOD (F/cc)	Results (F/field)	Results (F/cc)
		Pump No.	Location/Description/Interferences		Controls	On / Off / Total min	Pre / Post / Avg				

Personal Sample Codes
TWA = Time Weighted Average   EX = 30 minute Excursion
Number TWA sample sets: TWA1 = first set, TWA2 = second set
All personal samples are to be collected in the employee's breathing zone

Area Sample Codes*
OWA = outside work area   RR = pre-abatement   IA = inside regulated area
HE = HEPA exhaust   DE = outside decon   CL = Clearance
*Must use a location description: example - 3' north and 5' west of Column L1, approx 5' high

Respirator codes
HF = air purifying half face
FF = air purifying full face
PAPR = powered air purifying respirator
SAP = Type C pressure demand
SAC = Type C continuous flow
G = Glove bag
NPE = Negative pressure enclosure
ME = Mini-enclosure

Resp. cartridge codes
HE = HEPA
OV = organic vapor
AG = acid gas
ST = stack cartridge

Other PPE codes
CV = coverall
HCV = hooded coverall   HO = hood
B = boots   RG = rubber gloves
CG = cloth gloves
LG = leather gloves

Control codes
HV = HEPA vacuum   W = Wet methods
DV = Decon with vacuum   AM = Alternate means
DS = Decon with shower   PW = Prep Work
                          WTD = work area tear down

Calibration Data	Low Flow	Rotometer Mfg.	Model #	Serial #	Cert #	Cert Exp Date	Calibration date
	High Flow	Rotometer Mfg.	Model #	Serial #			Calibration date

I certify that the above samples were taken in compliance with applicable standards, regulations and project specifications.

Sampler Name _____ Signature _____ Sampler Firm _____ Date _____

FOR LAB USE ONLY

Lab _____ Analyst name _____ Signature _____ Analysis Date _____ Reviewer _____ Review Date _____

Glossary of Terms

Acoustical Insulation - The general application or use of asbestos for the control of sound due to its lack of reverberant surfaces.

Acoustical Tile - A finishing material in a building usually found in the ceiling or walls for the purpose of noise control.

Actinolite - One of six naturally occurring asbestos minerals. It is not normally used commercially.

Addenda - Changes made to working drawings and specifications for a building before the work is bid.

AHERA - Asbestos Hazard Emergency Response Act.

Algorithm - A formal numerical procedure for assessing suspect material; results are given a numerical score.

Alveoli - Located in clusters around the respiratory bronchioles of the lungs, this is the area in which true respiration takes place.

Amosite - An asbestiform mineral of the amphibole group. It is the second most commonly used form of asbestos in the U.S. Also known as brown asbestos.

Amphibole - One of the two major groups of minerals from which the asbestiform minerals are derived - distinguished by their chain-like crystal structure and chemical composition. Amosite and crocidolite are examples of amphibole minerals.

Anthophyllite - One of six naturally occurring asbestos minerals. It is of limited commercial value.

Asbestos - A generic name given to a number of naturally occurring hydrated mineral silicates that possess a unique crystalline structure, are incombustible in air, and separate into fibers. Asbestos includes the asbestiform varieties of chrysotile (serpentine); crocidolite (riebeckite); amosite (cummingtonite-grunerite); anthophyllite; tremolite, and actinolite.

Asbestos Bodies - Coated asbestos fibers often seen in the lungs of asbestos-exposure victims.

Air Sampling Technician- The "Restricted Handler II" certificate applies for those individuals who perform related air sampling activities. The AST course includes information on methodology for representative quality assurance for both area and personal sampling for Phase Contrast Microscopy (PCM) and Transmission Electron Microscopy (TEM). The course includes practical exercises utilizing the various types of air sampling equipment and concludes with a 50-question multiple choice examination. NYSDOH approval is to EEA.

Asbestos-Containing - Material (ACBM) Surfacing ACM, thermal system insulation ACM, or miscellaneous ACM that is found in or on interior structural members or other parts of a school building (AHERA definition).

Asbestos-Containing - Any material or product which contains more than one percent asbestos (AHERA, OSHA definition).

Glossary of Terms

Asbestosis - A non-malignant, progressive, irreversible lung disease caused by the inhalation of asbestos dust and characterized by diffuse fibrosis.

ASHARA - Asbestos School Hazard Abatement Reauthorization Act. U.S. EPA regulation enacted November 28, 1992 which extended accreditation requirements for inspectors, contractor/supervisors, designers, and workers to public and commercial buildings.

Breeching - A duct which transports combustion gases from a boiler or heater to a chimney or stack. Also called a flue.

Building Inspection - A building inspection involves (1) an investigation of records (including previous surveys, plans, specifications, and other documents) for the identification of ACBM, (2) a physical and visual inspection of the building for suspect materials, (3) sampling and analyzing suspect materials to test for asbestos, and (4) assessing the condition and location of the ACBM and other characteristics of the building.

Building Inspector - A person who conducts a survey of a building for the presence of asbestos-containing materials. Must be accredited under AHERA and ASHARA regulations.

Bulk Sample - Sample of bulk material; in the case of asbestos, suspect material.

Category I -
Non-friable ACM Asbestos-containing packings, gaskets, resilient floor covering and asphalt roofing products containing more than 1% asbestos.

Category II - Any material, excluding Category I non-friable ACM, Non-friable ACM containing more than 1% asbestos that, when dry, cannot be crumbled, pulverized, or reduced to powder by hand pressure. Example: asbestos cement products.

Cementitious ACM - Asbestos-containing materials that are densely packed, granular and are generally non-friable.

Chain-of custody - Formal procedures for tracking samples and insuring their integrity.

Change Order - A change to construction documents after a contract for construction has been signed.

Chrysotile - The only asbestiform mineral of the serpentine group. It is the most common form of asbestos used in buildings. Also known as white asbestos.

Certified Industrial -
Hygienist (CIH) An industrial hygienist who has been granted certification by the American Board of Industrial Hygiene.

Cilia - Tiny hair-like structures in the windpipe and bronchi of the lung passages which beat upward and that help force undesirable particles, fibers and liquids up and out of the lungs.

Claims-Made -
Insurance A form of insurance in which a claim is allowed only if the insurance is in effect when the claim is made, that is, when the injury or effect is observed.

Contract Documents - Legally binding building drawings and specifications. Also called construction documents.

Crocidolite - The strongest of the asbestos minerals. An asbestiform mineral of the

Glossary of Terms

amphibole group. It is of minor commercial value in the U.S. Blue asbestos

Damaged Friable - Surfacing (Miscellaneous) Material — Friable surfacing (miscellaneous) ACM which has deteriorated or sustained physical injury such that the internal structure (cohesion) of the material is inadequate or, if applicable, which has delaminated such that the bond to the substrate (adhesion) is inadequate or which for any other reason lacks fiber cohesion or adhesion qualities. Such damage or deterioration may be illustrated by the separation of ACM into layers; separation of ACM from the substrate; flaking, blistering, or crumbling of ACM surface, water damage; significant or repeated water stains. Gouges, mars or other signs of physical injury on the ACM Asbestos debris originating from the ACBM in question may also indicate damage (AHERA definition).

Damaged or Significantly Damaged Thermal System Insulation — Thermal system insulation on pipes, boilers, tanks, ducts, and other thermal system insulation equipment which has lost its structural integrity, or whose covering, in whole or in part, is crushed, water-stained, gouged, punctured, missing, or not intact such that it is not able to contain fibers. Damage may be further illustrated by occasional punctures, gouges, or other signs of physical injury to ACM, occasional water damage on the protective coverings/jackets; or exposed ACM ends or joints. Asbestos debris, originating from the ACBM in question may also indicate damage (AHERA definition).

Dose-Response Effect — The relationship between the amount of pollutant a person is exposed to (dose) and the increase risk of disease (effect). Usually the greater the dose, the greater the effect.

Electrical Systems — The system of wires, lights, power generation equipment, and related facilities to produce, convey, and utilize electrical power in a building.

Encapsulation — The use of an agent to seal the surface (bridging encapsulant) or penetrate the bulk (penetrating encapsulant) of ACM.

Enclosure — A resilient structure, built (or sprayed) around ACM designed to prevent disturbance and contain released fibers.

Epidemiology — The study of causes, occurrence and distribution of disease throughout a population.

Errors and Omissions Insurance — A type of insurance, which protects professionals for mistakes they may make in contracted plans and recommendations.

Excursion Limit (EL) — A level of airborne fibers specified by OSHA as a short term excursion level. It is currently 1.0 fibers per cubic centimeter (f/cc) of air, 30-minute time-weighted average, as measured by phase contrast microscopy.

f/cc — Fibers per cubic centimeters of air.

Fireproofing — Spray or trowel applied fire resistant materials.

Friable — Any materials that can be crumbled, pulverized, or reduced to powder by hand pressure when dry.

Functional Spaces — Spatially distinct units within a building, which contain identifiable populations of building occupants.

Glossary of Terms

General Liability Insurance — A type of insurance which covers the insured for damage to property and person caused by his or her own negligence.

Hazard Assessment — The interpretation and evaluation of physical assessment data in order to set abatement priorities and rank areas for response actions. These priorities and rankings are based on anticipated exposure to asbestos fibers.

Heating, Ventilating, & Air Conditioning (HVAC) System — The system of pipes, ducts, and equipment (air conditioners, chillers, heaters, boilers, pumps, fans) used to heat, cool, move, and filter air in a building. HVAC systems are also known as mechanical systems.

High Efficiency Particulate Air (HEPA) — A type of filter which is 99.97% efficient at filtering particles of 0.3 micrometers in diameter.

Homogeneous Sampling Area — An area of ACBM or suspect ACBM which appears similar throughout in terms of color, texture, and date of material application.

Indemnify — To pay for or pay back. Indemnification clauses in contracts are intended to cover the cost of judgements and/or legal defenses in the event of litigation.

Industrial Hygienist — A professional qualified by education, training, and experience to recognize, evaluate, and develop controls for occupational health hazards.

Latency Period — The time between first exposure to a disease causing agent and the appearance of the disease.

Liability — Being subject to legal action for one's behavior.

Lung Cancer — A malignant growth of abnormal cells in the lungs, specifically of the bronchi covering.

Macrophage — White blood cells, which attack foreign substances in the body. The release of enzymes from these cells as they attack undigestible particles, such as asbestos, contributes to the creation of scar tissue in the lung.

Management Plan — A plan for each LEA to control and manage ACBM (AHERA definition). Must be prepared by an EPA or state accredited Management Planner.

Management Planner — An individual that has completed an EPA or State approved course and passed an examination covering the development of management plans.

Mechanical Systems — See HVAC systems.

Mesothelioma — A relatively rare form of cancer, which develops in the lining of the pleura or peritoneum with no known cure. It is almost always caused by exposure to asbestos.

Micrometer — One millionth of one meter

Miscellaneous Material — Interior building material on structural components, structural members or fixtures, such as floor and ceiling tiles, and does not include surfacing material or thermal system insulation (AHERA definition).

MSHA — Mine Safety and Health Administration

Glossary of Terms

Negative Pressure Respirators — Respirators which function by the wearer breathing in air through a filter.

Negative Pressure Respirator Fit Check — A form of qualitative fit testing in which the wearer covers the filters of a negative pressure, air-purifying respirator to check for leaks around the face seal.

NESHAP — National Emission Standards for Hazardous Air Pollutants - EPA Regulation 40 CFR subpart M, Part 61.

NIOSH — The National Institute for Occupational Safety and Health which was established by the occupational Safety and Health Act of 1970.

NIOSH/MSHA — The official approving agencies for respiratory protective equipment who test and certify respirators.

Occurrence Insurance — A form of insurance in which a claim is allowed regardless of when the claim is filed. For asbestos insurance, the "occurrence" could be the time of first exposure.

Operations and Maintenance Plan (O&M) — Specific procedures and practices developed for the of asbestos-containing materials in interim control buildings buildings until it is removed.

OSHA — The Occupational Safety and Health Administration which was created by the Occupational Safety and Health Act of 1970; serves as the enforcement agency for safety and health in the workplace environment.

Permissible Exposure Limit (PEL) — A level of airborne fibers specified by OSHA as an occupational exposure standard for asbestos. It is currently 0.1 fibers per cubic centimeter of air, 8-hour time-weighted average, as measured by phase contrast microscopy.

Phase Contrast Microscopy (PCM) — An optical microscopic technique used for the counting of fibers in air samples, but which does not distinguish fiber types.

Physical Assessment — Assessing suspect material to determine the current condition of the material and the potential for future disturbance.

Plenum — A horizontal space designed to transport air in a building. Plenums are commonly the space between a dropped ceiling and the floor above.

Pleura — The thin membrane surrounding the lungs, and which lines the internal surface of the chest cavity.

Pleural Plaque — A fibrous thickening of the lining of the chest cavity. Associated with asbestos exposure.

Plumbing System — The system of pipes, valves, fittings and related components designed to convey liquid or gas fluids throughout a building. Some piping may also be part of the HVAC system.

Glossary of Terms

Point Counting - A method of analyzing bulk samples whereby the sample is homogenized, placed on microscope slides and examined under a polarized light microscope. A point counting stage (or mechanical stage) and cross hair reticle are used for counting with only the particle(s) directly under the cross being counted (void space is not counted). A minimum of 400 counts should be made for each slide (several slides are examined).

Polarized Light - An optical microscopy technique for analyzing bulk

Microscopy (PLM) samples for asbestos in which the sample is illuminated with polarized light (light which vibrates in only one plane) to distinguish between different types of asbestos fibers by their shape and unique optical properties.

Positive Pressure - Respirators Respirators which function by blowing air or providing pressured air to the wearer.

Positive Pressure Respirator Fit Check A form of qualitative fit testing in which the wearer covers the exhalation valve of a negative pressure, air-purifying respirator to check for leaks around the face seal.

Protection Factor (PF) A number, which reflects the degree of protection provided by a respirator. It is calculated by dividing the concentration of contaminant outside the mask by the concentration inside the mask.

Presumed ACM - Asbestos-containing thermal system insulation and surfacing materials found in a building constructed no later than 1980. (OSHA regulations)

Project Monitor - Any person other than the asbestos abatement contractor/supervisor, who oversees the scope, methodology, or quality control on an abatement project, must maintain a valid project monitor certification. The Project Monitor is responsible for satisfactory operation of abatement activities. This includes those who shall act in a "third party" and/or owners representative capacity. Completion of this course allows an individual to also obtain an air sampling technician certification. The course incorporates extensive practical exercises, a project site visit, and concludes with a 100 question multiple choice examination. NYSDOH approval is to EEA.

Quality Assurance - A program for collecting and analyzing additional samples of suspect material to check on the reliability of procedures.

Qualitative Fit Test - A method of testing a respirator's face-to-facepiece seal by covering the inhalation or exhalation valves and either breathing in or out to determine the presence of any leaks.

Quantitative Fit Test - Testing Testing the fit of a respirator by calculating concentrations of contaminants inside and outside the mask. This requires the use of instruments.

Rales - Cracking sounds in the lower half of the lung; symptomatic of progressing asbestosis.

Random Sample - A sample drawn in such a way that there is no set pattern and is designed to give a true representation of the entire population or area.

Record Documents - Drawings and specifications, which should reflect the way a building was actually constructed (sometimes referred to as "as-built drawings")

Glossary of Terms

Regulated Asbestos Containing Material (RACM) — a) friable asbestos material, b) Category I non-friable ACM that has become friable, c) Category I non-Friable ACM that will be or has been subjected to sanding, grinding, cutting or abrading, or d) Category II non-friable ACM that has a high probability of becoming or has become crumbled, pulverized, or reduced to powder by the forces expected to act on the material in the course of demolition or renovation operations regulated by subpart §61.141 of 40 CFR Part 61 (NESHAP Revision; Final Rule)

Respiration - The exchange of gases in the lungs

Respiratory Protection Program — A set of procedures and equipment required by OSHA to be established by an employer, which provides for the safe use of respirators on their job sites.

Respiratory Tract — The organs of the body, which convey air to the blood, allow exchange of gases, and remove carbon dioxide.

Serpentine — One of the two major groups of minerals from which the asbetiform minerals are derived; distinguished by their tubular structure and chemical composition. Chrysotile is a serpentine mineral.

Shop Drawings — Detailed drawings of selected items used in the construction of a building that are drawn by the contractor, but reviewed by the architect/engineer responsible for designing the project.

Significantly Damaged Friable Surfacing (Miscellaneous) Materials - Friable surfacing (miscellaneous) ACM in a functional space where damage is extensive and severe. (AHERA definition)

Specifications - A written set of standards, procedures, and materials for the construction of a building

Structural Member — Any load-supporting member such as beams and load supporting walls of a facility

Submittals — Drawings or descriptive literature such as operating manuals transmitted to the building owner upon construction completion

Substrate — The material or existing surface located under or behind the asbestos-containing material

Surfacing Material — Material that is sprayed-on, troweled-on or otherwise applied to surfaces, such as acoustical plaster on ceilings and fireproofing materials on structural members, or other materials on surfaces for acoustical, fireproofing, or other purposes (AHERA definition).

Synergistic — The combination of two effects which is greater than the sum of the two independent effects.

Thermal System Insulation — Material applied to pipes, fittings, boilers, breeching, tanks, ducts, or other interior structural components to prevent heat loss or gain, or water condensation, or for other purposes.

Tort — A legal wrong, sometimes referred to as negligence.

Glossary of Terms

Trachea – The main air tube into the lungs. Made up of cartilage and supported by cartilage rings, the trachea divides into two bronchi which lead into the lungs.

Transite™ - A trade name for asbestos cement wallboard and sheeting

Transmission - Electron Microscopy (TEM) A method of microscopic analysis which utilizes an electron beam that is focused onto a thin sample. As the beam penetrates (transmits) through the sample, the difference in densities produces an image on a fluorescent screen from which samples can be identified and counted. Used for analyzing air samples for asbestos.

Tremolite - One of six naturally occurring asbestos minerals, Tremolite has few commercial uses

Working drawings – A set of drawings, which reflect the intended construction and appearance of the building. Also known as building plans.

U.S. EPA – United States Environmental Protection Agency. Created in 1970, the U.S. EPA is the federal promulgator and enforcement agency for environmental regulations.